P.U.L.L.

Pop Up Lending Libraries

Together Kennett Square

Take A Book, Read A Book, Leave a Book

For more information about P.U.L.L., Contact:

www.AHHAH.org

BEVERLY HILLS SPY

BEVERLY HILLS SPY

The Double-Agent War Hero
Who Helped Japan Attack
Pearl Harbor

RONALD DRABKIN

WILLIAM MORROW
An Imprint of HarperCollins*Publishers*

HarperCollins books may be purchased for educational, business, or sales promotional use. For information, please email the Special Markets Department at SPsales@harpercollins.com.

Images in the photo insert are courtesy of the author, except:

p. 1, (*top*) Photo © Imperial War Museum; p. 2, (*top left; bottom*) Photo © Imperial War Museum; p. 3, (*top*) Photo courtesy of WING Aviation Press Co., LTD; p. 4, (*top*) Photo © KEYSTONE/HULTON ARCHIVE/GETTY IMAGES, (*bottom*) Photo © 1936, *Los Angeles Times*. Used with Permission; p. 5, Departure of Hawaii Clipper, Fang family *San Francisco Examiner* Photograph Archive Negative Files, BANC PIC 2006.029--NEG box 687, sleeve 096350_02, © The Regents of the University of California, The Bancroft Library, University of California, Berkeley; p. 6, (*top*) Photo courtesy of Glendale History Room, Library, Arts and Culture Dept., Glendale, CA; p. 7, (*top; middle*) Photo courtesy of Harvard-Westlake School; (*bottom*) Photo courtesy Southern California News Group / Press-Telegram; p. 8, (*top left*) The National Archives of the UK (TNA), KV2/331

FIRST EDITION

Designed by Bonni Leon-Berman

Library of Congress Cataloging-in-Publication Data

Names: Drabkin, Ronald, author.
Title: Beverly Hills spy / Ronald Drabkin.
Description: First edition. | New York : William Morrow, an Imprint of HarperCollins Publishers, 2024. | Includes bibliographical references and index.
Identifiers: LCCN 2023046767 (print) | LCCN 2023046768 (ebook) | ISBN 9780063310070 (hardcover) | ISBN 9780063310094 (epub)
Subjects: LCSH: Rutland, Frederick, 1887-1949. | Espionage, Japanese—United States—History. | World War, 1939-1945—Secret service—Japan. | World War, 1939-1945—Secret service—United States. | Spies—United States—Biography. | British—Japan—Biography. | British—California—Los Angeles—Biography. | Pearl Harbor (Hawaii), Attack on, 1941. | Hollywood (Los Angeles, Calif.)—Biography.
Classification: LCC D810.S7 R833 2024 (print) | LCC D810.S7 (ebook)
LC record available at https://lccn.loc.gov/2023046767
LC ebook record available at https://lccn.loc.gov/2023046768

ISBN 978-0-06-331007-0

23 24 25 26 27 LBC 5 4 3 2 1

This book is dedicated to my father and grandfather. I never did fully find out what they did in "the service," but in trying to find out, I happened across the Rutland story. If the FBI declassifies the rest of the Rutland files, perhaps I will find a mention of them.

The majority of the dialogue and conversations in this narrative nonfiction book are not meant to be a word-for-word transcript. Rather, the author leaned on diligent research, interviews, and the inclusion of information from personal records, declassified documents, and consultations with native speakers of Japanese and British English. Every effort was made to ensure that this work is as factually accurate as possible.

CONTENTS

x   Contents

CHAPTER 1

PEARL HARBOR

December 6, 1941

Admiral Husband Kimmel, the commander in chief of the United States Pacific Fleet, granted a rare interview to reporter Joseph Harsch of the *Christian Science Monitor*. Harsch asked whether Kimmel believed the Japanese would attack the United States.

"No, young man. I don't think they'd be such damned fools."

This was the day before the Japanese attack on Pearl Harbor.

The United States had double the population, vast natural resources, and an economy five times larger than Japan's. It wasn't that the Japanese couldn't attack. It was that they wouldn't. Like many Americans, Kimmel thought that if the Japanese were to attack the far more powerful United States, it would be tantamount to them committing national suicide.

Despite his flippant attitude, Kimmel did have clues that an attack could come. The US Army and Navy were reading many Japanese codes, under a top secret program called Magic. US Navy headquarters had recently sent Kimmel war-warning memos.

On November 27, Kimmel received a message that included, "This dispatch is to be considered a war warning."

On December 3, the navy sent Kimmel a note that Japan had ordered consulates to destroy codes and all but one code machine, a strong hint that a war was imminent.

On the morning of the attack, at six thirty a.m., US destroyer *Ward* reported that they had just sunk a submarine outside of Pearl Harbor. An hour later, US Army operators saw a large mass of airplanes coming toward Honolulu on their radar scope. They assumed that what they saw on their scopes were American planes.

Just then, the lead Japanese pilot, Mitsuo Fuchida—who was circling just north of Oahu—slid back the canopy on his Nakajima torpedo bomber. He fired a single flare out the window from his Kayaba signal pistol. The flare lit up the early morning sky, giving the pilots the "final go" signal. The weather was favorable with spotty clouds. They dropped altitude and approached the target from the southern side of the island.

A few minutes later, Fuchida saw the American ships in Pearl Harbor. It was a quiet Sunday morning, and many of the American sailors were asleep. Within an hour, thousands of them were dead and the US Pacific Fleet was in ruins.

...

In the days after the attack, much of America was consumed with three thoughts: *What happened?*; *How do we get revenge on the Japanese?*; and *Whose fault was it?*

A few days later, J. Edgar Hoover wrote to President Roosevelt, saying the surprise was the fault of the commanders on the ground, and of the US Navy's Office of Naval Intelligence (ONI, the part known today as NCIS), the agency in charge of anticipating threats from foreign navies. Hoover pointed out, correctly, that ONI *was* in chaos. The director had just started his job three weeks before, and he was the fourth director just that year.

With the press and the American people crying for blood, the US government kicked off the initial investigation into what happened. However, a thorough investigation wasn't possible because of the need to keep secret the existence of the Magic program. As Hoover had hoped (and intended), the conclusion pointed fingers at the commanders on the scene, Admiral Kimmel and Army General Walter Short, as practically the only guilty parties. They were removed from command and lowered in rank.

In 1944, the secretary of war kicked off a larger investigation led by Henry Clausen of the Judge Advocate General (JAG) Department. Clausen published an eight-hundred-page report that spread the blame beyond just the two men on the scene. To come to this conclusion, he had full access to the Magic files, and he interviewed or had access to over one hundred people, including the heads of the navy and US Naval Intelligence, the army, General Douglas MacArthur, the secretary of state, the Office of the President . . . but, strangely, no one from FBI headquarters.

In 1982, John Toland asserted in his book *Infamy* that much of the blame for the surprise at Pearl Harbor lay with unnamed higher-ups in Washington. There wasn't much public evidence at that time that would have pointed any blame at the FBI.

However, a recently released FBI file shows that an agent wrote a memo about a Japanese spy known as "Agent Shinkawa." In the file, the FBI agent says that this mysterious Japanese agent had flipped and become a spy for the United States Navy. A message came directly from Hoover, saying to not talk about Shinkawa to anyone outside the agency, because it was highly embarrassing to the FBI.

Only now can the full story of Agent Shinkawa be told. The FBI has recently released about two-thirds of Shinkawa's files—in Britain, MI5 has transparently released over one thousand pages of files on the man. In 1945, Japanese Navy Intelligence officers burned their files on Shinkawa and others, with clouds of smoke billowing for days over their headquarters in Hiyoshi, but stories of his accomplishments still exist in the unpublished (and still untranslated) memoirs of several Japanese admirals.

It turned out that Japanese spy Agent Shinkawa had indeed turned double agent and was attempting to help US Navy Intelligence anticipate the Japanese attack. The FBI didn't trust him and had him removed from the scene.

Shinkawa was not Japanese—he wasn't American either. In fact, he was British, and a VIP. And despite his late attempts to help the US stop the attack on Pearl Harbor, he had personally helped redesign the Japanese aircraft carriers that led the attack. He had helped the Japanese Navy update the famous Mitsubishi A6M Zero. He was even the lead investor in Kayaba, the company that made the signal pistol that kicked off the attack. For many years, this charismatic British war hero had been living in a house now worth $14 million in Beverly Hills. Newspapers of the period, which have only just gone online in 2023, show he often hosted parties and other events with the likes of Charlie Chaplin, Boris Karloff, Nigel Bruce, Amelia Earhart, Douglas Fairbanks, and the father of Yoko Ono.

This is the story of Frederick Rutland, also known as Agent Shinkawa of the Imperial Japanese Navy, and Rutland of Jutland, and who has certainly been called many other names over the years. It's a story of high ambition, daring greatness, and world-changing events—but mostly, it's a story of missed chances.

CHAPTER 2

THE BATTLE OF JUTLAND

July 31, 1916

Admiral David Beatty, commander of the British battle cruiser squadron, stood anxiously on the bridge of his flagship, the HMS *Lion*. The North Sea was pewter blue and choppy, an inhospitable and angry tub of fog and swells, and, as the afternoon unfolded, smoke. At two fifteen p.m., Beatty received a message: *Enemy in sight*. The sender was Edwyn Alexander-Sinclair, on the *Galatea*, head of the light cruiser squadron that was ahead of the fleet.

Galatea was the first of the British ships to see the enemy and quickly started taking fire. *Galatea* fired on a German destroyer from extreme range, briefly, before switching its fire to a cruiser. A shell from the cruiser slammed into *Galatea*, but miraculously didn't explode. Between the fog, weather, and general confusion that followed the exchange of gunnery, *Galatea* wasn't adequately able to communicate the locations and makeup of the German fleet. At 2:40 p.m., she radioed that "there was a large amount of smoke as though from a fleet bearing East Northeast."

Beatty ordered his ships to "head for the sound of the guns." It was risky. He didn't really know where the enemy was, or how many there were—so he had decided to try using a plane to search for the Germans. Of the 150 ships in the British fleet, there was exactly one that carried planes: the *Engadine*. He ordered *Engadine* to send out one of its four seaplanes to help find the German fleet.

The pilot selected for the mission, Frederick Rutland, had barely suppressed a yelp of delight when he heard the mission was a go. This would clearly be the most important air mission in British naval history, and he'd been selected.

He paced on the deck of the ship, worried his risky mission might be canceled because of the weather. Indeed, in normal times, the mission would certainly have been canceled, but the stakes were too high now. In theory, if he was able to convey the location of the Germans, he—a junior officer, flying in a Short Brothers wood-and-canvas biplane that was said to be "made of sticks and string"—could change the course of the battle, or even of the war itself.

Launching a seaplane was a risky affair even in fair weather. The engines broke often, which could easily be fatal if the plane happened to be over water and out of sight of the fleet. These early seaplanes didn't take off from the deck of the ship. Instead, they were lowered by crane from the ship's deck into the water and took off from there. Rutland thought back to a mission a month earlier that had failed when high waves crashed a couple of planes into each other. Oddly, this brought a smile to his face, as he considered there wouldn't be any other planes to worry about on this mission. Today, the glory would be all his.

Rutland watched the deck crew efficiently execute the laborious process to prepare his plane for takeoff. First, the crew opened the unwieldy hangar doors. As the ship was rolling in the heavy swells, he ran down to help the crew wrestle the plane onto the deck. The Short seaplane had no wheels, just large floats, so it took several minutes of extreme effort to get the 3,500-pound plane into position. The deck crew then turned a crank to unfold the wings and lock them into place. From there, they checked the airframe and 245-horsepower engine, and then adjusted the crane to gently lift the plane and place her, her pilot, and Rutland's observer, George Trewin, into the water next to the ship. Rutland noted that the deck crew got the plane ready in under twenty minutes, which was a new record—highly impressive, considering the prior record had been set in fair weather and in port.

As Rutland watched the crew get his plane ready, he calmed himself by remembering that he had been selected due to his smarts, effort, and over-all excellence, and that he had constantly beaten all of the odds. His fellow pilots had been mostly commissioned as officers after graduating from the Royal Naval Colleges, Oxford, or Cambridge. Rutland, on the other hand, was an elementary school dropout, the son of a day laborer who had initially joined the Royal Navy with the rank of "Second Class Boy." He came from a family that was desperately poor; he was so undernourished as a child that, when he first enlisted in the navy, he was only five feet, two inches tall and weighed just eighty-five pounds.

Rutland and Trewin performed final checks on the floatplane before gunning the engine and turning toward the wind to take off. In the dis-tance, there were clear, alarming sounds of explosions as the battle heated up. Bouncing along the swells, he pulled back the stick and was relieved when the plane eased into the air. He rapidly took the plane to its top speed of eighty-eight miles an hour and flew just below the low clouds at only nine hundred feet of altitude. Heading toward the smoke, he sighted the German ships about ten minutes later. Given the poor visibility, he needed to fly very close to the German light cruisers and destroyers, and guided the plane in for a closer look. As he approached, he saw puffs of smoke coming from below—it seemed every gun on the enemy ships had opened fire at him.

Rutland described the German shooting as "fairly good, with shells ex-ploding on my wing, before and behind me." Trewin started the process of sending the report back to the fleet. Rutland called out to him the number and types of ships. Trewin wrote them down and read them back to con-firm. He then translated the information into code and tapped the letters in the dots and dashes of Morse. As he was transmitting, Rutland turned the plane and, being sure to fly out of range of the German guns, looked for other German ships.

Rutland could sense just how terrified Trewin was, but was confident he'd successfully relayed the makeup and coordinates of the German ships to the British fleet. As soon as Trewin had finished radioing his report, the

German ships performed a 180-degree turn. Rutland needed to do it all over again. He flew back around, and as the German ships again opened fire, Trewin transmitted the new location and heading of the enemy.

Rutland's mind wandered to the topic of the radio. Rain was falling into the open cockpit, but he knew the radio would work well—he had updated the design of the radio himself. Two years earlier, when he was a brand-new pilot, the radios on the navy planes had been shorting out in the rain. He set up a workshop where he experimented with the electronics, working late into the night on his own time, after his regular war duty was over. He discovered the radio's power supply had insufficient waterproofing. He implemented a fix and documented it in a detailed report to the Admiralty.

The Royal Navy promptly implemented his improvement to all the radios in all of the planes in the fleet. He received an official commendation, which stated that it was highly unusual for a new officer to improve the entire fleet. He chuckled, enjoying the praise, but to him it'd been easy. A decade earlier, as a seventeen-year-old enlisted sailor, he had been both a diver and an electrical system expert, so waterproofing electrical systems was something he had done many times. Rutland had a drumbeat of similar incremental improvements to the planes, electronics, and tactics, and that was a reason he was chosen for interesting missions. His brilliance had led him to flying that day at Jutland.

Rutland didn't see other German ships, so he turned the plane back toward the British fleet, excited about the successful mission. He checked the wings of the plane, noticing that the German shells seemed to have miraculously missed them. He spotted the British ships just a few miles away—but just at that moment, his engine sputtered, stalled, and died. Rutland tried to glide the plane farther away from the German fleet, toward the approaching British, but he was forced to put his seaplane down on the water.

He climbed out of the cockpit and onto the seaplane's float and clambered to the front to try to fix the engine. The swells were high, and it was challenging for him to keep his balance as he looked up and, just for a moment, took in the majestic yet terrifying scene. The fleets were closing with each other in what was shaping up to be the biggest naval battle in history, and through a stroke of bad luck, his plane had come down smack in the middle of the battle, right between the British and German fleets. The shells flying over his head in both directions weighed up to two thousand pounds each—not much less than his entire plane. He popped open the engine compartment and started examining the engine, hoping he could find a quick fix. He worried that the engine had taken a hit. But no, it was a mechanical failure. Because he had been flying the plane at the extreme of its capabilities, the stress on the fragile engine had popped a hole in the fuel line. A problem, no doubt, but one he could fix. Gripping the float of his plane, Rutland concentrated on the task before him as the swells kept him off-balance.

He started searching his flight suit for anything that would let him patch the hole, and fashioned a piece of rubber from his flight suit into a stopper, which he used to plug the fuel line. *That should do it*, he thought, *at least for now.* He closed the engine compartment and jumped back into the cockpit, ready to get back in the air and take another pass by the German fleet. The battle lay in the balance, and he was ready to continue to do his part.

He reported the repair to *Engadine* as he headed back toward the ship. He placed his floatplane alongside *Engadine*, and the plane and its two crew were recovered aboard with no further issues. Just as Rutland and Trewin were being pulled aboard their ship, a nearby battle cruiser, the *Indefatigable*, exploded under German fire. Within minutes, the *Queen Mary* fell to the same fate, with over 1,200 British sailors and one Japanese Navy observer killed. Admiral Beatty turned to his flag captain and said, "Chatfield, there seems to be something wrong with our bloody ships today."

From his place on the deck, Rutland watched in horror as the two battle cruisers burned. Smoke was everywhere, which prevented the gunners on the remaining British ships from accurately targeting their weapons. He lobbied the captain, saying that if he could take off again, he could radio the exact coordinates of the German ships to the gunners. The answer was no, as the weather had gotten considerably worse. Furious, Rutland could do nothing but watch impotently as the largest naval battle in history continued to unfold around him.

The *Engadine*, lacking any significant guns or armor, had been staying out of the way of the main fight, pulling back just behind the line of battle in case it was needed again. In the meantime, yet another British battle cruiser, the HMS *Warrior*, was suffering heavy pounding from eleven-inch shells. It was on fire in multiple places and was taking on water. The *Engadine* was ordered to go forward and tow the *Warrior* to safety, and did so, attaching a thick steel hawser cable and slowly heading toward Britain.

As the sun rose the next morning, Rutland and his shipmates could see that the deck of the *Warrior* was only four feet above the water—the cruiser's bulkheads were giving way, and it was obvious the ship would sink before they could reach a friendly port. The crew started transferring the roughly eight hundred surviving sailors from the *Warrior* to *Engadine*, an extremely difficult operation in heavy seas and with so many wounded sailors laid out on stretchers. Fortunately, as a former channel steamer, *Engadine* was still equipped with a rubber fender, which allowed its crew to get the ships close enough to facilitate the rescue. Together, the sailors first pulled the able-bodied men across by their arms and hands. Once those men were safely aboard, the crew started passing the wounded across in stretchers. Just as the captain and his remaining officers boarded *Engadine*, a wounded sailor fell out of a stretcher and dropped into the water.

Rutland ran over to the side of the ship and started tracking the wounded sailor. A couple crew members were trying to lasso the man with a bowline knot, which the drowning sailor might have been able to grab on to, even in his infirm state. Rutland, who had a habit of talking to himself in challenging moments, talked through how it would work before he ordered the men on the deck to hold one end of the rope, while he grabbed the other end. Before they could stop him, he started rappelling down the side of the ship before submerging himself into the cold water. He swam over to the man and wrapped the bowline knot around himself, shouting at the crew back on deck to pull them up.

As the two men rose from the water, the steel hawser cable used by *Engadine* to tow the *Warrior* cut against the rope. "Sorry, me lad," Rutland said to the now-unconscious man, "I'm afraid we have another dip coming." After the ship steered clear, Rutland was pulled up on the deck, gasping for breath with the wounded man. The sailors unhooked the cable, and *Engadine* pulled clear before *Warrior* slipped under the waves.

The *Engadine* was crowded with the *Warrior*'s crew, which included about one hundred wounded sailors and many dead bodies. Reaching the English port of Rosyth, it landed the wounded first. The captain of the *Warrior* made a speech at the port, with a passionate thank-you to Rutland for the rescue. Rutland found the praise a bit embarrassing. He thought the rescue was just something he should do, his duty even. Besides, Rutland acknowledged that, although his actions may have looked dramatic, he was an experienced navy diver who had jumped over the side of a ship dozens of times before. Other than the brief time when the steel cable came close to the rope, his life had never really been in danger.

But he also noted those who had watched him go over the side didn't know that, and the crew of the *Warrior* were in a very emotional situation. Hundreds of their shipmates were dead or wounded, and they themselves realized they were lucky to be alive. They could have easily gone the way of *Queen Mary* and *Indefatigable*, where almost the entire crews had perished. Perhaps it was natural that the captain had made so much of Rutland risking his life to try to save one of his sailors.

In the following days, the British press, eager to claim bravery and action for their side, christened Rutland with a new nickname: "Rutland of Jutland." He was nominated for the Distinguished Service Cross, so that he would thereafter be officially known as "Frederick Rutland, DSC." In that event-filled month, he also welcomed the birth of his first child, a boy, whom he named Frederick. Then, on August 18, the *London Gazette* reported that Rutland, "whose bravery was said to be magnificent," had also been nominated for another award, the Albert Medal, First Class, in gold. It was a medal for lifesaving, which was only for "cases of extreme and heroic daring." The Albert Medal was almost always awarded posthumously, and Rutland was the only living man who could wear it. Rutland was invited to an audience with King George V twice within the month, once for each medal.

Rutland was cool and confident when he met the king. He was now a national hero, but not a particularly modest one. He lapped up the praise and looked for more. Later, one of his subordinates, William Dickson, who eventually became Marshal of the Royal Air Force, said that "Rutland was greedy with the limelight. When a reporter came on the ship, he ensured the other officers wouldn't be noticed."

Later in life, Rutland was discussing how this one deed of lifesaving earned him a gold medal and an audience with the king with his son, Frederick. He told Frederick that similar feats of bravery must have happened thousands of times during the war; what was different about his case was that the reporters found out about it and were looking for a story. In other words, he told his son, heroism was not so much about doing something unusual, but simply doing your job when someone just happened to be watching.

From that point forward, many of the top admirals—including John Keyes, Herbert Richmond, and William Pakenham—started to contact him directly for suggestions on how to operate the Royal Navy's aircraft. To Rutland, this indicated that future promotions to the top ranks were certain—until all of a sudden, they weren't.

CHAPTER 3

SPURNED BY THE RAF

1917–1922

The Battle of Jutland was the first battle in which an airplane took off from an aircraft carrier. The one airplane in this battle, Rutland's, had a straightforward task: to be launched from the ship, find the location of the enemy, and radio back where the enemy was. Rutland accomplished this feat at the Battle of Jutland in just fifty-two minutes. Yet when Rutland's feat was trumpeted in the press, visionaries realized that it was only a matter of time until airplanes would begin to determine the outcome of the naval battlefield. The planes would keep getting faster, fly farther, and become armed with increasingly more powerful weapons; eventually, it was speculated, they would get so strong that they would make battleships obsolete. And indeed, the moment the era of the battleships was finally over was the attack on Pearl Harbor, nearly a quarter century later, when the Japanese aircraft sank American battleships. The story of Frederick Rutland spans Jutland to Pearl Harbor and every major advance in between. And, perhaps uniquely, Rutland advised all three of the most advanced navies of the world—the British, the American, and the Japanese.

Of course, in 1916, the vast majority of the people who read about Rutland's exploits in the *Times* and elsewhere didn't understand the future implications of his feat. What they did know was the name of the newly famous "Rutland of Jutland." This was partly by design. The Battle of Jutland was, at best, a draw. The British Royal Navy was the strongest navy in the world, and it was embarrassing and bad for popular morale that they couldn't defeat the Germans. Hence, the Royal Navy was eager to popularize the news of Rutland, who became a symbol of both British heroism and technological supremacy, all in one. Plus, the name "Rutland of Jutland" was catchy. The British who read the papers wanted to know more about their new hero, who, it turned out, had a very atypical background.

Frederick Rutland was not, as his biographer Desmond Young noted, "one of those dashing young naval officers of good family who go fox hunting, play polo in Malta, and are the life and soul of cocktail parties in a foreign port."

Rather than being from a "good family," he was the son of a desperately poor day laborer in the port city of Weymouth, England. The town was adjacent to a major Royal Navy base. Like the other poverty-stricken boys in Weymouth, Rutland grew up seeing the navy officers, dressed in their formal white uniforms and attended by servants, coming and going from their ships. From an early age, he had dreamed of nothing but joining them. As an uneducated boy from the lower class, however, becoming an officer was impossible—but he knew he could join the navy as an enlisted man, or what was more commonly known as "the lower deck."

In 1901, at age fourteen, he left school and started work at a local hotel, where he made sweets for wealthy patrons as a confectioner. The position initially suited him, because he got to eat enough food for the first time in a long time, but before long he decided to apply to the Royal Navy.

The application was challenging. Rutland had many traits the navy looked for in a boy sailor: he was bright, ending each school year near the top of his class, and very mechanically oriented. His teachers also recommended him, noting his natural charisma and likeability. The teachers noted that he did try their patience with his tendency to fool around with the boys in his class, but that wouldn't be an issue; the Royal Navy was good at introducing discipline to its sailors.

However, the small and undernourished Rutland had a difficult time passing the minimum standards for fitness. Rutland had hoped that the Royal Navy would take one look at his baby face and just assume he would continue to grow. Another problem was that he was too young; the minimum age to apply was fifteen. But he simply lied about his age, had his father sign his approval, and submitted his application. He was overjoyed a week later when he found he had been accepted.

The Royal Navy's philosophy at the time was to invest in these young sailors, teaching them everything there was to know about every part of a ship. The training ship, HMS *Boscawen*, originally built in Weymouth as a sailing ship, was still partially rigged with sails when Rutland joined the crew. There were no longer any regular navy ships that used sails, but the training included having the boys learn how to rig the sails anyway. Learning how to use a ship under sail was not practical, but it was believed that it would help the boys understand the fundamentals of naval life and the ways of a British sailor.

Ironically, learning how to operate sails later turned out to be one key to Rutland's success in the pioneering of planes safely taking off and landing on ships. The early biplanes that Rutland flew were made of wood and canvas, just like the masts of a sailing ship. His understanding of wind, canvas, and water was a bonus sixteen years later, when he was the leader of the Royal Navy's elite flight group, in charge of deciding how to land planes on a ship in a gusty wind.

Just as Rutland won over his primary school teachers, he impressed his superiors in the navy with his excellence. He displayed a high technical aptitude and quickly became an expert on every machine he touched. Because torpedoes required electricity to fire, he mastered the ship's electrical system, and he threw himself eagerly into the new field of wireless communication, learning the ins and outs of radio technology. He was quickly promoted to First Class Boy, then left the training ship when he was assigned to be a diver on HMS *Minotaur*.

By 1910, nine years into his service, while attending diving school near Portsmouth, Rutland watched, mesmerized, as aircraft from the naval wing of the Royal Flying Corps flew in and out of a nearby airfield. Smitten by the allure of flight, he was determined to transfer to the RFC.

However, only officers could become pilots. There was a test to become an officer, and the written part of the test was close to impossible for someone who had dropped out of school. Yet, assisted in studying by Dorothy Norris, a twenty-year-old schoolteacher who would later become his wife, Rutland passed.

A November 1911 Royal Navy report about Rutland commended his performance and described him as "zealous and loyal." Another noted his "outstanding" performance and his top-notch ratings. He was transferred from a torpedo boat to the recently formed Royal Naval Air Service (RNAS), reporting at the age of twenty-eight to the Royal Navy flying school at Eastchurch, on the coast of Kent, fifty-five miles east of London, where he learned the basics of flight on a Short pusher biplane. Technically, he did well. But he felt like, and was, very much an outsider among the other pilots in his class. He was almost a decade older than the others, only five foot seven, and the son of a day laborer.

Rutland rapidly became known for his flying prowess, but even more so his technical skills. The planes the pilots flew had engines that broke frequently. His dozen years in the lower deck of the Royal Navy left him able to fix or improve just about every part of the planes, and his fellow pilots didn't have the experience to match him. One day, he watched, somewhat amused, as a fellow new pilot tried unsuccessfully to fix an engine. He helped the man, but his air of superiority delivered in a lower-class accent irked his fellow pilot. Or, perhaps more accurately, the other pilot—who was of a superior class, and had read classics at Cambridge—realized his skills were no match for Rutland's for the task at hand. Yet, despite some of these issues with his peers, Rutland's excellence impressed his superiors. His personnel records were soon full of glowing commentary about his performance and potential.

On completion of flight training, he was assigned to Calshot Naval Air Station for seaplane training before finally getting posted to the *Engadine*, a channel-steamer-cum-seaplane-tender equipped with two Short 184 scout planes and two Sopwith Babys.

Rutland drew positive attention from several admirals yet again after the Royal Navy's failed aircraft carrier attack on a series of German zeppelin hangars in Tønder, just a few short weeks before the Battle of Jutland. Eleven seaplanes took off after being placed in the water by HMS *Vindex* and *Engadine*, including one piloted by Rutland. Several planes collided on the surface of the Atlantic, while others had their propellers destroyed by waves. The attack was a spectacular failure, and Rutland and a few other pilots were called before a board of inquiry. Rutland alone gave a confident report, full of revolutionary but actionable suggestions on how to prevent a similar failure in the future and launch a successful attack.

Following his heroism during the Battle of Jutland, Rutland continued his rise up the ranks. He was promoted to flight commander and assigned to the HMS *Manxman*, which had recently been modified to carry four airplanes.

Rutland was also placed on a committee with Rear Admiral Richard Phillimore to decide on the design of a new aircraft carrier. His design was one with a large, flat deck. He said that "an expert pilot could land on a small deck, but the only way to get large numbers of planes in the air is to have a large, flat deck so that non-experts can land safely," envisioning a design similar to the eventual carriers of World War II and today.

Rutland's initial design proposal was rejected. The Royal Navy took a half measure, taking the light, fast battle cruiser HMS *Furious* and modifying it into half of an aircraft carrier. They ripped out the front gun and put a flat deck on just the front half of the ship. Planes could take off from this front deck, avoiding the need to be lowered into the water for takeoff, but the planes would need to either land in the water or attempt to reach a land base on completion of the mission.

However, E. H. Dunning, the senior flying officer of *Furious*, thought it was possible to land planes on this very small deck. It was initially thought to be suicidal, but in reality the planes could fly as slow as forty miles per hour—not much faster than the ship could sail—so, in theory, one could slowly fly alongside the ship, cut the power, and simply drop the plane onto the small deck. Eager to prove the critics wrong, Dunning expertly demonstrated a landing, becoming the first person to land an airplane on the deck of a moving ship.

Confident that he had solved the problem, Dunning started training his pilots in carrier deck landings, starting by having them practice in a chalked-off area on land. To perfect the technique, Dunning successfully landed on *Furious* a second time. But, on his third try, the plane bounded just slightly back in the air, and a gust of wind blew the plane off the deck and into the water. Dunning was killed.

Rutland, newly promoted to squadron leader, was the obvious choice to replace Dunning as head of *Furious*'s air group. He was positive that landing on this mini deck was a terrible idea, but he knew that, to establish his credibility with his men, he would need to perform this risky landing himself. He made one successful landing, but deemed Dunning's method impossible to use. He stopped the exercises and sent "the shortest report of his career." It said, "It would be possible to train non-expert pilots to land on the front deck of *Furious*. If we did so, I would expect their life span to be about ten landings. In bad weather, their life span would be shorter."

Rutland continued to show brilliance in driving technical improvements as well, shocking the fleet by demonstrating that a plane could safely take off in less than twenty feet. Based on this success, the Royal Navy added a scout plane to many of its battleships, dramatically increasing the ability of the fleet to find the enemy.

However, Rutland continued to struggle with people issues. Dickson said that "we admired Rutland for his record and undisputed guts. But we really didn't get to know him, or he us. He seemed too busy to take us into his confidence and inspire us, as Dunning had done." Another, Geoffrey Moore, admitted class issues played a role, and that "the pilots didn't like being bossed around by an ex lower deck." Rutland also clashed with the captain, who found it threatening that the admirals consulted Rutland directly, bypassing the chain of command.

In April 1918, Britain merged the RNAS with the Royal Flying Corps to create the Royal Air Force; Rutland and the other pilots were given new ranks in the RAF, meaning they were no longer in the Royal Navy. The Royal Navy had tagged Rutland as a "capable and zealous officer, who with more experience, would do well in higher ranks. Recommended for promotion." However, his new superior officers from the RAF knew (or cared) less about his naval heroics. They saw him as lower-class, a loose cannon, and not a team player. Rutland was moved to a shore-based position where he headed a committee, giving him authority over carrier and plane design—a very important and influential position that let him exert his world-class knowledge of ship and plane design. He enjoyed being the expert, but the job had zero glamour and no chance for more coverage in the newspapers.

...

During the war, the British had invited Japanese observers onto their ships. When these men went back to Japan, they explained just how good the British were, particularly in naval aviation. For example, they brought statistics showing just how much more often their own aviators crashed than the British.

The Japanese Navy formally asked the postwar British government for help in creating its naval air forces. Britain had provided help to the Japanese Navy for a few decades, and this was, in theory, no different. There was controversy in Britain about the wisdom of passing such cutting-edge technology to any foreign country. But, ultimately, the British agreed to send a mission to Japan—a major reason for the approval was that the British wanted to sell planes to the Japanese Navy.

In September 1921, Japan welcomed a group of thirty British naval aviation experts: pilots, engineers, and salesmen from several British aircraft firms. Leading the group was Scottish nobleman William Francis Forbes-Sempill, who had also been a squadron leader with the Royal Navy during World War I. On the trip, Sempill brought several of the latest-model RAF planes with him, and he and his team spent well over a year showing the Japanese Navy the latest British tactics in torpedo bombing, flight control, carrier landing, and takeoffs. The collaboration was technically successful, but voices in Britain continued to question the wisdom of arming Japan with the latest military technology, and the merits of continuing the Japanese-British alliance in general. As Japan's navy grew in strength—quickly becoming one of the top three navies in the world—Britain eventually decided to call off the alliance. The mission ended after eighteen months, along with the wrapping up of the formal alliance between the two countries.

The Japanese Navy knew they needed more help. Though the Japanese launched the *Hosho*, the first purpose-built aircraft carrier, they were still dependent on British pilots, their planes were designed by British expats, and the *Hosho* itself still had far too many pilots crashing and dying when trying to land. Japan still needed British technology, and it was no longer for sale.

The only real option, then, was to steal it.

...

Rutland's life and career were hitting major headwinds. By 1920, his marriage with Dorothy had run its course. Any hope of saving it vanished when Dorothy started having an affair with a British officer named Gerald White. In response, Rutland started an affair with White's wife, who also happened to be named Dorothy. Rutland found the new Dorothy attractive for several reasons. She was childless, had the straight dark hair that he found attractive, was from a wealthy family, and was much more interested in adventure than his current wife, who he deemed to have a typical schoolteacher personality.

While postwar affairs and divorces were not uncommon after World War I—or after any war for that matter—wife swapping in this manner with a fellow officer was a bridge too far. Whispers among fellow officers continued about Rutland betraying his wife in other ways as well. She had dedicated herself to supporting him in becoming an officer and a pilot, tutoring him on the material on the officer qualification test for hours each night. The Rutlands also had two small children, Fred and their daughter, Barbara. But by 1922, Rutland and Dorothy were living together as an unmarried couple, and the two children were bouncing back and forth between the two homes. It was hardly appropriate behavior for a British officer.

Rutland's new superior officers began giving him lists of reasons why he wouldn't be in line for promotion. To start, he was over thirty years old, which was considered too old. He was world-famous for his bravery in the navy, but his peers—who were mostly from the army—were combat pilots, aces who had shot down German planes during the war. In one meeting, a superior officer reminded Rutland that he'd never shot down a single German, but assured him he would always have a midlevel job in the Royal Air Force due to his technical expertise. The officer noted the poorly concealed anger in Rutland's eyes, and his inability to conceal this anger reinforced the notion that Rutland was a talented officer but one who was of a lower social class, and who acted as such—unfit for higher rank.

...

In late 1922, Rutland walked into the Imperial Japanese Navy office in Westminster. He introduced himself to the Japanese officer on duty, who was named Kobayashi, saying "My name is Rutland," and added that he was interested in exploring new opportunities.

Kobayashi's jaw dropped. He, and everyone else in the office, knew exactly who Rutland was. He and the other Japanese officer on duty, Commander Goro Hara, couldn't believe their luck. They were tasked with obtaining the latest in British naval aircraft and carrier technology, and the most accomplished British aviator in the field had simply dropped into their lap.

A few weeks later, attaché Shiro Takasu, who'd helped organize the Sempill mission, contacted Rutland to formally discuss how he might help. It seemed obvious that the British would not allow Rutland to take a job with the Japanese Navy directly. However, Takasu proposed an arrangement where Rutland would, on paper, work for Mitsubishi, a private Japanese company.

Rutland needed the permission of the Royal Air Force to retire. Until then, Rutland wouldn't be free to take the job with Mitsubishi or even leave the country. While he waited for his application to travel through the military's bureaucracy, he accepted a job with a company called Wireless Services, which made radio broadcasting equipment. Rutland proved a great ambassador for the company. He hosted demonstrations in a posh Piccadilly showroom to potential customers, including several from the BBC. The technology was so new that even the BBC wasn't entirely confident in being able to maintain it; an equipment failure could knock them off the air. One of the BBC engineers asked Rutland how a broadcaster could maintain the radio equipment. Rutland replied with a big smile, saying the device is made so that parts are easy to replace. He then opened up the equipment, disassembled it, replaced some parts, and put it all back together. This was enough to close the deal with the BBC.

Rutland continued to meet with Takasu, and after each conversation, Rutland grew even more excited about working with the Japanese. Takasu shared with Rutland the latest about the construction of the *Hosho*. The Japanese needed help exactly in the areas where Rutland was strongest, such as aircraft takeoff and landing and carrier design.

Rutland stressed to Takasu that landing on a moving deck was always going to be the biggest challenge in naval aviation. Even though the *Hosho* had a large, flat deck, the pilots needed to deal with the rocking of the ship, smoke from the ship's smokestacks, occasional bursting tires, and the known issue of the planes bouncing on landing with the inherent risk of the plane being caught by a gust of wind and thrown overboard, as had happened to Dunning. Rutland had spent considerable time working on all of these issues with quite good success and told Takasu he was confident he could help.

A man named Herbert Smith had designed Rutland's now-famous Sopwith Pup when he was the chief designer for Sopwith, which had since filed for bankruptcy. Smith, out of a job, had been hired by and was now working for Mitsubishi as their head aircraft designer, unrelated to the Sempill mission. The Sempill mission had ended, but Rutland realized, in addition to Smith, there were dozens of other Britons in Japan. And in fact, several members of the Sempill mission, including a friend of Rutland's named CHC Smith, had been hired back by the Japanese on a private basis. The Japanese would be getting British naval aviation technology one way or another, and there was absolutely no doubt in his mind that if he did not give it to them, they would find some other way.

Though there were many Britons going back and forth from Japan, Rutland caught the eye of RAF and MI5, partly because the British codebreakers had read the Japanese radio traffic about Rutland's recruitment by the Japanese. The name of the world-famous Rutland drew their attention. Thanks to the codebreakers, Rutland's superiors knew exactly which of Rutland's statements were exaggerations and untruths. Once Rutland had been tagged as a possible traitor in his files, he drew more attention, and the file started to grow bigger.

The MI5 file profiling Rutland's security risks includes various catty comments such as referring to Dorothy as his "so-called wife."

A month after he submitted his request to retire, Rutland noticed he was being followed. Bemused, he dropped a note to Dorothy saying maybe someone was tailing him due to his upcoming divorce from his first wife, likely trying to confirm if he and Dorothy were living together, unmarried. But he then noticed that there were actually three men following him, which would be far more than would be needed in a simple divorce case. He concluded it must be something to do with his negotiations with the Japanese. Rutland decided to have fun with the men following him on multiple occasions—a couple of times, he doubled back to see them try to hide themselves, and once hit the gas at a dangerous yellow light to see if they would risk their lives to follow him. In any event, he concluded to Dorothy, there was nothing at all wrong with anything he was doing, so it was fine.

The British didn't take any action against Rutland. They knew he was being somewhat untruthful with them about his plans, but he was not a big enough fish to take action and thereby risk alerting the Japanese that their codes were not secure. In May, the Royal Air Force relented: a passport showed up in Rutland's mailbox, and they begrudgingly allowed him to leave the country unimpeded.

· · ·

Rutland promptly moved to Paris with his family, where he continued to work for Wireless Services. The Rutlands rented an upscale house in the Garches district for themselves and the two children. The house came with a cook and a nurse. Rutland then worked with the Japanese naval attachés in Paris to figure out the details of his future employment and residence in Japan. He was double-dipping in salary, getting funds from his current employer and also from his future employer, Mitsubishi, which, in addition to aircraft manufacturing, had a bank branch in Paris.

Living now in a different country, Rutland assumed that the British government would forget about him. He secured a visa from the Japanese embassy, convinced that no one would notice he was heading to Japan. Everything he did was legitimate, he told everyone, but he also knew it was probably best not to draw too much attention to himself in the meantime.

The very social Rutlands hosted numerous English, French, and Japanese guests at their house. One day, when a pair of Japanese attachés came to visit Rutland, he invited them to stay for dinner, and had his French servant try to make Japanese food. The polite Japanese praised the efforts of the servant on the cooking, but the part of the dinner they enjoyed most was—after they had all downed a bottle of wine—their unsuccessful effort to teach Dorothy how to use chopsticks.

Rutland was completing the plans to move the family to Japan, with a sticking point being how to have Mitsubishi lease his family a house big and luxurious enough to match the one in Paris. Soon after they had settled on a property, Rutland picked up a local newspaper. The headline said that Japan had been hit by a massive earthquake. Hundreds of thousands of houses had burned, including the one they had rented. It seemed their move would need to be pushed back a bit further.

CHAPTER 4

DEAD US MARINES

1923

The earthquake hit just before lunch.

Ellis Zacharias, a young US naval officer and Japanese language student, was at the pier to see off the *Empress of Australia*, which was scheduled to depart from Yokohama Port exactly at noon. Astern of the *Empress* and moored alongside the end of the pier was the *Steel Navigator*, a small freighter of the US Steel Corporation. Already, a larger-than-expected crowd had gathered, a scene of feverish activity: multicolored streamers fluttering in the breeze, travelers boarding, stewards loading luggage and provisions, people bidding farewell to their friends and loved ones.

Zacharias liked what he saw. The joy-filled smiles of welcome and teary-eyed goodbyes of impending absence moved him in a way he couldn't fully articulate. It reminded him a bit of his boyhood in Jacksonville, Florida, by the port and the navy base.

At that moment, the earthquake hit. Zacharias and everyone else nearby were knocked off their feet by the shaking of the pier. People who had been only moments before hugging their loved ones scrambled to hold on to each other for dear life. Though they were right next to him, Zacharias couldn't hear their cries of terror because they were drowned out by the din of falling structures and the continued roar of the earth.

Years later, recalling the moment the earthquake struck, he recounted that it was strange to notice that all of the different faces, the smiles, the tears, all the gamut of emotions, had changed into one look, of stark terror, in an instant.

Even after the ground settled, fire threatened to burn the city into a gigantic heap of rubble. Zacharias ordered bystanders to fill buckets of water to try to put out nearby flames. The Japanese were slow to get started on rescue, since they didn't have instructions. However, once he and the others directed them to help, they all proved more than up to the task, working dispassionately as one, assisting with emergency after emergency through the night. It was an impressive work ethic and discipline, he thought, and he'd seen that same dedication mirrored in the Japanese Navy.

Zacharias was one of the most promising young officers of the US Navy's Office of Naval Intelligence. A brilliant and driven officer, he was assigned to Japan three years earlier to learn the language and cultivate contacts with the Japanese Navy. Zacharias initially moved to the seaside town of Zushi, the next town over from where Rutland initially lived. He also regularly visited the foreign settlement in Yokohama. Though he struggled to give voice to why the harbor calmed him, he understood his mission in full by this point and knew all too well how to communicate his incipient concern about Japan's intentions. Spend enough time with the enemy and you'll start to perceive everything they do as a threat, especially when you're one of a handful of people who even consider them an enemy.

Zacharias and others who warned about a Japanese threat felt they were mostly ignored. The US and Japanese Navies had thought of each other as potential enemies ever since Japan defeated the Russian Navy in 1905. Some in the US press also highlighted the Japanese threat, notably William Randolph Hearst, whose newspaper editorials brought a racist element to the narrative, stressing the threat of the "Yellow Peril" to the Caucasian race. However, the idea of an actual war starting with Japan was still considered by most to be ludicrous. The more likely threat to US security, according to consensus, was from radicals and insurrectionists already inside the country—anarchists, communists, union leaders. Other than its strategic location in the Pacific, Japan was hardly a priority. But

Zacharias headed a small cadre of naval officers convinced that Japan was not only an emerging threat but a likely ruthless, unrelenting enemy, and that the United States needed to ready itself for a conflict, both with military preparation and intelligence.

He and a few others in the US Navy were highly interested in some islands in the Pacific that the Japanese had recently conquered. This group of islands, known as the "Mandates," had been owned by Germany—but when Japan joined World War I to support its British ally, the Japanese Navy had occupied them. The Mandates quite quickly afterward became a crucial element in the emerging distrust between Japan and the United States.

Zacharias and others suspected the Japanese Navy, which they believed had ambitions of empire, was fortifying the islands, or possibly even making submarine bases, but there was no way to prove it because the Japanese didn't allow visitors.

In the spring, Zacharias became aware of an American who had arrived in Yokohama and "frequented shabby drinking places and geisha houses." The man didn't visit actual geisha houses, since those were for a higher-class clientele, but the Americans typically referred to any house of entertainment as a geisha house. The man, Pete Ellis, announced to anyone who would listen that he was a retired Marine Corps intelligence officer on a secret mission to visit the Mandates under the guise of an innocuous traveler "to find out what the hell was going on down there." Zacharias had Captain Lyman Cotten, the other naval attaché in Yokohama, investigate what the man was doing. In his report, Cotten noted to Zacharias that this would be the first time he had met an American on a secret mission who was telling people in bars that he was on a secret mission.

Ellis, like Zacharias, was highly concerned about the potential of Japanese aggression against the US. Despite battles with alcoholism and depression, Ellis was a well-respected marine. In addition to his strong combat record, he had helped start the Marines Officer Candidates School and the new Marine base in Quantico. In 1921, two years before he arrived in Yokohama, Ellis wrote a report titled "Operations Plan 712," which predicted that Japan would start a war with the US. Ellis stressed that in that war, the islands in the Mandates—Palau, Truk, Saipan, Ponape, and others—would be a major battleground. In his report, he laid out the "island hopping" strategy the Marine Corps would eventually adopt to great effect in World War II. Ellis proposed a plan to Marine commandant John Lejeune to use the cover of being a traveling businessman to get onto the islands to find out what the Japanese Navy was doing there. In doing so, he could also inspect the beaches on these islands and decide which were best, which would be very helpful for the Marines when they did end up assaulting them.

Lejeune clearly had some reservations, not least of which were Ellis's mental state and alcoholism, but in the end, approved the mission. Lejeune arranged for Ellis to take leave from the Marines. Because he would be going as a civilian, there was no need to get approval from higher-up officers or run it by the State Department, and ONI would also not know what Ellis was doing. Lejeune also prepared an undated resignation letter from the Marine Corps for Ellis, so if for some reason things went south, the Marines could claim they knew nothing about Ellis. Ellis established his cover as a merchant who was buying copra, dried kernels from the coconuts that are plentiful on these islands.

When Ellis arrived in Yokohama, he stood out. Cotten and Zacharias were puzzled by how such an irresponsible individual, who "violated every rule and principle of proper intelligence could be entrusted with the mission of this serious nature." For several days, Cotten watched him toboggan rapidly in the Yokohama bars, where every visit revealed more about his proposed trip—not only to ONI, but to Japanese counterintelligence that happened to be listening as well.

Soon thereafter, an agitated Cotten called Zacharias. "We have real trouble with this fellow Ellis."

"Drunk again," remarked Zacharias. "I know."

"Not *again*," replied Cotten. "He is in a state of permanent drunkenness." Even in an emergency, Cotten maintained a sense of humor, one of the many things Zacharias liked about his colleague.

Then Pete Ellis disappeared.

Cotten searched the local bars, but they weren't able to find him anywhere. After a few days, they notified the Japanese missing persons bureau, but neither saw nor heard anything about Ellis for several weeks.

Then, in May, Cotten received a call from an officer from the Japanese Navy Ministry, telling him that Ellis was on the island of Jaluit—exactly where he had told bar patrons he was planning on going. The Japanese officer told Cotten that Ellis had died, and that he had immediately been cremated. He added that they would be happy to return Ellis's ashes.

Zacharias and Cotten suspected the Japanese had killed him. They decided to send an American to the island to get Ellis's ashes, and while there the man might even be able to see what was happening on the islands from a military perspective. The Japanese agreed, and Zacharias decided to send Lawrence Zembsch, a pharmacist, who left and then returned to Yokohama on August 16 on a Japanese ship.

Zacharias and Cotten arranged to meet him at the ship, eager to hear his report. As the passengers filed out, there was no sign of Zembsch. Alarmed, they approached the ship's captain, who escorted them belowdecks to a cabin. Zembsch was very ill, clutching the box of ashes as he lay in the bunk. Zacharias immediately suspected the Japanese had poisoned him, and that the Japanese were sending a clear message not to mess with them.

These episodes reinforced in Zacharias's mind just how ruthless the Japanese could be. Soon after, he met a Japanese officer, Isoroku Yamamoto, who was recently back from a stint at the Japanese embassy in Washington, DC. Yamamoto—who was the eventual head of the Pearl Harbor attack—occasionally invited Zacharias and other American naval officers to a game of cards.

As he got to know more Japanese people, he decided they were a paradox. They were highly risk averse and absolutely terrified of making the slightest mistake. He found it annoying that the waiters in his favorite bar would always check his order twice, and when he paid, they would count out the change twice, then confirm with him it was correct before handing the coins over. But on the other side of the coin, the heads of the Japanese military certainly didn't appear to be preternaturally averse to risk or afraid of bold action. In fact, their last two wars, against Russia and China, had both started with Japan executing a surprise attack.

Indeed, the more he talked to these officers in the Japanese Navy, the more impressed he was at their diligence and risk-taking. Thinking about the dead marine, he was alarmed at their ruthlessness. He concluded they would be a surprisingly challenging adversary, should they decide to fight the United States. He also concluded that, given their expansionism, a fight was bound to happen sooner or later. Preparing the US for this war—and trying with all of his might to make the right people take this threat seriously—became his life's mission.

CHAPTER 5

THE WORLD'S FIRST AIRCRAFT CARRIER

December 1923

The earthquake had devastated the housing stock all over the Tokyo region, including the area where most of the foreigners lived in Yokohama. But eventually, late in the year, the Rutlands finally arranged to go to Japan. They took the train to Marseilles, where they boarded the *Kaisar-i-Hind*. Trailing them was a British agent, who confirmed Rutland's plans by calling the steamboat company. In his report sent back to London, the agent included disparaging comments about Rutland in general, noting that he was traveling with his "supposed wife."

When the *Kaisar-i-Hind* arrived in Yokohama harbor, the Rutlands, coming down the gangplank, were immediately overwhelmed by the sights, sounds, and smells of this new and very foreign land. Rutland thought it seemed like a fascinating sort of orderly, clean chaos. With bicycles and rickshaw taxis whirring about everywhere, the Rutlands were greeted in style, with several Mitsubishi employees waiting to take them to the Yokohama Grand hotel for their first night in Japan.

...

For the short term, Mitsubishi rented the Rutlands a large villa in Kamakura. The house had room for their two children, and more space for the additional children they planned to have when they were able to be legally married. Rutland had an upstairs office that served as a home workshop for his wireless sets. Kamakura is just across the hill from the main Japanese naval base in Yokosuka, and many Japanese naval officers lived there; it is still popular with today's naval officers. If anyone asked, Rutland could say that he lived there because of the limited availability of suitable housing in the foreign colony due to the earthquake. What he didn't mention was that living near the Japanese naval officers allowed him to meet with them frequently, and since it was far from Yokohama, the British likely wouldn't notice these meetings.

Rutland and Dorothy did go to the foreign colony in Yokohama almost every weekend. It was an hour away by car, but Rutland enjoyed the drive behind the wheel of a Chrysler, cruising around at speeds that rivaled the Short Pusher seaplane he'd piloted early in the war.

The first director of MI5, Colonel Sir Vernon Kell, was referred to in the British Intelligence fashion simply as "K."* K assigned a British military officer, Francis Stewart Gilderoy "Roy" Piggott, to watch Rutland after his arrival. Piggott was immediately suspicious. Zooming around Japan in his new imported car, Rutland gave the distinct impression that he was a wealthy man—wealthier than one would expect. Piggott noted that Dorothy was from a very accomplished family and was potentially subsidizing their lifestyle, but Rutland's conspicuous display of affluence convinced him someone other than Mitsubishi was also paying Rutland. In his report, he noted with disdain that Dorothy referred to herself as "Mrs. Rutland," even though they were not married. Piggott also noted that "Rutland talks a lot and will no doubt be giving himself away soon."

Soon, Dorothy was expecting a child, a boy whom they named David. And later that year, Rutland's divorce came through, finalized on grounds of adultery, which allowed the couple to finally marry. The youngest child, a girl named Annabel, was born in 1926. One day, Rutland had a

---

* "M" in the James Bond series was partially modeled on "K."

photographer take a picture of year-and-a-half-old Annabel in a kimono. He treasured this picture, carrying it with him for much of his life. While Dorothy was busy with the children, Rutland went to the Mitsubishi office in Tokyo two or three times a week.

It would have been illegal for Rutland to have been working for the Japanese Navy; hence, Rutland's agreement with the Royal Air Force that he was working for Mitsubishi. Despite this, Rutland was indeed working for the Japanese Navy. He was coaching them on how to make their carriers better.

To keep it secret, Torao Kuwabara, the head pilot of the Japanese Navy, visited the Rutland house at least once a week with other colleagues for the better part of a year. In his memoirs, which are far out of print and appear to exist in just a few copies, he explained that, by having Rutland live far away from Yokohama, and by having him and his colleagues visit Rutland while wearing civilian clothes, they were able to avoid attention. These tactics appear to have worked, as the British never learned about this work with the Japanese Navy. Rutland coached Kuwabara and his staff on how to update the design of aircraft carrier *Hosho* and two new carriers being constructed, *Akagi* and *Kaga* (the two ships that Admiral Yamamoto would eventually use to lead the Pearl Harbor attack). The planes were getting faster and heavier, and the design of the ships needed to solve the existing problems with crashing on landing and adapt to a different kind of plane.

In his memoirs, Kuwabara noted that "Rutland's help was invaluable."

Kuwabara also introduced Rutland to an impressive young entrepreneur. Shiro Kayaba, only twenty-two years old, had started a company that was making landing gear for the Japanese Navy planes. After the deaths of Dunning and others on carrier landings several years before, Rutland had performed experiments with manufacturers such as Oleo, becoming perhaps the world's leading expert on landing gear. Rutland took the train to Kayaba's new workshop in eastern Tokyo, and the two of them had a great time playing around with prototypes in Kayaba's workshop. Rutland concluded that Kayaba was one of the best engineers he had ever met—even better than himself. Kayaba had lost his first workshop in the fire after the big earthquake the prior year and needed cash to expand. Rutland made an angel investment in Kayaba's company, pulling in a Mitsui company for some extra funds. Kayaba used those funds to expand his manufacturing.

One of the few wireless stores in Japan was located just across from Tokyo station in the upscale Marunouchi Building, which had been recently built by a real estate division of Mitsubishi. After his workday at Mitsubishi was finished, Rutland often visited the shop to see if any new radios had come in. On one visit, a Japanese man approached him and said hello in English. Rutland assumed the man simply wanted to practice a few words of English, an experience as familiar to English-speaking foreigners in Japan in 1923 as it is in modern times. But it turned out the man already spoke fluent English. The man introduced himself to Rutland as Mr. Kikuchi and told Rutland he was interested in getting into the wireless business. The conversation concluded with an agreement to have Rutland import wireless sets, which Kikuchi would distribute locally. Kikuchi was one of four brothers from Nagoya, two of whom also founded a predecessor firm to Fujifilm.

After a year, the Rutlands finally moved to Yokohama, after building an extremely impressive house on one of the best locations on the bluff, with a commanding view of the harbor half a block up from the foreign cemetery. Rutland's secret meetings helping the Japanese Navy design its carriers had mostly wrapped up, so he no longer needed to live somewhere where the British wouldn't notice who he was meeting. His work with Kayaba on landing gear was in the open and legitimate. The Rutlands rapidly became good friends with their next-door neighbors, who were also a young British couple. The wife was very impressed with both and wrote about them to her mother in England. She said that Rutland and Dorothy made an impression—Rutland, not tall, but strong, with his piercing blue-green eyes and dimples. Dorothy was striking, with jet-black hair and dark eyes, giving her "the look of an Italian." She also added, "If Rutland was with you in England, I'm sure he would flirt with you."

...

On March 8, 1925, the British agent F. S. G. Piggott visited a Japanese military parade in Yoyogi and was rather surprised to see the Rutlands there, and Rutland sitting with Kuwabara in the VIP seats. Piggott later visited the Rutlands and asked some piercing questions. He wasn't entirely satisfied with the answers and sent a report to MI5 in the UK. K thanked Piggott for the report on Rutland, and inquired into the status of the tortoiseshell eyeglass frames that Piggott was trying to find for him.

K eventually got his Japanese eyeglass frames. He also now had a good idea of Japan's espionage strategy, and it was concerning. The Japanese Navy appeared to be pulling out all the stops to use espionage, bribery, and legal methods to obtain technical information on the most advanced and newest ships and planes. The Scottish noble William Francis Forbes-Sempill, back in the United Kingdom, seemed to continue to be passing secrets to the Japanese. But Rutland was still there in Japan, in person, and appeared to be a key player in modernizing the Japanese Navy. Knowing Rutland's reputation as a genius designer of aircraft carriers and parts of planes, it was a big concern. K noticed that Rutland's file was getting larger and larger, but there was nothing the British found that was illegal.

For now, there was nothing the British could do about Rutland.

The publicity-loving Rutland was back on that very delicate tightrope that he liked. He was working with visionary admirals, impacting future world events, and tricking most people into thinking he was a high-class, respectable, upstanding person.

CHAPTER 6

GEISHA PARTY

July 1924

Rutland was on the deck of the newly renovated aircraft carrier *Hosho* as it steamed into the wind. The men watched the four biplanes take off uneventfully, but that wasn't surprising. The takeoff was almost always smooth. The hard part was the landing. Landing a rickety wood-and-canvas plane safely onto a moving ship's deck was not easy. All of the men had lost friends in landing accidents.

The other men on the deck were in Japanese Navy uniforms, including Rutland's business partner, Shiro Kayaba, who had been temporarily commissioned into the Japanese Navy for this project. Rutland was also there, in his double-breasted suit.

The planes didn't go very far or very fast, but they didn't need to. The purpose of this exercise was to see if they could land safely in the light wind that was blowing. The planes circled around a bit before briefly going out of sight as they looped back around to land on the ship from the stern.

The men moved toward the back of the ship and looked into the sky. It wasn't long before they saw the lead plane as a speck in the distance—a couple of the men pointed and gave a shout. The line of four biplanes gradually approached at landing speed, not much over forty miles per hour. They were new Mitsubishi 2MT1 biplanes. The planes had been designed by Herbert Smith, and they had British Napier Lion engines, but they were otherwise all Japanese, fresh from the Mitsubishi factory in Nagoya. The pilots were also all Japanese.

The first plane came in slowly, easily, and touched down, coming straight down the centerline of the deck. Rutland's eyes were briefly pulled up to see the red circle logo, the same circle on the Japanese flag, seeming to glow on the side of the plane, before noting with satisfaction that the shock-absorbing landing gear worked perfectly. The plane barely bounced at all as it caught the horizontal wires, slowed, and then stopped. Rutland's mind briefly flashed back to the Great War, when pilots like his late rival Dunning had been killed by their planes bouncing and blowing overboard.

The men on the deck helped pull the first plane to the side to make way for the next three—they all came down for perfect landings in quick succession. The pilots climbed out of the open cockpits. The first pilot was Rutland's friend Kuwabara, who was exuberant as he swung his legs over the side and onto the lower wing before he climbed down onto the deck. All the planes looked good. Later, Rutland, Kayaba, and Kuwabara would inspect the planes, with special attention paid to the landing gears back at Kayaba's workshop. But first, the officers and men lined up on the deck and gave the traditional raised-arms shout of "Banzai!" three times.

The Hosho docked back at Yokosuka with the officers and men in high spirits. That evening, a navy driver brought a small party a short way and pulled up to a newly renovated and luxurious private restaurant. Emerging from one of the cars were Rutland, Kayaba, and Kuwabara. Emerging from another car was Captain Isoroku Yamamoto, now commander of the Yokosuka district, the leading proponent of air power in the Japanese Navy. As one might expect for a restaurant beloved by the navy, it was on a bluff overlooking the ocean.

As they emerged, Kuwabara said, "Rutland-san, I am happy to be able to take you here. This is your first time at Komatsu since its reconstruction, right?" Rutland nodded, commenting that it was an honor to be taken to such a famous place.

As they walked in, they were greeted by two kimono-clad women. Rutland knew the elegant woman of about seventy to be the owner. Her name was also Komatsu; she had named the restaurant after her geisha name. He didn't know who the other woman was, but in looking twice, she was actually a girl who appeared to be about fifteen years old. The girl was clearly working with Komatsu and was of higher status than the servants. The men removed their boots, which a servant took away. As they stepped up into the restaurant, Komatsu escorted them to the large room on the second floor and closed the shoji screen, giving them complete privacy.

As the men sat down on the floor, the shoji screen on the other side slid open, and a younger woman appeared, kneeling with a tray. She bowed deeply, touching her head to the tatami floor as she apologized for bothering them. She and another servant brought in the first round of drinks and light food, then backed away to where they had entered, again touching their heads to the floor as they closed the shoji screen behind them.

Kuwabara explained to Rutland that the young hostess was Komatsu's grandniece. In the fashion of Japanese family businesses, Komatsu had adopted her as her daughter, and was grooming her to take over the place when Komatsu retired.

Kuwabara explained to Rutland about the renovation of Komatsu and the decorations in the room. One of the hanging scrolls on the wall, he mentioned, was written by Admiral Tōgō. As the drinks and food arrived, little by little, the party started to get more and more boisterous. Kuwabara repeated that he was so happy that the planes landed on the ship. The men laughed, a bit nervously. It was emotional. Landing was still going to be the most dangerous part of carrier aviation, but it would be an acceptable risk going forward. Yamamoto then stressed that, thanks to the contributions of the men there, including Rutland, the future of the Japanese Navy was now clear. The next war would not be fought by battleships, but by aircraft flying from ships. The current planes may be small and slow, he said, but that would improve step by step—it was inevitable. The Japanese Navy, with Rutland's help, was to be a key influencer in global events. They toasted to their success.

Yamamoto had Rutland tell them a World War I story about attacking

German airships. In return, Rutland asked Yamamoto about his time at Harvard. Yamamoto's English was stunningly good after two years in the US, and Rutland asked what the key to his mastery of English was. Yamamoto told him that it was all because of poker.

"Poker?" asked Rutland.

"That's right," said Yamamoto. "Not only did I learn a lot of very basic English from playing poker with my Harvard classmates, but I learned even more when I won all of their money, and more than that when I used their money to subsidize my hitchhiking trip across the USA, before heading back to Japan!"

The men had a toast to Rutland and Kayaba for their hard work on the landing gear. Kuwabara also made a toast to Rutland for his advice on the redesign of the carriers. Kuwabara added that, now that the project was done, he wouldn't need to visit Rutland's house as often. Chuckling, he said, "I bet your wife will likely be happy about that."

A group of geisha had joined the party, pouring drinks for the men and encouraging the conversation. None of the geisha spoke English, although during pauses in the men's conversation, several tried the one phrase they knew to use on foreign clients, *Ai rabu yu* (I love you), which was a hit with Rutland as with everyone else. Rutland wondered idly if the geisha understood their pronunciation of "love" sounded like "rub" to an English speaker.

Kuwabara confirmed that based on this success, the navy would be increasing their orders from Kayaba. Kayaba and his main investor, Rutland, would be profiting handsomely from the navy sales. Rutland and Kayaba had jointly filed a patent on landing gear, ensuring that these contracts with the Japanese Navy would be locked in and the company would scale.

Kuwabara leaned over to Rutland, looking approvingly at one of the geisha. "Rutland-san," he said, "what do you like better? Japanese women or English women?"

Rutland replied, "I like all of them!" The men all laughed. "The only problem with English women here in Japan, though, is there are so few, and they are all married!"

Yamamoto chuckled. After a couple of years in Boston, Rutland's English accent sounded funny to him. He turned to Rutland and said, "Well, in that case, why don't you have a Japanese one?" Yamamoto chuckled again, as he said, "You can choose one. But not here. It would have to be a different class of establishment." Yamamoto explained, somewhat conspiratorially, "It is possible, in theory, for a foreigner to have a relationship with a real geisha. But perhaps it would not be wise to try. Furthermore, the young woman is the adopted daughter of the owner. Don't look at her! Komatsu-san might not like that. And by the way, don't look at Komatsu either. She is too old!"

More laughter rang out, and the drinks flowed until the sun rose over the Land of the Rising Sun.

CHAPTER 7

THE POKER GAME

1928

"Gentlemen do not read each other's mail," said the US secretary of state, Henry Stimson. The officers of the US Navy's Office of Naval Intelligence, on hearing this, would perhaps have just decided they were not gentlemen. Or they might have noted that their star cryptanalyst, Agnes Meyer Driscoll, was not by any means a gentleman—in fact, she was a woman. Driscoll and Joseph Rochefort had just broken yet another Japanese Navy code, known as the Red Book Code, in 1926, and the information they got was outstanding. The navy would not stop trying to read Japanese mail, no matter what the secretary of state said. Right after they broke the Red Code, the codebreakers in room 2646 at the Navy Department got a new superior officer—Commander Ellis Zacharias, who was most recently captain of the destroyer USS *McCormick*.

Zacharias found codebreaking fascinating, and rather different than he expected. It sounded glamorous on the surface, but he rapidly found that codebreakers, an introverted lot, were just quietly hammering away at puzzles all day long. They worked on stacks of indexed sheets, with the quiet look of concentration of those doing a crossword, full-time, nights, weekends, forgetting to eat, all in service of trying to crack some very high-stakes puzzles. Some of them had electronic machines, running numbers, others just pencil and paper. The stacks of paper with random figures looked disorganized, but they were not.

Zacharias stressed that even the best codebreakers can't tell everything about an enemy just from intercepting their radio communications. There was context, understanding the situation, understanding about the people quoted in the intercepts, that was needed to paint the entire picture of the enemy's movements. This need for context was why Zacharias was assigned to the job. It was a perfect fit: Zacharias was a fluent speaker of Japanese, ex-resident of Yokohama, poker-playing partner of Japanese admirals, and experienced navy sailor. With these talents, he took messages that Driscoll had decoded and used his knowledge to fill in the background, interpret what the Japanese were doing in context, and add actionable insights for the navy.

The chatty and extroverted Zacharias was initially taken aback by the codebreaking office being so quiet. They were content to work for their country quietly and intensely, knowing they would likely forever remain anonymous. Zacharias's wife, Claire, joked that she was impressed that he was able to successfully tone down his personality to work in an office where barely anyone talked. Postwar, Zacharias reverted to his more natural style, even hosting a TV program on espionage, but he was able to restrain his natural style short-term to make his stint overseeing codebreaking a success.

On a couple of occasions, Zacharias and Claire were invited to parties at the Japanese embassy. The parties were formal, and the Japanese there were traditional, a bit stilted, and liked to ask Zacharias obvious, transactional questions. *What is your new job, Commander Zacharias?* or *How is the accuracy of the new American battleship guns?* He chuckled at the interrogation. Their lines of questioning were unoriginal and unlikely to get him to give them any secrets.

One day, Zacharias went home after a tiring day at the office. He wanted nothing better than a peaceful dinner and to play a bit with his son, Ellis Jr. But Claire greeted him at the door, saying, "There was an unusual phone call for you. A Japanese named Yamamoto, who said you were old friends from when we were in Yokohama."

"Yamamoto?" he replied. Yamamoto was a somewhat common name, and he knew more than one. But he realized which Yamamoto it must be. "The navy captain?" he asked.

"I believe so. He was very chatty, and we had quite a long conversation. He said to apologize for calling you here at the house, but that it was the only way he could find you. He also wanted to invite you to his place for some drinks and a card game."

"Oh . . ." Zacharias took this news in. Of course, there was no phone number listed for the codebreaking office, so that was why Yamamoto couldn't have reached him at work. It was clear the Japanese had been observing him and knew what type of role he played.

He called Yamamoto back to see what he had in mind. Yamamoto and Zacharias didn't know each other all that well in the past, but Zacharias knew that Yamamoto had a reputation for being smarter, a freer thinker, and even more aggressive than the other Japanese naval officers, and he also knew he was destined to be one of the top leaders of the Japanese Navy. Yamamoto was also committed to aircraft, when many of his peers in the Japanese Navy could only think about battleships. The party, said Yamamoto, would be different from those hosted by Yamamoto's predecessors, since Yamamoto had come to DC on his own, leaving his wife and child back in Japan. Therefore, Yamamoto explained, he was not inviting Zacharias to a formal party, since he had no wife there to act as a hostess. So it would be a more intimate gathering—just a few men, cocktails, and a deck of cards.

Other US Navy officers had already noticed that Yamamoto asked piercing and insightful questions, in a very different way from his predecessors. Instead of asking about numbers of ships or range of guns, Yamamoto—a firm believer in the power of aircraft carriers, back to his days overseeing Kuwabara and Rutland's efforts—would ask strategic questions on topics like carrier operations strategy or the merits of torpedo bombers versus regular bombers. Yamamoto didn't bother with low-level questions, since he had assigned those to his junior staff.

Zacharias approached Yamamoto's apartment in the Alban Towers with a bit of trepidation. Yamamoto opened the door, and sure enough, it was the same stocky, dark-browed man he had met in Japan a decade earlier. Yamamoto greeted him with his wide smile, but Zacharias felt a note of condescension visible even when he was smiling. Yamamoto escorted him inside and offered him cocktails. The drinking was moderate. A junior officer put out a mixture of Japanese and American dishes. Yamamoto looked eager to play—the table was barely cleared when the card game started. Yamamoto's bids and bluffs were interspersed with questions about naval matters, but at first the inquiries were subtle.

Yamamoto was missing two fingers on his right hand. The way Yamamoto flipped through the cards with the remaining fingers was uncanny. He seemed to revel in showing off this skill. One of the other Americans complimented him on it, and he laughed out loud, explaining that the missing fingers were the result of a Russian shell that hit the Japanese flagship, *Mikasa*, during the Russo-Japanese War. Zacharias noticed Yamamoto's smirk as he reminded the Americans that this was the battle where they "sent the enemy ships to the bottom."

Zacharias's mind wandered back to discussions he had in Japan with Japanese naval officers. Yamamoto was more aggressive than the others, but in a way, all the Japanese naval officers were aggressive. It was the training they received at the Japanese Naval Academy at Etajima, he thought, that focused on the history of the Japanese Navy, proper etiquette, and offense. The lessons also emphasized that it would be an honor for a Japanese naval officer to sacrifice his life for his country. In some countries, those lessons might have been just for show. Zacharias, however, knew the Japanese did everything to an extreme, and it didn't bode well for a future of peace.

Zacharias was extremely good at poker. His game with Yamamoto was different. He noted, "Unlike most Japanese, who feel that they lose face when defeated even in a harmless card game and are usually embarrassed, Yamamoto appreciated my attempts to beat him. I found him a man of open challenge and a lover of combat."

Zacharias added that in these games, "I first recognized the direction Japan was taking in her naval development. The aircraft carrier, the combination of sea power and air power, was an obsession with Yamamoto. Even at this early time, it was easy to see exactly how Yamamoto would attack an enemy, such as the US, with carrier aircraft."

Later, when Zacharias mentioned the Japanese threat to his superiors in the navy or elsewhere in the US government, he felt ignored. He thought they were totally blind to the possibility of war, and it was eating at him.

A month later, upon returning to his office after another card game, Zacharias's mind returned to how best to counter Japanese espionage threats. Yamamoto and his staff at the Japanese embassy asked questions to learn about the US Navy. They didn't do anything egregious, but even if they did, they had diplomatic immunity and therefore couldn't be arrested. However, he anticipated the Japanese would send spies to the US, and the navy wasn't particularly staffed or chartered to deal with them. When this did happen, he would need the help of the FBI to address it.

Zacharias requested a meeting with FBI director J. Edgar Hoover to discuss the topic. Hoover would reign in this job for over fifty years but, at the time, was still new to the position.

Zacharias opined to Hoover that "Japan is going to emerge as the largest threat to the United States."

Hoover laughed at the comment. He asked if Zacharias really thought the US was more at risk from Japan than it was from the communists? From gang warfare in Chicago? Or the bank robbers running across the United States?

Zacharias felt his blood boil and he leaned forward. He was used to having to convince people about Japan, but he was not used to being laughed at. Getting heated, he replied that "bank robbers were a problem, but not a threat to the United States like Japan would be."

After a minute of this exchange, Hoover summoned one of his larger assistants. Just ten minutes into the scheduled hour-long meeting, the man grabbed Zacharias's arm and escorted him out of Hoover's office.

Zacharias didn't forget this insult, and Hoover's low opinion of Zacharias percolated through the FBI a decade later when the navy and the FBI should have been working together to anticipate a coming Japanese attack.

CHAPTER 8

THE ATTEMPTED ASSASSINATION OF CHARLIE CHAPLIN

May 1932

Charlie Chaplin was visiting Japan with a group that included his brother Sydney Chaplin, and Chaplin's Japanese personal secretary, Toraichi Kono. Chaplin had been to Japan a decade earlier for work, when he and Fatty Arbuckle performed in a silent comedy show. This time, the purpose of the trip was purely pleasure. The group spent their time in Japan seeing traditional Japanese art, attending performances of Japanese dance, observing traditional craftsmen at work, and viewing the natural beauty of locations such as Miyanoshita and Mount Fuji.

Japan's prime minister, Tsuyoshi Inukai, had arranged for his son to take Chaplin and his party to watch a sumo wrestling match. They took a place of honor in the front row and marveled at the spectacle of the immense men in their loincloths crashing into each other. During one bout, they heard screams and commotion from an entrance above. Turning around, they saw armed soldiers pushing their way through the mass of spectators toward their seats. The soldiers looked serious and surrounded them but didn't appear threatening. Everyone was shouting. Not understanding anything being said, the Chaplins were a bit scared, but it ultimately seemed that the soldiers were there to protect them. As they were being escorted toward the exit by the soldiers, Chaplin demanded, "Kono, what on earth is happening?"

Kono said, "They say we are in danger, sir, and we need to come with them for our safety." Chaplin saw shock on the face of their host, the young Inukai. It was the face of a young man who has just been told his father has been killed. The Chaplin party was promptly escorted back to the Imperial Hotel via taxi. As they looked out the car window, they saw soldiers running around all over the city.

Prime Minister Inukai had been assassinated in an attempted coup. The prime minister's assassins were a group of young officers from the Japanese Navy. They thought the prime minister needed to die because he didn't believe enough in militarism and hadn't funded the navy enough.

The coup attempt went no further, and the assassins were arrested. Later, they told the court more about their goals. They wanted to start a war between Japan and the United States, immediately—believing that if they had been able to kill Charlie Chaplin, the United States would be so angry it would have caused a war to erupt between Japan and the United States.

Chaplin was rattled that he had been targeted for assassination. He was also very confused, because he thought the assassins made no sense at all. He couldn't see America fighting another country over any celebrity. But it made no sense on a more basic level. He noted that "they wanted a war with America, but I'm British. I'm not even American." He wasn't sure that most Japanese understood that point. It was clear that the assassins didn't like the twin foreign influences of Hollywood movies and jazz music. They wanted the populace angry at the West, and that narrative was threatened by a wildly popular Westerner—Chaplin—coming to Japan to make people laugh.

Chaplin and his party briefly remained in Japan to give further statements to the police and personally pay his condolences to the prime minister's family before taking a ship home to Los Angeles.

The assassins' plot illustrated that, at this early date—almost a decade before Pearl Harbor—many in Japan were seeing war with America as inevitable. Strikingly, the assassins were members of the Japanese Navy. It seems the Japanese Navy—the organization that eventually led the attack against the United States at Pearl Harbor—was mentally preparing itself for war, so much so that some young officers had decided it was worth committing political assassination to help make that war happen.

Another alarming sign was how much enthusiastic public support the assassins received. The court received a petition with tens of thousands of signatures to have them declared innocent. A group of youths offered the court to take the place of the assassins in the courtroom—an offer coupled with one finger of each petitioner pickled in a jar, as a demonstration of their sincerity.

The light sentences the assassins eventually received were an indirect sign that Japan's march toward war would continue, and that the government's control over the military was not strong.*

Zacharias was at sea when he first heard about the incident, and it made further alarm bells go off in his head. The incident was evidence that Japanese society was taking a step forward toward the consensus that war with the United States would come—a sentiment that would snowball, little by little, until war finally broke out.

Before leaving Japan, Chaplin's mind wandered to the dinner he had with his brother Sydney and Kono the night before the assassination. During the meal, six young men entered. One sat next to Kono. There was some talk of dishonor and insult, something about ancestors and pictures painted on silk—Chaplin couldn't quite recall. What he did remember was how scared Kono looked. Kono—tall, distinguished, well-dressed— was normally cool as a cucumber. Chaplin wondered if this incident was related to the assassination attempt.

The Hiroshima-born Toraichi Kono had been hired by Chaplin fifteen years before and had driven Chaplin's car and acted in a couple of films

---

* As this chapter was being written, ex–prime minister Shinzo Abe of Japan was assassinated. Abe's assassin's stated goal was to stop the Japanese ruling party from being influenced by a cult with ties to North Korea, and strikingly the assassination appears to have achieved its goal.

before Chaplin made him his personal assistant. He fit the image Chaplin wanted to project to the world. When Kono had first arrived at Chaplin's house for a job interview, dressed in a double-breasted suit and hat, Chaplin took one look at him and exclaimed, "You are smart!"

By the early 1920s, Kono was managing Chaplin's household, bringing in Japanese maids, butlers, gardeners, and chefs. Chaplin's reliance on Kono only increased his fondness for the Japanese. People would ask Chaplin why there were so many Japanese around, and he explained that Japanese servants were superior. For example, Japanese servants got the broom into each corner of the room, unlike their American counterparts, who merely moved the dirt around by sweeping in a circle in the middle.

There was another reason Chaplin preferred Japanese servants: their loyalty and discretion. There seemed to be very little risk that Kono or his Japanese staff would talk to the press. Chaplin perceived Japanese people to be inherently loyal—much more so than Americans, who would sell someone out to the press for a few bucks. In the case of Kono, perhaps his loyalty stemmed from the fact that he was the younger son of a samurai family. Kono himself spoke excellent English, but most of the servants could not. Ambitious gossip columnists were constantly trying to bribe servants to get information on Chaplin and other actors. But it was almost impossible for them to get information from his non-English-speaking staff, who lived in the closed Japanese society in the Little Tokyo section of Los Angeles.

The power of the press to bring down celebrities was terrifying to most of Hollywood. A decade earlier, Chaplin had been shocked at the media circus around his friend Fatty Arbuckle, who had been the second-biggest star in Hollywood after Chaplin. Arbuckle's movie career was destroyed when he was accused of murder after a young woman died in his hotel room after one of his parties. Arbuckle was eventually acquitted, but it didn't matter. His murder case had been front-page news for months, and no movie studio would give him a contract again.

Chaplin was himself the victim of a media frenzy during his divorce from Lita Grey, but his career somehow survived. Lita's accusations had been so salacious that newsboys sold pamphlets on the street describing her side of the story. The stories seemed to be exaggerated, but the basic facts of the situation were bad enough. Chaplin and Grey had gotten married when she was just sixteen. And it was worse than just that—it turned out they had gotten married because she was pregnant. Even more scandalously, the wedding had taken place in Mexico because underage marriage was legal south of the border, but was not legal in California. But somehow, Chaplin emerged from the Grey divorce as big a star as ever.

To date, Chaplin had escaped a career-ending scandal through a combination of good timing and even better luck. But it seemed like it might be just a matter of time. Chaplin's affair with Grey was not an aberration. He had a reputation for liking young teen girls. Chaplin, like many celebrities in Hollywood, had no trouble finding romantic partners, but even the most untouchable celebrities normally wouldn't pursue sexual liaisons with minors, which risked not just scandal, but potential arrest. Chaplin's focus was how to prevent media leaks. For that, he was able to lean on the discreet Kono and his non-English-speaking staff.

There had been other close calls. A decade earlier, Chaplin had been a guest on William Randolph Hearst's yacht when one of the other guests, a movie producer named Thomas Ince, mysteriously died. No one seemed to know how the man had died, and the other guests weren't talking. Some of the gossip columnists wrote that it was an accidental shooting, at the hand of Hearst himself, who was really targeting Chaplin over an affair he'd had with Hearst's paramour, Marion Davies.

Kono yet again helped Chaplin make the best of a potentially disastrous situation. Amidst the confusion of the dead man on the yacht, Kono appeared at the dock after racing down from Los Angeles, collected Chaplin, and escorted him away before most of the press could appear. The official cause of death of the movie producer was that he was eating salted almonds with a peptic ulcer. Scandal handled.

Chaplin kept Kono extremely busy, working him seven days a week.

At first, Kono was thrilled to work for Chaplin. He had left Japan fifteen years earlier after a dispute with his father, and now he was a player in some of the most privileged circles in the entire world. He himself was a minor celebrity in Hollywood and in the smaller community of Little Tokyo. However, Chaplin was known to be detail-oriented to the point of perfectionism in his films, and he was similarly demanding on Kono around every last detail of his work. Slowly, the demands of working for Chaplin began to eat at him. At some point, he started to feel he wouldn't be able to take the abuse anymore.

CHAPTER 9

THE 1932 SUMMER OLYMPICS

Summer 1932

Two months after Chaplin left Japan to come back to Hollywood, he was one of over one hundred thousand excited spectators cheering the opening ceremony of the tenth Olympiad, the 1932 Los Angeles Summer Olympics.

Kono dropped Chaplin and a female companion at the VIP entrance of the Los Angeles Coliseum where they met newspaper publisher William Randolph Hearst and his mistress, Marion Davies. They walked over and took their places in the front row, but Chaplin felt strangely anonymous for a brief moment. Most people in the massive stadium didn't know they were there, because they were mixed in a mottled sprawl of athletes, dignitaries, singers, soldiers, and actors. Somehow, Hearst had gotten over the issues involving the love triangle with Davies, and the two celebrities enjoyed each other's company.

Chaplin repeatedly looked around in wonder at the spectacle and pageantry brought out by the Olympic games. He'd spent his entire career pursuing this sort of opulence.

Years in the making, the 1932 Summer Olympic Games were a coming-out party for the rapidly growing city of Los Angeles. The studio heads and real estate developers wanted desperately to turn Los Angeles, once a backwater of a city of back lots and naval bases, into a metropolis worthy of London, Paris, and New York. What had started as impromptu conversations at the Los Angeles Athletic Club, where Chaplin had briefly lived, had come to life. Billy Garland, the club's president, couldn't stop selling the Olympics—forcing it into existence through a combination of adman and mobster tactics, all flair and flex, the only way to get anything done in this city. Garland couldn't talk about anything else, insisting to Chaplin and other club members—Douglas Fairbanks, Rudolph Valentino, and Al Jolson among them—how he was going to turn the frontier into a fantasy. And, by God, he'd done it.

Everything Chaplin saw, everything he felt, was the pinnacle of the past decade, a period of maneuvering and muscling when his adopted city oversaw a period of rapid development and burgeoning industrialization. Los Angeles was alive, shiny, and new, a star on the red carpet, bursting with excitement and possibility. And, like everything else in Hollywood, it was a masterful mirage, a temporary distraction from a more disquieting reality. Outside the walls of the Coliseum, the crown jewel of the tenth Olympiad, the Great Depression was impossible to ignore. Nearly one-third of the entire population of California was unemployed, and evicted families dragged their belongings up and down city sidewalks, past soup kitchens, and, increasingly, shantytowns. They were unaware of a world beyond these issues—still far away, across the Atlantic and the Pacific Oceans—and rising militarization.

Looking across the infield of the stadium, Chaplin could see the flags of fifty different countries, flapping proudly above the crowd. The white banner stamped with a red circle caught Chaplin's eye. It was the handsome standard of Imperial Japan. Many of the European countries found it hard to send large numbers of athletes all the way to Los Angeles. However, the relatively close country of Japan had been able to send a large contingent to the Los Angeles Olympics.

Prior to the 1932 Summer Olympics, Japan was somewhat of a mystery to Americans—so far away, so different. Many Americans only thought of Japan as a romantic, beautiful place of geisha and Mount Fuji. Despite being the recent target of an assassination plot, Chaplin was still in that camp. He thought the appreciation for beauty and the perfection of the artisans of Japan was unmatched anywhere in the world. His tramp character carried a cane, which was always Japanese-made, because he felt Japanese artisans simply made better canes than any other country. He loved the Japanese tea ceremony because it revealed a philosophy of life that beautifies the simple action of preparing tea to please the senses. More than anything, he still believed these kinds of things revealed the peaceful character and soul of the nation. But maybe this was true only of old Japan, and modern Japan was a terrible beauty still waiting to be born.

To those in the US Navy and some government circles, Japan was considered a distant, but approaching, threat. The loudest and most influential voice warning Americans about the threat from Japan was the man sitting with Chaplin at the Olympics, William Randolph Hearst. Hearst's editorials on the subject were occasionally objective coverage of possible Japanese militarism mixed with speculation about what Japan was doing in the Mandates, the islands where the American marine had mysteriously died. But Hearst often devolved into ugly racial attacks. Even during World War I, Hearst had financed a movie that had as its plot Japanese officers leading Mexican soldiers in an invasion of California, with an even uglier underlying theme of the nonwhite soldiers threatening the virtue of white women. Hearst's stated opinion at that time was that it was wrong for America to join a war against the Germans, who were white, and that the country should save spending American blood and treasure for future wars with the nonwhite races.

Following the Olympics, from faraway London, was Frederick Rutland. Rutland was working a fairly uninteresting desk job, and the Olympic coverage on the BBC hit on the sorts of high-class spectacles he found exciting—with sport, that enviable California weather, movie stars, and even the Japanese.

In addition to Chaplin, Hearst, and their dates, the one hundred thousand people at the opening ceremony of the Olympics included a Japanese man named Takuya Torii. Torii had arranged to stay in Los Angeles for a few months, after which he would move to Palo Alto to begin his studies at

Stanford University in the fall semester. He had been hand selected by the Japanese director of naval intelligence, Shigetarō Shimada, to be the first agent to be sent to America in a new effort to prepare for the upcoming war between Japan and the United States.

Torii was a surface warfare officer and destroyer captain, not a spy, so he had no real training on how to do the job. It wasn't just Torii who was unprepared; actually, no Japanese naval officer had formal training in espionage. Since he had no trained spies, Shimada decided to do something similar to what he had done himself in England. He selected naval academy graduates who he assumed were bright and flexible and who he believed would be able to figure out what was needed to do effective espionage.

The curriculum at Japanese Naval Academy at Etajima was influenced by the British advisors to the Japanese Navy, so was similar to what Royal Navy cadets had received—this didn't include instruction on espionage. However, the Japanese naval cadets did have one notable class that was rather different from anything British cadets learned. They had a class on ninjutsu, the art of being a ninja. Ninjas in popular culture seem to be similar to spies in some ways, but the class was more about stealth and weapons, rather than intelligence itself.

Shimada had empathized with the young naval officers that had assassinated the prime minister two months before. He was also now convinced Japan would eventually enter a war with the United States, and he was keenly aware that espionage had been barely resourced until now and wasn't respected within the Japanese Navy. He noted that when Japanese Navy ships planned an exercise, the plans were approved by the emperor himself, but espionage was so low status that there weren't even any plans to show the emperor.

To prepare for war, the Japanese Navy would have to know its enemy better. To start, Shimada assigned Torii to what he considered to be the most important espionage target, Los Angeles, with its naval base and aircraft factories.

Shimada mentally reviewed the reasons why war with the United States was inevitable. America, it was felt, had insulted Japan many times. For example, in the formation of the League of Nations, there was the stated ideal that all nations were equal, but the US (and Australia) had blocked the proposed racial equality clause in the formation of the league. The United States had blocked immigration from Japan in a racially motivated policy in the 1920s. After Japan invaded Manchuria in 1931, the United States published the Stimson Doctrine, which stated Japan's invasion of Manchuria was illegitimate. The US later pursued this policy in the League of Nations, leading Japan's representative, Matsuoka, to give a fiery speech and lead the Japanese delegation in a walkout from the League.

The US also threatened to terminate its long-standing trade partnership with Japan, a threat the United States would eventually carry out before the close of the decade. The US Navy transferred its Scouting Force from the East Coast to the Los Angeles port of San Pedro, where it joined the Battle Force as part of the United States Fleet, the country's principal naval force.

Immediately after moving to Los Angeles, Torii stayed in Little Tokyo with Dr. Takashi Furusawa and his wife, Sachiko, who jointly ran the local branch of the Japanese Navy Association. Known for her hospitality to visiting sailors, Sachiko earned the nickname "Mom of the Japanese Navy." Furusawa took Torii apartment hunting in San Pedro. There was a Japanese colony in the area at a location called "fish harbor." Japanese fisherman operated their fishing boats out of the harbor, so Torii would blend in, be able to find Japanese food, and meet fellow Japanese people for support.

From his apartment in San Pedro, Torii could walk out of the door and head over to the harbor to observe the US Navy ships. Like all of the Japanese agents, Torii was discouraged from working with Japanese Americans, but some casual chats with Japanese citizen fishermen wouldn't hurt anyone.

Despite his inexperience, Torii was able to walk around the naval docks freely and unnoticed, checking out the US warships as easily as, he often joked, stepping into a movie theater to watch Clark Gable and Jean Harlow in *Red Dust*, or Johnny Weissmuller and Maureen O'Sullivan in *Tarzan*. How unlike his youth in Nagasaki, where the police monitored what everyone was doing, everywhere, at all times. The United States was, indeed, a strange concept, a country built almost entirely on the contradictory impulses of a shared national identity and personal privacy. A grand experiment in self-determination and free enterprise available to most anyone, the freedom of America made it a good place to be a spy, whether its leaders and citizens realized it or not—and Torii was all too willing to capitalize on the situation.

Late on the night of August 22, 1932, just a few days after the closing ceremony of the tenth Olympiad, Torii sped south on the thoroughfare between Little Tokyo and San Pedro, outside the port of Los Angeles. He was returning home from a dinner with Masaki Ogata, a classmate and commander in the Japanese Navy who had been part of a large delegation in town for the Olympics. The two of them had a great time at dinner; Torii was drunk, his brain soaked with sake, and, increasingly, convinced of his own invincibility. He pressed his foot against the accelerator and raced through the vacant streets of Los Angeles County, rushing past the markets, dry-goods stores, and pool halls along the way.

Passing over a raised trolley track, the car went airborne briefly, before landing again in a cloud of dirt. Instinctively, Torii reached across the front seat for his briefcase, which was stuffed with pages of encrypted notes, pictures, and blueprints of the US Pacific Fleet. Regaining control of his car, Torii placed the briefcase on his lap and wiped the sweat beginning to pool on his neck, considering again what exactly he held in his possession.

Torii and Ogata took great pride in their countrymen's showing in the Games, claiming seven gold medals and eighteen medals in total. Japanese swimmers, led by the fifteen-year-old Yasuji Miyazaki, performed exceptionally well. In his semifinal of the 100m freestyle, Miyazaki broke American champion Johnny Weissmuller's Olympic record with a time of

58.2 seconds. After taking home gold in the final, he competed the next day in the 4x200 freestyle relay event. The team set a new world record of 8 minutes and 58.4 seconds, claiming back-to-back golds for Miyazaki. The Japanese felt their success at the Olympics was symbolic of their arrival on the world stage. It was the medals, to be sure, but also the newspaper pictures of the handsome gold-medal winner Baron Nishi mixing at parties with Chaplin, Douglas Fairbanks, and Will Rogers. It all conveyed a new respectability for Japan.

Torii's dining partner, Ogata, was ostensibly in Los Angeles to cheer on the more than one hundred Japanese athletes competing in the Olympics, but the real reason for his visit was far more nefarious. The old shipmates arranged to meet at the Ichifuji restaurant in Little Tokyo. Over food and several rounds of sake, Torii relayed what he had gathered about the US Navy and passed documents to Ogata for him to hand carry to Japanese intelligence back home. In return, Ogata left Torii with an updated list of information he was ordered to find out. The list included the state of training of the US Navy sailors, what new ships were being launched, the accuracy of its gunnery, the attitudes of the US Navy toward Japan, and any new tactics the US was developing.

It was a heady time for Torii. He was growing delirious with the responsibility placed on him. Like never before, he felt aligned with his country and an active participant in its destiny, which stretched out in front of him, as wide open as the deserted streets he now drove through. Excited, he thought about how he would start his mission. First thing in the morning, he would reach out to his mentor and handler, Dr. Furusawa. He would first explain about his dinner with Ogata, then update Furusawa about his new directives and go over plans for reaching out to the people to gather the needed information. Rehearsing what he would say, he took his eyes off the road and, just like that, let destiny slip through his fingers.

A few miles from home, he lost control of his car and crashed into an embankment.

CHAPTER 10

THE FBI AND THE DEAD SPY

1932–33

A phone call about a dead Japanese spy was not something FBI special agent John Hanson was expecting. A native of Minnesota, Hanson defied the stereotype of the taciturn Midwestern Scandinavian and had thrown himself eagerly into the rather glamorous life of a California FBI agent. The FBI seemed to be getting more and more well known all the time; the year before, the agency had been on the lips of much of the United States for its work on the arrests of Al Capone and the kidnapper of the one-year-old son of famous aviator Charles Lindbergh. Hanson noted the impressed look on people's faces when he pulled out his Federal Bureau of Investigation business card.

The focus on press and the image of the FBI came from the top. FBI director J. Edgar Hoover correctly realized that fawning press coverage was good for both his budget and his job security. Every FBI agent was required to be strictly professional, in part to protect the FBI's image.

Hanson needed to ensure his agents wouldn't do anything that would cause negative press for the bureau, and there were any number of reasons his job was more challenging from a PR perspective than his counterparts in other FBI offices. For one, Hoover was not a fan of Hollywood, with its many left-wing and communist-leaning actors. Regardless, the FBI agents needed to tread lightly in Hollywood—with dozens of paparazzi following the actors around, any misstep could hit the national press instantly. The press was always on the lookout for a new story, and

the many foreign spies that the FBI was monitoring in the area were potential catnip for the press as well. An arrest and trial of foreign spies would
need to be done quietly to avoid pulling in the media.

Hanson's agents did occasionally go to the port of San Pedro and its US
Navy base, for reasons that usually didn't include spies. FBI agents near
the harbor were mostly chasing the gangsters that were smuggling cheap
whiskey by ship from Canada into Los Angeles. Sometimes the whiskey
would be off-loaded into small boats; other times it would just be hidden
in a cargo vessel and unloaded with the other cargo in San Pedro, to be
distributed to the raging party scene at places like the Venice speakeasy
the Del Monte or the Belasco or Mayan in the theater district, often via
nearby pharmacies such as Wallgreen Drugs on Broadway.

Hanson's office also spent considerable time chasing anarchists, communists, and other subversive characters who seemed to thrive in the
warm California sun. There was a large office for Intourist, the official
travel agency for anyone who wanted to go visit the Soviet Union. It appeared that office was used more by Soviet spies than actual tourists.

Hanson didn't completely ignore Japan. He had read the frequent anti-
Japanese coverage in newspapers such as William Randolph Hearst's
Examiner, and had followed recent world events, such as the US condemn-
ing the recent Japanese invasion of Manchuria. But, overall, Japan was far
away, Hearst's newspapers were more sensational than anything else, and
the Japanese in San Pedro, like those in Little Tokyo, were largely hard-
working and law-abiding people who kept to themselves.

Hanson's lack of interest in Japan was mainstream in the United States.
To be fair, though, World War II was quite far off. Japan was still eight
full years away from joining the Axis powers, and, for that matter, Hitler
hadn't even come to power in Germany yet.

The Los Angeles Police detective who called Hanson, "Heinie" Heinritz, had quite a tale. They had pulled a dead Japanese person out of a
crashed car, and the man had a briefcase containing all sorts of information about the US Navy. It appeared they'd found a dead Japanese spy.

Heinritz arranged a meeting at the precinct around the corner so that Los Angeles Police, FBI, and the Office of Naval Intelligence could address the issue.

The navy was the most interested in the issue, since they were the ones being spied on. However, the FBI needed to be involved, because the navy had no jurisdiction off of the base. If the navy found a spy stealing information on a ship, or on a naval base, the navy could arrest them—however, anywhere off base, the navy wouldn't legally be able to arrest them, so the FBI was needed. In theory, the Los Angeles Police could also make an arrest of a spy, but they didn't have the means to handle an arrest of that scale—so all parties leaned on Hanson's FBI office.*

The police officers on the scene had followed normal procedures, sending Torii's body to the morgue and taking his possessions to the police station to release to his next of kin. But, the next morning, looking through Torii's wallet and identification, it appeared there was no clear next of kin. Torii lived alone in an apartment and had just come to the US recently. So the LAPD called the Japanese consulate to report a deceased Japanese citizen. The embassy staffer had told the police officer that he needed to consult the consul general, Kageyama, and then would reply.

A few hours later, the precinct got a curious call. It was from Takashi Furusawa, the Japanese doctor who had helped Torii find his apartment. Furusawa, in demanding words, told the lieutenant who answered that he was coming to pick up Torii's briefcase. The officer was immediately suspicious—the tone of the call was rather rude, Furusawa's accent was very strong, and most strangely, Furusawa seemed to be very interested in the briefcase only, but not at all interested in the body. He asked Furusawa exactly who he was and under what authority he was calling.

Quickly realizing that Furusawa was neither a relative nor an official at the consulate, but simply a civilian doctor who said he was a friend, the

---

* Fans of the TV show *NCIS* know that in the 2000s, navy investigators do have jurisdiction to arrest people outside of navy bases. Their predecessors in ONI in the 1930s did not.

lieutenant asked him again exactly who he was and on what authority he wanted to get the briefcase back. There was a proper procedure that the LAPD followed, and items belonging to deceased persons were not released to random callers. If there was no next of kin, they needed to hear from the Japanese consulate itself.

Ignoring this direction, Furusawa called several more times, sounding more and more irate and frantic each time. The officers in the station found the repeated calls rather humorous. Eventually, the police gave Furusawa the briefcase back—but when they did, it was empty. He was angry, but there wasn't anything he could do about it.

Hanson assigned a couple of agents to conduct a formal investigation into Furusawa. They reported that Furusawa was an ob-gyn who had first come to the US in 1906, arriving in San Francisco just before the great earthquake—thousands were killed and some accounts say that nearly 80 percent of the city was destroyed. With his housing in San Francisco caught up in the devastation, he moved to Los Angeles.

The agents confirmed quickly by reading the local Japanese press that Furusawa was head of the local branch of the Japanese Navy Association, which brought together local Japanese VIPs along with visiting Japanese naval officers. His wife, Sachiko, was even more of a die-hard supporter of the Japanese Navy than her husband. She had recently come back from Shanghai, where she delivered presents to Japanese sailors who had been injured in a recent confrontation with Chinese troops. Visiting sailors would very often stay with the Furusawas—or, if they did not, they stayed at the Olympic Hotel, just around the corner.

The conclusion of the agents was twofold:

1. Furusawa was head of a courier system, which allowed mail to be hand delivered from any agent to any other agent, or to do mail delivery to and from Japan. By doing hand delivery, there was no chance American counterintelligence would be able to intercept the mail. Torii's briefcase contained letters and memos to and from Furusawa.

2. The Japanese Navy Association that Furusawa headed had, as
   one of its subcommittees, a "research division." This was where
   the Japanese naval attachés could assign tasks to local Japanese,
   researching everything from shipbuilding to US naval base status.
   The local Japanese in the group were not typically military, but could
   handle many basic tasks.

It was also notable that the Japanese Navy Association was for Japanese
citizens only. Japanese Americans were not invited in almost all cases.

The problem for Hanson was: What to do with Furusawa? The evidence
found in Torii's briefcase was damning and might have held up in a court
of law. But Torii was dead, and therefore he couldn't be arrested. He was
sure that Furusawa was involved in Japanese naval espionage, but the evidence was lacking. The briefcase showed that Furusawa was passing letters to and from Torii, but that by itself didn't prove a case against him. In
theory, Hanson could have pushed it further to try to get more evidence.

However, Japanese espionage was not high up on the priorities of the
FBI. The decision was made to close the case. Furusawa's file was put in
a filing cabinet in the FBI office on Spring Street with a duplicate sent to
Washington.

...

Shimada, back in Imperial Navy headquarters in Hibiya, received a hand-
carried letter from the USA. Opening it, he was floored. Torii—dead? He
had all of two naval attachés/agents on the ground on the West Coast of
the United States, and the leader, whom Shimada had personally selected,
was dead, because he drank too much. It was very frustrating.

After collecting his wits and consulting with his staff, Shimada thought
about what they had learned, and tried to decide the best path going forward. He discussed these issues and his ultimate decision in his memoirs,
which went undiscovered and unpublished until 2017. Therein, he wrote

that at a high level, nothing had changed. He expected a war between the US and Japan—not in the short term, but it would happen. This war would be, for the most part, a naval battle, with Japan's fleet fighting America's. To win this war, Japan would need to know more, a lot more, about the US Navy. As an example, the Japanese Navy knew very little about the latest in American battleship gunnery, and, without that, it would be hard to understand what tactics to use in this future battle. Specifically, how accurate were the American guns at different ranges? How well-trained were the crews? Would the Japanese battleships do better firing at the American ones at long range? Or would they do better sailing into close range and firing point-blank? With Torii's death, these questions were still unanswered.

Shimada also heard from Yamamoto, who had a request for a small change in the mission. Yamamoto agreed with most of Shimada's espionage goals, with one exception. He disagreed that learning about American battleship guns was the highest priority. The future war, stated Yamamoto, would be decided by aircraft carriers and their planes. Recent Japanese exercises had shown that planes would soon be able to strike ships farther away from the carriers than ever, so it would be even easier for aircraft carriers to stay far away from battleships and send planes to attack them again and again with no chance of the battleships catching them.

Yamamoto requested that Shimada find out more about American warplane manufacturing and naval aviation. The Japanese Navy was still flying biplanes, which could fly for less than three hours and would go under 150 miles per hour. However, the first all-metal monoplanes were being designed, and it was clear that in a few years the planes would have double the range and speed, at which time, Yamamoto stressed, the Japanese fleet would be able to attack enemy ships from even farther away. Coupled with a surprise attack, Japan would be able to defeat the enemy without their ships even seeing them.

Shimada told Yamamoto that the one agent in Los Angeles could easily look at both ships and aircraft production, because Los Angeles produced over half of America's warplanes. A majority of American aircraft companies had moved to Los Angeles, because the habitually great weather helped to speed up airplane development. There was little rain and no snow to interfere with test flights. Lockheed, Douglas, Northrop, North American, Hughes, and Kinner were all in the area, with their plants interspersed among the beaches, palm trees, and movie stars.

Shimada wanted to simply send a new agent to Los Angeles, but he didn't have the budget to send anyone else yet. So he gave orders for the agent currently in Seattle, Lieutenant Nakazawa, to move to California and take over espionage for the entire West Coast. He ended up in San Mateo.

Shimada and the intelligence staff had learned some helpful things from sending Torii to Los Angeles. The Americans could have cracked down on Furusawa and others, but they didn't. Also, unlike Japan, American society was quite open. Japanese agents could drive over to San Pedro and look openly at the US Fleet. Information on the US military was available in the newspapers, and congressional debate on budgets was freely available from the government printing office. Torii had even found that Americans liked to talk and could easily be bribed. It wouldn't be so hard.

Shimada and Yamamoto also had some other key learnings. A junior Japanese officer, like Torii, was good at some parts of espionage, it seemed. Information on ship sailings, gunnery accuracy, and ship construction was all available. What was missing, however, was the higher-level context. Yamamoto, when he was posted to Washington, DC, five years prior, had focused on this. What was the American strategy? How well did Americans train their crews? What kind of guns would new battleships have? How about the new dive-bombing tactics that the Americans seemed to be focusing on—what was the future of that?

During discussions, Yamamoto mentioned the help the Japanese Navy had received from Frederick Rutland in the early 1920s. Not only had Rutland assisted with tactical items like landing gear and carrier design, but he had helped with the big picture, telling his Japanese counterparts the higher-level evolution of British carrier aviation, how the pilots were trained, what kind of ships would be developed in the future, and more.

Shimada thought about all of this and said, "I wonder where Rutland is now?"

CHAPTER 11

THE ATTACHÉ AND THE SLEEPER

November 1932

On an overcast morning in November 1932, Rutland received a letter that shook up his quiet life in England. He had a cushy sales job at Scammell and Nephew, where his brother-in-law was an executive. His family was intact and had adjusted well to life back in London after their yearslong sojourn in Yokohama. To his surprise, he was getting comfortable with his quotidian life, yet in private moments, he recognized how deeply he missed the public's adulation and how much he had enjoyed the admiration of the Japanese Admiralty he once regularly impressed. And, presumably, once you've flown a rickety eighty-horsepower plane off of a large board placed on a battle cruiser turret, a quiet life as a salesman doesn't give you the same rush.

Rutland's employer made the largest and most striking vehicles on British roads in the prewar period. Scammell vehicles may be familiar to many modern readers because, in the *Thomas the Tank Engine* cartoons, the "bad guys" are a pair of devious trucks made by Scammell named Max and Monty, who are trying to steal away business from the trains.

The letter Rutland received was from Shiro Takasu, the same Japanese naval officer who had recruited him to Japan in 1923. Takasu was back in London, stationed again at the Japanese embassy. Takasu suggested they get together if Rutland was interested. Rutland wrote Takasu back immediately, stating he was "most agreeably surprised to get the letter, and that in fact, he hadn't heard from anyone from Japan for several years." He suggested either lunch that Friday, or if that didn't work, perhaps they could spend the day together on Sunday at Walton-on-Thames.

While awaiting Takasu's response, Rutland considered what this letter might mean. He had been dreaming about something much more interesting than his sales job and thought that Takasu might indeed bring him a new opportunity. The other thing on his mind was money, specifically how to get the proceeds of his spectacular £3,000 investment in Kayaba Industries from a decade earlier. The company was selling warplane parts to the Japanese Navy at such a large scale that he estimated his investment might now be worth close to £100,000. However, Kayaba explained in a letter that he couldn't send this much money to the UK because of Japanese foreign exchange controls. But, if Rutland could find his way back to Japan, Kayaba would gladly give him at least some of the money that was owed to him, handing it over in cash if need be.

Rutland was also considering starting his own trading company. During his time in Yokohama, Rutland had become friends with many traders in Japan, most notably his friend Augie Manley. He also knew many reputable traders based in China. If he got the money from Kayaba, he could easily roll that over into the seed capital for his trading company.

Rutland and Takasu agreed to meet at Walton-on-Thames on Sunday. Takasu showed up, not in his Japanese Navy uniform, but in a suit and tie so as to not draw attention. The men chatted over a pleasant meal and continued their conversation as they strolled down the path in Riverside Park. Over the last decade, Takasu had rotated through various roles, from instructor at the naval war college to captain of the light cruiser *Isuzu*, but was back helping with intelligence.

Takasu explained that they were looking for a friend who could help them find out information and who they could trust for sound advice. Both he and Shimada, head of the navy's intelligence operations, thought that Rutland could fit the bill nicely. "Many of the Japanese naval officers that you worked with in the early 1920s are being promoted into very high positions. These officers are influential and powerful, and they respect you and your expertise greatly. You are the obvious choice. Actually, you are the only choice! Are you interested?"

Rutland was ready to say yes, when Takasu added that they wanted him to work in America, likely somewhere like Hollywood, to prepare, in his words, "in the event of war between America and Japan."

Momentarily stunned, Rutland asked, "In America, you say? Please explain why that would be."

"Well, war between the US and Japan seems unlikely. But lately, the US has been very aggressive toward Japan. We need to prepare for the worst case. And, if war was to occur, we would need to know what is happening on the West Coast of the USA. To do so, nothing could be better than someone from Japan's historical ally, Britain. Plus, we notice Hollywood is full of successful British people. You would fit in quite well there."

Rutland slowly took this all in, momentarily pausing to look at the river and gather his thoughts. He thought the chance of a war between Japan and the US was not really worthy of consideration. He couldn't imagine Japan would be so foolish as to attack the US—his position had always been that, if they did, it would be national suicide. It would never happen. This was not an uninformed opinion. He knew the top officers of the Japanese Navy—he had been drinking with them at places like Komatsu, and he had even been to their houses. These men, he knew, were dedicated to their craft, competent, and aggressive. But they were also practical and wouldn't do anything stupid.

Takasu stopped, leaning against a railing, and stared out across the Thames. The sun was overhead, and the river reflected the light into his eyes. "You know, Rutland-san, the Japanese Navy is Kayaba's biggest customer, which puts us in a particular place of influence. But this works the other way too. There are situations when we wouldn't be inclined to exercise this influence."

Rutland realized he had just been threatened, in a roundabout, Japanese way. He knew that if he didn't take the job, he would never get the money he was owed from Kayaba. He asked for a few days to consider the offer and to consult with Dorothy. Relocating to the US would have him far away from his two children from his first marriage, who would no doubt remain with their mother in England. He was particularly proud of his oldest son, Fred, who was a star student and already aspiring to have a career in medicine.

Dorothy seemed excited, but she also knew her husband could be a bit impulsive, and asked about the safety and legality of the work. He replied, "That is also the beauty of this arrangement. I shall simply be an advisor conversing with people and then informing others of our discussions. Not only is it perfectly safe, but it is also legally sound. In addition, as a British subject in the United States, I would legally be able to do many things that an American would not be able to do."

After a pause, he added, "They are eager to pay generously for almost no work at all. My old friends in the Japanese Navy simply desire some legally obtainable information. And also, trust me, there is no possibility of a conflict between Japan and the United States."

Further influencing his decision was how this Japan connection could kickstart Rutland's proposed Asian trading company. As part of the offer, Takasu agreed to bring Rutland back to Japan, where he could reconnect with friends in the trading industry and, if everything lined up, he could even launch his business before relocating to the States. Creating the trading company would make an excellent cover for espionage. People involved in trading could easily travel about without suspicion. Specializing in naval and airplane-related products, he would have the perfect excuse to visit US naval bases and stop by arms manufacturers. As far as Rutland was concerned, however, the best part was that the Japanese would subsidize his lifestyle and business ambitions almost entirely, and he would get his money from Kayaba too. They could be living a highly upscale life in glamorous Hollywood.

The following Sunday, Takasu treated Rutland to a dinner at a Japanese restaurant off of Shaftesbury Avenue in Piccadilly. He laid out in general terms how their agreement would work. Rutland would relocate to the West Coast of the USA, where he would gather information, primarily about the US Navy. The immediate goal would be to get situated and embed himself into society in the United States, giving them occasional updates. "That way," Takasu said, "if a war were to start, you would be positioned to give us essential information about the country's war efforts."

The conversation could only go so far with Takasu alone, however. Rutland and Takasu agreed that Rutland would return to Japan to visit Admiral Shimada and others at the Kai Gun Sho, the Japanese Admiralty, where they would finalize the details of Rutland's work.

Rutland was a bit surprised when Takasu gave him some other news: Takasu would be heading back to Japan in the near future. However, Takasu assured him, it was actually a plus, because he had been promoted to director of Naval Intelligence, taking the job currently held by Shimada. He would be replaced as Rutland's key contact by a young officer named Arata Oka, whom Rutland would soon meet. Takasu passed a letter of introduction from Oka to Rutland.

Realizing how much Takasu had helped him, and how much he was depending on Takasu in the future, Rutland purchased a gold cigarette case and had Takasu's initials engraved on it. He gave it to him in their last meeting before Takasu went back. Takasu was shocked once he realized that the case was made of real gold. He thanked Rutland and said that he looked forward to seeing him in Japan soon.

The new Japanese attaché, Oka, was just as aggressive and dedicated as other Japanese naval officers, but he immediately left an impression with his style, which was different from other Japanese officers; he was outgoing, bold, and a bit impulsive. It wasn't that Oka spoke English that perfectly, it was just that he had no hesitation in getting out there and using it.

Oka was also intensely critical of his predecessors in London, stressing that the state of Japanese intelligence gathering was so poor because "the Japanese in England only talked amongst themselves in Japanese." He told Takasu that the way to do espionage was to immerse yourself in British society, foster relationships, and thereby discover actionable leads. Oka popped into pubs and had a couple of pints with the locals just about every night. He genuinely enjoyed chatting up the Englishmen he met. He was extremely arrogant, with an aggressive attitude, but the British found that interesting. More often than not, after a few too many rounds, the British would feel comfortable verbally sparring with him, sometimes sharing more information than they might have under different circumstances.

Another British agent Oka recruited while drinking at an upscale club was Herbert Greene, who he dubbed Agent Midorikawa. Greene was from a prominent family; his uncle was secretary of the Admiralty, and he was the brother of novelist Graham Greene. Several of the Greene family ended up working in British Intelligence, and Graham wrote slightly fictionalized books about the topic, such as *Our Man in Havana*.

Being able to drink a lot of alcohol was thought of as *otoko-rashii* (macho) in the Imperial Japanese Navy of the time. Drinks were available aboard ships, and pilots would take a shot before missions. But, as in many things, Oka went beyond. Late one night, while he was drinking at Von Salzmann's German restaurant, one of the other guests replied to one of Oka's typically aggressive statements by making a racist comment about Japanese people. Instantly angered, he shoved the man down to the floor, and yelled for all to hear that soon "Japan will kick the white man out of every corner of Asia," which left quite an impression on the British who overheard it.

...

Rutland and Oka arranged their first meeting via letters. Rutland suggested they meet in St. James's Park, between Big Ben and Buckingham Palace. Rutland told Oka he would be easy to spot; he just needed to look for the man with bright green eyes. For the first meeting, they simply just walked by each other and nodded. For a second meeting, they met at Ham Common, a more discreet outdoor location by the Thames, before moving on to dinner.

Rutland ordered a whiskey soda. Oka ordered a double shot of whiskey, neat, and drank it very quickly. Oka confirmed, "I will be your key contact, even after you go to America. There is no need to talk with anyone from the Japanese embassy in Washington. It is more secure to handle things ourselves."

Taking a sip of his whiskey soda, Rutland acknowledged and listed some of his requirements. He said, "I'd like to confirm the budget for this trip with my family to the US. The Japanese Navy has always been very generous, and I expect my family would be provided first-class passage tickets and train fare across the US, and at least two thousand dollars for rental housing in Los Angeles." Oka countered with a slightly lower bid, explaining he didn't think the family needed to go first-class everywhere, but that he would need to get authorization from Tokyo for this kind of sum anyway.

Rutland reiterated that all of his trips for the Japanese Navy in the 1920s had been first-class. Slightly annoyed, Oka ordered another double whiskey and promptly downed it. Starting to get drunk, he ordered another and clearly started tuning out Rutland's demands. Changing the topic, he asked Rutland if he was good at singing.

The dinner had gone worse than expected. Oka thought Rutland a prima donna. Rutland was used to the VIP treatment from his Japanese hosts, and certainly wanted to keep it that way. On Rutland's side of the table, he didn't like Oka trying to cut costs. He also was trying to figure out how to negotiate with someone who was too drunk to remember their discussion the next morning. Rutland's solution was for them to have their next meeting in a park during the daytime, figuring Oka would be more likely to be sober that way.

But Oka had heard and understood Rutland's demands. After consulting with Tokyo on budgets, he agreed to send the Rutland family on their trip with first-class tickets and provided a healthy budget for a house rental for when they arrived in Los Angeles.

Rutland told his children in excited tones about their upcoming trip to the United States. After arriving in New York, they would then cross the country by train. After getting to Los Angeles, he would get Dorothy and his children settled before heading over to Japan. The slow trip across the US by train was beneficial to the Japanese Navy too. Rutland bought an expensive new German camera and would appear to be exactly what he was—a British tourist father showing his kids the US—while being able to take pictures of sites of naval yards and factories to add to the report that he would bring with him to deliver to the Japanese Navy.

Initially, Oka and Takasu had considered communicating with Rutland through the Japanese Navy's "White" code. However, Shimada overruled them, warning that if the British found out that Rutland was using a Japanese Navy code, they would figure out he was spying. Letters and telegrams were best, they ultimately decided, written in a very basic cipher with code names for each person.

The code names chosen by the Japanese Navy were so basic they were quite easy to figure out. For example, Rutland addressed letters to Oka, "Dear Arthur." Oka's first name was "Arata," and he occasionally introduced himself as Arthur. No great mystery there. Takasu's code name was "Susan," a bit harder to crack, though hardly impossible. In Japanese, "Mr. Takasu" is pronounced "Taka-Su-san"—hence, "Susan." In their communication, they all referred to Japan as Denmark, no doubt because of Rutland's appreciation for that country.

To start his trading company, Rutland had previously met with a safety razor company and a range finder company, entering into deals with both to serve as their sales agent in the States. He had also arranged to represent a Japanese firm that wanted help purchasing railway signals and military equipment from the US government. With these agreements, he obtained a six-month visa for his family to the USA and a two-month visa to Japan for himself. Rutland also made arrangements to take some Australian opals and Japanese pearls with him on the trip, which he would then try to sell in either the United States or Japan. Before he departed, he placed an ad in the *New York Times*, offering his import/export services.

The most difficult part of moving to America for Rutland was his older two children from his first marriage, Fred and Barbara. He visited them at their mother's house to say goodbye, told them he was proud of them, and promised he would be back to visit. Afterward, he went back to prepare for his big voyage.

CHAPTER 12

HOLLYWOOD

1933

On August 31, 1933, Rutland and family boarded a train from Waterloo Station in London to Southampton. One of the men sending him off was H. T. M. Bell, an import/export expert who went by one of his middle names, "Montague." He had helped Rutland make plans to start a trading company, and his daughter, Doris Montague Bell, was accompanying the Rutlands as a nanny. The party—Rutland, Dorothy, Miss Bell, and Rutland's children David and Annabel—boarded the RMS *Olympic*, the sister ship of the *Titanic*, and waved goodbye to the crowd gathered on the dock. The whistle blew, and they settled into their long journey.

Just a couple of hours later, before Rutland could fully relax, a steward knocked on the door of their cabin. Opening the door, the steward delivered to Rutland a troubling telegram. It was from Oka, who had signed his code name, Arthur. The telegram simply said, *Bon Voyage. Susan [Takasu] wants you to stay in America three weeks more. Please confirm new itinerary.*

Rutland was quite surprised. As the *Olympic* carried farther away from port, Rutland worried that the Japanese—perhaps under advisement from Oka—were suddenly getting cold feet about their arrangement. He had sold his house in London and staked his future on an enterprise and lifestyle almost entirely funded by the Japanese. Without them, he would be lost.

When Rutland tried to send a telegram back to Oka, it bounced back, which only heightened Rutland's concern. Rutland, realizing he may have just had the wrong address, tried to keep calm. He sent a second telegram to Oka via the Mitsubishi office in London, and waited.

The reason Oka had requested Rutland delay his arrival was the sudden discovery that the British Far Eastern Squadron was scheduled to arrive in Yokohama on the very same day as Rutland, October 4. This would have been a nightmare scenario for Rutland's mission. British warships would be docked all around Yokohama Bay, and the clubs and restaurants would be crowded with British naval officers and men. A passenger liner filled with British and American civilians arriving would be a noteworthy arrival, and officers would surely note the famous Rutland of Jutland among the Westerners visiting Yokohama. Rutland didn't know this. But, as he thought about it, the delay would be a good thing. It would mean a longer summer vacation in the US with his kids, hopefully still paid for by the Japanese Navy.

The extra time also meant Rutland would have the chance to schedule additional work. On the back end, he could add Vancouver to his itinerary, which would allow him to report more detailed information to the Kai Gun Sho in Tokyo.

But Rutland wasn't safe from prying eyes even while at sea. An MI6 counterintelligence agent was on board, sent to keep an eye on them. The agent approached the family and started playing with David and Annabel. Initially, Dorothy was more friendly than Rutland, but midway through the voyage Rutland and the agent were regularly playing deck tennis and chatting on about Rutland's proposed businesses. To win Rutland over, the agent went so far as to offer Rutland connections to American jewelers and friends of his in the US Navy. The more they spoke, however, the more the agent grew confused by Rutland and his situation.

Rutland told the agent his trading company was focused on opals and pearls, train signals, razor blades, aircraft landing gear, aircraft instruments, radios, Scotch whiskey, leather, silk shirts, and pumping machinery. The agent was left wondering if Rutland really intended to make such a complicated business, how Rutland was connected to each product, and whether these activities were just a cover for something else.

The Rutlands' arrival in New York went poorly. Custom agents found a visiting Englishman dripping with expensive opals and pearls, no license to import them, and, apparently, no interest in paying duty on them either. Being stuck in a customs office with small children having tantrums was hardly the grand arrival in America that Rutland had hoped for, but he eventually arranged to pay customs duties and was released with his goods.

In New York, the Rutlands stayed in the newly constructed Hotel Tudor by Grand Central Station. Now that he had extra time to spend in the States, Rutland made day trips to several navy yards, including Boston, Washington, Newport News, and others, taking notes and pictures for the Japanese Navy. He failed to sell the opals and had to arrange to keep most of them in New York, storing them in a secure location for the duration.

The Rutlands then left on a circuitous route for Los Angeles via Niagara Falls, Chicago, St. Louis, and Colorado Springs. For the family's stay in Los Angeles, he rented a place on Holmby Avenue, just south of the university that had recently been given the name "UCLA." As Dorothy set up their rental home, with her first priority a couple of purebred cocker spaniels, Rutland surveilled the port of Los Angeles in San Pedro and the navy ships there before leaving for Japan, with stops in San Francisco and Vancouver.

Rutland arrived in Yokohama on October 21, with a full agenda for his three weeks in the country. From Yokohama, he took the train to Tokyo, where he stayed at the Frank Lloyd Wright–designed Imperial Hotel, just across from the Imperial Palace. When he checked in, the clerk handed him a letter that was addressed to him for delivery on arrival. He opened the letter, and realized it was from his friend and business partner Kayaba. The letter said, "I am so happy to hear about your safe arrival in Japan. I will visit you at your hotel on the evening of twenty-sixth."

The meetings at Kai Gun Sho found Rutland heavily engaged in discussions to design his job structure with Takasu and a handful of others. Takasu gave him a new code name, "Agent Shinkawa," meaning "new river." Going forward, Rutland would be eyes only for the director of naval intelligence (Takasu) and Oka in London.

Shimada and Takasu had some disagreement with each other on what Rutland's role would be. Shimada had originally wanted Rutland to be a sleeper agent—meaning he would basically do nothing other than put his network in place until a war was to start, hiring informants and creating a communication network. Takasu had a different suggestion. Rutland was asking for a lot of money, so why not put him to work short-term for some light espionage? It made plenty of sense. They needed the help—Rutland was extremely knowledgeable and had already brought them pictures of many US naval bases.

It was increasingly clear that Rutland could do things for Japan that no one else could do. As expected, the Japanese attachés couldn't operate at a high level of American society, and by definition, neither could the lower-level Americans who were being recruited as spies. For example, not long after a Japanese attaché recruited a drunk ex-sailor named Harry Thompson to find out information on the US Navy, Thompson tried to get information by going aboard ships and buying sailors drinks at waterfront bars. He was discovered and sentenced to jail in 1936. Thompson was deemed by Shimada not to have obtained great information, but perhaps it was obvious from the beginning that Rutland's ability to hobnob at higher levels would get far more valuable information than a cashiered ex-seaman would be able to get at any bar frequented by enlisted sailors.*

Eventually, Shimada agreed with Takasu on the scope of Agent Shinkawa's work. Takasu asked Rutland to monitor the US Navy on its West Coast bases, including its base in Pearl Harbor. Rutland replied that he could find "a suitable man" to hire in Hawaii to work in his import business, which would both pay for itself and help in intelligence. Accordingly, Rutland changed the route of his trip home to stop by Hawaii.

---

* Thompson was initially exposed by Agnes Driscoll's US Navy signal intelligence team, leading to his arrest.

Kayaba came by the hotel as scheduled on the twenty-sixth. The two old friends greeted each other with a warm handshake. It felt like old times to Rutland for a moment, when he and Kayaba were tinkering with aircraft parts in Kayaba's workshop. Rutland's concern about finances were immediately addressed, as Kayaba told him, "I am so happy to pay you the sum for which I have too long been indebted." He presented Rutland with a stack of US dollars and some gold. He apologized for the mix of methods of payment, explaining that it wasn't easy to get foreign currencies from the banks in Yokohama.

However, Kayaba had a new proposal for Rutland. Kayaba's company had grown, but still had Mitsubishi and the Japanese Navy as his largest customers by far. He wanted to diversify. He told Rutland that Rutland was "someone he trusted deeply, and would like to work with again." Kayaba proposed an agreement where Rutland would be Kayaba's exclusive agent in the US, the UK, and France for the next five years. Kayaba was particularly interested in selling some of his new products, such as an aircraft engine starter and a range finder, but there was a question as to which products would be most suited for export.

Rutland liked Kayaba's plan. He mentioned his plans to be in Hawaii on the next leg of his trip, and he would be able to chat with the American aviators he would meet there to understand if there would be a need for Kayaba's new products. And he also showed Kayaba how they could communicate by wire, via the account of his good friend Augie Manley in Yokohama.

After the time in Japan, Rutland headed for China, where he met his friend Lionel Howell to discuss gem importing. From China, Rutland went back to Yokohama before catching a ship to Hawaii, where he spent a week looking into the navy base at Pearl Harbor, looking into the possibility of exporting Kayaba's products, and investigating hiring a man as a representative of his future trading company there. From Hawaii it was back to Los Angeles to meet his family. From there, Rutland took a ship back to New York, which let him examine the US naval bases in the Panama Canal before heading back to London.

After arriving in London, Rutland incorporated his import/export company, Marston Barrs, named after his wife's two maiden names. He hired an office worker named Olivia MacDougal to run the office from London. Surveillance from MI5 indicated she didn't do very much or, at least, came to the office late and left early. The stock of the company was set up as one hundred shares: ninety-eight for Rutland, one for MacDougal, and one for then-seventeen-year-old Fred Rutland.

Back in Los Angeles, Rutland had everything he needed to set up his trading for great success—or so he thought. Rutland believed he had a good head for business. He relished the excitement of the buying and selling, even if he didn't love its fine-print details, and he had demonstrated an acumen for selling radios in the 1920s. But his past success was a bit of an anomaly. He had never before had to deal with the minutiae of bookkeeping, running profit and loss reports, or how to account for import duties and sales taxes.

Another problem was that Rutland missed being popular. He picked up the check everywhere, which was great for networking but less helpful for making a business work.

On an early trip back to New York, Rutland took a sample of pearls from a Japanese company called Omori to the Fifth Avenue flagship store of the famous Japanese pearl cultivation company Mikimoto. Rutland talked his way into a meeting with Mr. Mikimoto himself, and showed him the pearls he had to sell, all of which were emblazoned with the logo of Mikimoto's competitor. Mr. Mikimoto politely declined Rutland's offer to purchase product from his competitor and quickly escorted Rutland out. A British agent was trailing Rutland and noted that this failed transaction showed there was something not quite right with Rutland, or at least exposed his limits as a capable businessman.

Soon thereafter, the peripatetic Rutland tried to bulk export Hollywood hair grease for men, which required a large amount of capital to hire a crew to package and sell the hair grease to retail channels in England. The idea went nowhere.

By the late summer of 1934, Rutland had been traveling around so much that he had only been on the ground in Los Angeles for about two months total. What was becoming more evident to Oka was that Rutland was more interested in living well and travel than gathering information or working in any capacity. Flush from his visit to Japan, Rutland still had a significant slug of money from Kayaba, and the Japanese Navy was subsidizing his Hollywood lifestyle and business start-up. But, as he continued to tell Oka, he needed more funds to get the business off the ground. In reality, he wanted more money so that he could purchase a house that he felt suited him.

While Rutland was away, Dorothy had been looking at homes for sale in Beverly Hills. Rutland told Oka that his mission required him to buy, not rent—using the excuse that, if a war broke out, there would probably not be any way to rent a house. Oka sent a message to Takasu, discussing Rutland's budget-busting demands. In the message, he admitted that of course he had no idea about prices of California real estate, but that it sounded like quite a dubious claim.

Earlier, Oka had sent his payments to Rutland via cash or check. The paymaster was Eisuke Ono, a patrician Japanese banker who had recently moved to San Francisco to run local operations for the Yokohama Specie Bank. That same year, in 1933, Ono welcomed a baby daughter into the world—Yoko Ono—who'd later have her own significant role to play in British-US relations.

Ono was concerned about the payments sent from Oka. As the amount of money increased, so did the chance the US authorities would notice. To avoid detection, Ono requested that £2,000 in US Steel stock certificates be sent to Rutland—then, to be even more cautious, had the certificates sent to Vancouver, Canada, so the US authorities would definitely not notice. Rutland could just drive to Vancouver from Los Angeles and pick them up.

Rutland liked that plan. It was summer vacation for the children, so great timing for a family getaway. He and Dorothy bundled up the two children and their two new dogs. They drove up past Crater Lake and enjoyed a stay at the Columbia Gorge Hotel. As they approached the Canadian border, they stayed at a campsite near Bellingham. A forest ranger picked them up for not putting out their campfire, and briefly took them in, but the rest of the trip was uneventful. Rutland picked up the stock certificates and planned to use them to buy a house. Later, he only briefly wondered if Oka was being sarcastic in a letter when he responded that he wished he had the time to take his family on a vacation in Canada.

Rutland discussed the housing situation with Dorothy. They decided that they would buy a house more expensive than they had originally thought, one that would let them host very upscale parties. Before they could buy it, he would just need a bit of time to squeeze more money from the Japanese to make the purchase. In the meantime, they rented an opulent house in Beverly Hills on Rexford Drive.

The stock certificate experience gave Rutland the idea of becoming a stockbroker himself. With a neighbor, he established the firm of Rutland, Edwards & Co. with an office on Sixth Street, near the Los Angeles Stock Exchange.

Close to a year later, the Rutlands bought a house on one of the Bird Streets, an exclusive area in the Hollywood Hills where the streets have names like Oriole, Mockingbird, and Nightingale. (Modern-day Bird Street residents have included Leonardo DiCaprio, George Harrison, Dr. Dre, Jodie Foster, and Christina Aguilera.) The Rutlands paid $25,000 in cash for the two-story house with a basement on Warbler Way, which featured an excellent city view, a pool, a large garden, and a two-car garage. The Rutlands fairly quickly threw their first garden party, which included British actors and a couple of US Navy officers. The guests noted the house was on a double lot, up some very windy roads in the hills, near a dead end. The streets themselves were not well lit, but the sparking lights of Hollywood and Beverly Hills below made the road visible. As they approached, guests took in the three visible stories made of wood and stone. The house, built into the side of the hill, had a staircase to the front door—from there, one could see a grand vista of Hollywood and Westwood below, with the ocean faintly flickering in the distance. The view from the upper floors at night must have been spectacular, they thought. The guests were let into the house by a butler. They had drinks, played badminton, swam, and ate Spanish barbeque. Rutland had the opportunity to discuss gunnery with a navy captain. Torii had been assigned to find out how accurate the American battleships were when they fired at different ranges, but was unable to accomplish this task before he died. Rutland simply asked one of the US Navy captains about it, mentioning his service spotting for the gunnery of British battleships at Jutland, and got every answer that Oka wanted—just like that.

Dorothy enrolled David and Annabel in the exclusive private Curtis School. Annabel later enrolled in the best girls' school in Los Angeles, the Westlake School for Girls, where her classmates included Phoebe Hearst and Shirley Temple. For Rutland, the schools were just one more way for him to embed himself among the rich and powerful of Los Angeles.

Much of the basement was entirely devoted to Rutland's photography interests, including a projector and a darkroom for developing film. The upstairs contained a workshop full of parts for radios. Many of the radios were now actually out of date, but with their bigger parts, they were easier for a child to take apart. David, who was thirteen years old in 1936, was as curious as his father, and they enjoyed tinkering with the radios together. David was an extremely apt pupil. He later became a star student at the California Institute of Technology and built some of the first computers. In a book he published in 1994 about radios, he credited his father's teaching him with helping kick off his engineering career.

Despite all of this, throughout the fall, Rutland continued to plead poverty with Oka, noting that his business was operating at a loss. Rutland requested more money from Oka, stating that not only was the business losing money, but also the cost of living in Los Angeles was quite high compared to London. In fact, in a perfect display of his lack of self-awareness, he told Oka he needed more funds because servants now cost $125 per month and steak was $0.49 a pound. Oka again found Rutland's requests for money not only unreasonable, but rather ridiculous.

Rutland was able to negotiate the pay he wanted. Two years later, Shimada not only noted in his diary that Rutland was the Japanese Navy's highest-paid agent, but jotted down his pay, which was roughly equivalent to ten times that of the highest-paid Japanese admiral.

Oka was impressed that Rutland seemed to be able to call any admiral or other VIP to get key information the Japanese Navy needed. However, he was a bit undependable, and wasn't making any progress on setting up the sleeper network, or indeed anything that called for any planning, focus, or organizational skills. He wired to Takasu a warning: *The idea of Japan being dependent on Shinkawa for its only information source in the US during a war is not advisable at all.*

CHAPTER 13

THE PRIVATE CLUB

1934

Rutland returned home after his first dinner with some Englishmen at the Masquers Club, a comedy club for actors on Sycamore Avenue. The more famous members appreciated the privacy of the club; no reporters or random fans were admitted.

"How was the dinner?" asked Dorothy.

"It was fascinating," Rutland replied. "I think we can say, we English are no different from everyone else who has come to Hollywood. They have come to reinvent themselves. Nothing is quite real." He continued, "The leader of the group, Alan Mowbray, is a good example. Do you remember his role as the butler in *God's Gift to Women*? He is not upper-class, but the Americans think he is, because he is tall, and has a strong presence with his emphatic accent."

Dorothy nodded, adding, "You also have a strong presence, so this is to our advantage here in Los Angeles."

"Yes, it seems so," continued Rutland. "But there is more. Mowbray's name is not actually Mowbray. His biography says he won the Croix de Guerre in the war. I don't believe that either. It's all done to look a certain way, really. But I don't mind. Mowbray is an influential man and enjoyable to have drinks with. It is just fascinating. And, as you imply, I fit in at this club far better than at an upper-class club back home."

"Indeed. Who else was at the dinner, then?" asked Dorothy.

"I enjoyed speaking with Boris Karloff about his potential sequel to

Frankenstein. Can you believe, the new movie will be called *Bride of Frankenstein!*" This got a chuckle out of Dorothy. "Charlie Chaplin and his brother Syd were at the last meeting, and come fairly often. But, apparently, Chaplin has stated that he is 'not a joiner,' meaning, he doesn't formally join clubs or groups. That is okay. He is welcome when he comes. I am sure you will meet him at some future formal dinner there."

Dorothy beamed at the thought of being able to meet famous actors.

Rutland continued, saying that Mowbray was a heavy drinker. He and his friends W. C. Fields, Errol Flynn, and John Barrymore, the "Bundy Boys," were known for their wild parties in clubs and on yachts. The others noted Mowbray had powers that they couldn't match. For example, only Mowbray could be driving drunk, rear-end the car of a young woman on Canon Drive in Beverly Hills, get out of the car, apologize, ask her for her phone number, and successfully ask her on a date.

Unusual for a Hollywood actor, Mowbray wasn't really a fan of seeing himself on the big screen, and never went to see his work. He spent more time making things happen off-screen—one of his more notable accomplishments in that respect was cofounding the Screen Actors Guild (SAG).

In the early 1930s, pay for Hollywood actors was low and working conditions were bad. The actors blamed the situation on the actors' union, the Academy of Motion Picture Arts and Sciences, which was "in cahoots" with the studio owners. Boris Karloff was particularly incensed about work conditions after a twenty-five-hour-long shoot on the set of *Frankenstein.* Mowbray, Karloff, and several other friends decided to create a new actors' union, called the Screen Actors Guild, with Mowbray as cofounder and vice president. Mowbray personally wrote a check to the lawyer to do the initial incorporation of SAG.

Mowbray had a hand in the creation of several other organizations. In 1935, he and a group of other Britons formally incorporated the British United Services Club (BUSC), a British military-themed club for actors in Hollywood. The BUSC was initially a private, all-male club with monthly meetings and formal balls. Dress code requirements were British military formal attire or black tie, with kilts acceptable for Scots. Women were not accepted as members until well into the 1980s, but were able to attend the balls as guests.

Formal membership in the club was and is limited to those who had been in the British military, including Canada, Australia, and New Zealand, plus Americans who had served under British command. Associate members can be other British subjects or American military members who didn't serve under the British. British diplomats were also welcome.

Mowbray was able to arrange for the BUSC to use the Masquers building for their club events. Mowbray continued to act in films, but he was annoyed that just about every role he was offered was for him to play the English butler. He enjoyed more his non-film pursuits, such as his work with the National Geographic Society—and, later, helping the FBI on the Rutland case. But Mowbray kept his activities with the FBI secret for the rest of his life, even though he was ironically an actor in some spy movies, like in the original *Man from U.N.C.L.E.* in the 1960s.

Mowbray and his fellows at the British United Services Club were happy to have the famous war hero Rutland as a member and occasional speaker. Part of Rutland's appeal was that, although he exuded confidence, he was not a boastful man. Rutland spoke only occasionally about his time as a war hero and test pilot. He didn't need to boast, because word very naturally got around about his heroics. He was also quite good at mixing and making friends, helping make the dinners more successful, and it was welcome that he always picked up the check.

Hiding in plain sight, Rutland spoke freely to Mowbray and others in and outside the club about his experience and work with Japanese companies. But the club members felt he was somewhat mysterious. When one of the other club presidents was interviewed after the war, one of them said, "Fred Rutland? Of course, I knew him. He was a fine chap, and I took to him at once. He was very popular and helped to make a success of our dinners." His friends said that Rutland enjoyed the good life and didn't really worry about the bills catching up to him later. They didn't know at that time, of course, that the dinners he bought were paid for by the Imperial Japanese Navy.

The BUSC played a key role in Rutland's espionage-related objectives. During his chats with handler Oka in London, Rutland referenced the club—telling Oka that, should a war break out between the US and Japan, "What better plan for Japan than to have a spy ring of British veterans, many of which had fond memories of fighting with Japan in the Great War, who could roam about Los Angeles fully above suspicion, pick up needed information, and feed it to Tokyo?"

The BUSC frequently invited prominent American military members as guests. Rutland found the Americans easy to impress. He was introduced as "Squadron Leader Rutland"—not just a fellow naval aviator, but actually, the man who had been the *first-ever* wartime carrier aviator. After a few drinks, the genuinely curious Rutland would ask the American airman about the capabilities of a new fighter or dive bomber. Rutland was then able to choose the most knowledgeable or influential US Navy officers that he met at the club to send an invitation to join the exclusive weekend badminton parties at his house in the Hollywood Hills.

However, as much as this schmoozing at parties was effortless for Rutland, the benefits of his work to the Japanese Navy were very clear. There was a clear racial color line in Los Angeles. A Japanese naval attaché would likely not be invited to the British club or to an upscale party in Hollywood, but even if one was, it would be highly unlikely a Japanese person would be able to get an American officer to share secrets about new American military capabilities. Rutland could get this information quite easily. Rutland wasn't working very hard, but that didn't really matter—he was able to get a lot of the information Oka needed through casual conversations. Once Oka saw the sort of information Rutland was able to extract, Oka started to warm to Rutland a bit.

Rutland's role kept expanding. Far from his being the sleeper agent that they'd first envisioned, the temptation to give him more work was too much to ignore, especially after Rutland demonstrated that he could get high-level information from Americans at parties. Not surprisingly, his reports on new American warplanes were accurate and very detailed. The Japanese airplane manufacturers wanted more of the same, so he started getting more requests for technical information. This was all well and good from the near-term perspective for the Japanese Navy, but it also exposed him to possible discovery from US counterintelligence. Oka was keenly aware that the Japanese Navy would absolutely need an information source in the US after the war started, and that Rutland was putting himself in the path of too much risk. He needed to derive a backup plan—but didn't have one yet.

Rutland's initial plan was to recruit other Britons at the BUSC by simply telling them about his work for the Japanese, mentioning that it was all legal, and letting them know it would be easy money and interesting. However, with the international situation getting more tense, the idea that anyone would sign up to help the Japanese Navy sounded less legitimate year by year. Plus, Rutland was also spending every bit of money he was getting from his Japanese handlers, who were not excited about laying out more cash to recruit more Britons. Recruiting other Britons as spies would ultimately be too hard to carry out. Rutland had many plans that never came to fruition, and this was no different—Rutland never recruited any other assets at the club.

...

Charlie Chaplin came by the club on occasion. There was something he enjoyed about being in a private location, with other Britons, many of whom were famous Hollywood stars. Plus, it was easy. The club was literally two minutes from his studio at Sunset and La Brea.

The Chaplin studio had a sign on the door. It said:

No admission
Don't ask it
No exceptions

Chaplin's butler, Toraichi Kono, knew just how much his perfectionist boss demanded privacy at his house and his movie studio. Anything that interfered with it was likely to bring a fit of anger from Chaplin.

At the Los Angeles Olympics two years prior, Kono had arranged the parties for Chaplin, Fairbanks, and Mary Pickford to meet Baron Nishi. The coverage of these parties in Japanese newspapers ended up putting Kono in a very difficult situation. Word got around the Japanese community that, if you wanted to meet Chaplin, you called Kono. For example, General Iwane Matsui of the Japanese Army came to visit Los Angeles. Matsui was a big fan of Chaplin and a brutal, authoritarian man. He later became infamous for leading the Japanese Army during the Rape of Nanking, when his troops massacred over one hundred thousand Chinese. Matsui had his assistant call Kono to arrange a meeting with Chaplin.

Kono was in a lose-lose situation. He couldn't say no to a visiting Japanese general. But he also couldn't betray the trust of his boss, Chaplin, who would have been furious if he found out Kono was setting up meetings with random groupies of any nationality. An extremely stressed-out Kono found a time on the calendar when Chaplin was traveling, and secretly let Matsui into the Chaplin studios at that time to look around. The pictures of Matsui at the Chaplin studios later surfaced at Matsui's war crime trial in an attempt to humanize him. It didn't work—he was sentenced to death along with wartime prime minister Tojo and several other Class A criminals.

Initially, Kono had loved his job, and still loved the association with fame. But by the mid-1930s, he felt that he was in hell. Kono didn't appear to have any moral quandaries about covering up a suspicious death or enabling Chaplin's taste in underage females. The problem was that Chaplin worked Kono seven days a week and demanded perfection in everything. With the added stress of fulfilling the demands of Japanese officials to whom he couldn't say no, Kono was ready to crack under the strain.

Things got even worse after Chaplin got married to his third wife, Paulette Goddard. Goddard didn't like Kono's grip on the household and found all of the Japanese quietly watching her to be creepy. When Kono tried to call out her excessive spending to Chaplin, Chaplin blew up at Kono. It was the last straw. Chaplin told Kono he was fired, to which Kono replied, "You can't fire me, I quit!"

Suddenly, Kono desperately needed to find a new job, and planned to leverage his connections in both Hollywood and Little Tokyo to find one.

CHAPTER 14

SPY WORK IS NOT
A BLANK CHECK

May 1935

The two London police officers arrived outside the pub in Piccadilly at seven a.m. The call had been about a Japanese man, passed out drunk—and indeed, there he was, spread-eagled on the sidewalk. He was a muscular man, midforties, in a suit that was looking the worse for the wear, who had apparently passed out after a hard night's drinking. Next to the man in the gutter was a briefcase that he had apparently dropped.

The police looked for identification in the suit pocket; not finding a wallet, they popped open the briefcase. Out spilled an alarming amount of classified documents in English and Japanese. One of the officers took the man to sober up; the other took the more incriminating-looking documents back to the police station.

Arata Oka, an elite Japanese Naval Academy graduate with no espionage training, had managed to lose a briefcase while drunk; his colleague Torii in Los Angeles, also an academy graduate with no espionage training, had done the same thing. Unbelievably, the Japanese agents had now lost briefcases containing top secret material in two cities.*

The documents and copies of Oka's identification arrived on the desk

---

* American agents would not have been so careless. This author's father was known to take his briefcase with him to the restroom to ensure it didn't leave his sight.

of K at MI5. The information found to be in Oka's possession was rather damning and contained many references to Rutland. K asked his staff to see if there was anything in these files that showed either Oka or Rutland were breaking any British laws. The answer was no. Rutland's espionage was completely focused on the United States. And, furthermore, it appeared from the documents that Rutland's primary activity in Los Angeles was asking Oka for more funds to support his upscale lifestyle.

Rutland appeared to be making a name for himself in Los Angeles society, as seen by quotes about Rutland in the Los Angeles newspapers that were in the briefcase. K idly realized that, should Rutland be discovered by the Americans, it would be embarrassing for Britain. But there wasn't really anything K could do about that at the moment. MI5 communication with the FBI was limited, partly because the US and Britain were not allies. In addition, many members of the British upper class, from which MI5 drew its agents, didn't really like Americans.

In Oka's mind, Rutland was a problem. The last year or so had Rutland asking for increasing amounts of money but having no success at all getting his business off the ground. Furthermore, aside from the technical details about US warplanes and battleships, Rutland hadn't been able to contribute significantly to war preparations.

Oka presented the problem to Takasu, stating, "Rutland is not, of course, Japanese, and therefore is working to maximize his own fortune, while not working very hard. It isn't that easy, but we can address by reducing the amount we pay him, while also specifying exactly what we want him to do."

Oka subsequently summoned Rutland to London to try to iron out how the job would be structured going forward. Rutland started his trip by meeting up with his children, Fred and Barbara, and from there went to meet Oka back at Ham Common for some very matter-of-fact discussion. Oka started by making it clear he was not happy with Rutland's progress, and laid out expectations on how much time Rutland would spend in Los Angeles, what kind of work he would do, and turnaround time on that work. Oka and Rutland came to some agreements. For example, Rutland agreed he would be responsive to requests for information. He would spend most of his time in Los Angeles but would meet annually with Japanese agents in various locations in the Americas and Asia to report.

Rutland lobbied to Oka to communicate more with Tokyo directly, saying too many telegrams to London might make American authorities come to believe he was acting as a British agent. But, in reality, Rutland—feeling that Oka wasn't a huge fan of his—wanted to be talking to others to help solidify his employment. Rutland also asked for more pay, and Oka forwarded that request on to Tokyo several times. Takasu, annoyed, replied to Oka that "constant repetition of Rutland's demands for pay are not only postponing the matter but may invite the suspicions of the British."

Takasu was correct to be concerned. K of MI5 had the Japanese-speaking Cambridge graduate Courtenay Young as his head of the Japan desk. Young and his team were reading not just this telegram, but most of the telegrams between Tokyo and the Japanese embassy in London. The telegram didn't just invite their suspicions—their suspicions were already well-formed, and they found the situation rather hilarious.

Oka would be moving back to Japan soon, but he would continue to be Rutland's point of contact. Initially for communication for when he was in Japan, Oka arranged to have Rutland send the letters to Japan addressed to his wife, Ikuko Oka, at her home address in Tokyo. Letters back from Oka to Rutland would be mailed from the return address of an "American friend who lives in Yokohama" and, later, if Oka was in the UK, using Rutland's then-eighteen-year-old son, Fred. Involving a teenager in international espionage was quickly seen as untenable, but the American friend emerged as the way to send letters to and from Japan. Rutland arranged for Oka to have Japanese intelligence instructions sent to him from the return address "A. Manley, 252 Yamate Cho, Yokohama," with the salutation "Dear Fred" and signed "Auggie." Rutland also maintained a post office box in Manley's name in Los Angeles. This surprisingly astute bit of spycraft by Rutland later confused the FBI. FBI reports, for instance, refer to Rutland as "Major Frederick J. Rutland, alias Augie Manley."

Yet "Augie Manley" was not an alias. Manley was a real person, a long-time friend of Rutland from his Yokohama days, who gave him the green light to use his name and address in this communication scheme. Manley was born in Yokohama, Japan, to American parents in 1880. He worked for Cornes & Company, which was established in 1861—still around in 2023, it claims to be the oldest foreign trading company in Japan.

It was also a perfect cover; as the employee of a trading company, it would not be unusual for Manley to have addresses in both California and Japan and to be in correspondence with business associates on both sides of the Pacific.

Finally, it was agreed that in the event of war between Japan and the United States, Rutland would head to Ottawa, Canada, and report to the Japanese embassy there—an arrangement that interestingly assumed that Japan and the British Empire would still be at peace. However, after Rutland moved back to Los Angeles, he decided that Mexico was a better outlet than Canada.

CHAPTER 15

IN PLAIN SIGHT

1936

Dorothy dropped her husband off at Los Angeles's Union Station, where he boarded a train to San Diego, and then took a trolley to the Mexican border. From the border, he walked over to the Molino Rojo on Avenida Revolución. The Molino Rojo was an all-in-one casino, bar, whorehouse, and meeting place. "Molino Rojo" is the Spanish translation of "Moulin Rouge," the famous club in Paris, but was far, far more downscale. For example, it attracted visiting American tourists by creative advertising that included a donkey with a Molino Rojo banner on the Avenida and sponsorship of a traveling baseball team.

Molino Rojo proprietor So Yasuhara had been born in California to Japanese parents, and later immigrated to Mexico to establish his business. When Rutland arrived at the door, Yasuhara greeted Rutland and escorted him into his office. Rutland pulled out of his briefcase a round, three-pound metallic object with a glass face that looked a bit like a very large thermometer. He told Yasuhara, "Please have this sent on a ship, hand-carried, and have it delivered to Sonoda-san at the Japan Aircraft Company." The device was the "phantom gauge," a new lightweight gauge that was being tested by the Electric Boat company in Groton, Connecticut. It would save weight and increase storage capacity for the fuel and oil tanks on submarines. Rutland suggested that, once the US Navy had proved the technology effective, these gauges could be licensed or copied for Japanese submarines as well.

Rutland could have sent that gauge by regular mail—buying an industrial part was not illegal. However, he wanted to test his communication route via Mexico, and also, sending it this way made him appear more valuable to his Japanese counterparts.

Rutland then caught an airline flight from Tijuana to Mexico City. After he arrived, he went to the headquarters of the Mexican Air Force, where he made a sales pitch for some new trainer airplanes made by the Security Aircraft Company. He stressed that the construction of the planes made them very affordable and a good way to train many Mexican pilots at low cost. Unfortunately, the Mexicans weren't ready to buy yet. He thanked them for their time and offered to host them for a visit to the Security Aircraft offices in Los Angeles and to a party at his mansion.

Rutland then visited the Japanese embassy in Cuajimalpa. The influx of Japanese Navy officers had recently doubled the number of staff from ten to twenty, and office space was tight. He was able to meet the new attachés and discuss how best to pass information to them in the future. After returning home to Los Angeles, he sent an invoice for his travel to Mexico to the Japanese Navy and a duplicate one to Security Aircraft, so that he had his expenses for the trip paid for twice.

The founder and CEO of the Security Aircraft Company was a minor celebrity named Bert Kinner, whose planes were well known among the aviation community for being easy to maintain and low-cost. He was also responsible for inventions that eventually helped the US Navy, such as the folding-wing aircraft. Above all else, he was most famous for his sponsorship of Amelia Earhart and other female flyers.

Rutland had been eager to meet Kinner. He liked the planes, and also liked how good Kinner was at PR. When Rutland was still in Britain, he read newspaper reports about a Kinner-sponsored, all-female, cross-country air race. Kinner had arranged for reporters to go to New Jersey to cover the end of the race. The reporters wrote that an all-female race was different, because as each of the female pilots touched her wheels down, you could see a puff of makeup fly up from her open cockpit. This was obviously sexist fiction, but it was the kind of PR savvy Rutland enjoyed.

In November 1936, Rutland made his annual trip to Japan. This trip to Japan was covered in the *Los Angeles Times*, which reported—correctly—that he would be attending to several business deals while there.

Rutland was again staying at the Imperial Hotel in Tokyo. The morning after he arrived, a Japanese naval officer came to meet him and escorted him over to the Kai Gun Sho for his meeting with Oka. He was thankful that Oka seemed recently to be happier with his work, but Rutland was still trying his best to get Oka fully on his side after their rocky start. He brought Oka an engraved gold cigarette case, identical to the one he had given Takasu.

The next day, Oka took Rutland with him to meet the new Yokohama-based Japan Aircraft Company or JAC, which was making trainer planes and seaplanes for the Japanese Navy. The navy was helping JAC get its business off the ground, seeding it with recently retired navy officers, providing funding, and now introducing them to technical advisors such as Rutland. This was part of the Japanese Navy's goal to be less dependent on Mitsubishi for aircraft—encouraging this new start-up was a way to diversify their supplier base.*

At the meeting, Oka introduced Rutland to his key contact at JAC, who was named Sonoda. Sonoda was an English speaker, and explained what kind of technology JAC wanted. Rutland gave a brief explanation of what he knew off the top of his head and took notes on things they wanted him to find out. Rutland told Sonoda that he would get him the full details on all his questions by the next time they met, and proposed that perhaps next time they meet in the United States.

The Japanese manufacturers were finding it a challenge to keep abreast of the advances in warplane technology in the 1930s because planes were getting better at a breathtaking rate. Rutland's Short seaplane had flown at

---

* Today, JAC is known for the high-performance parts they make for Boeing, Airbus, and various satellite manufacturers.

a top speed of 88 miles per hour and could barely go 200 miles before running out of fuel. By 1930, the US, Japan, and Britain were flying biplanes like the Fairey Flycatcher, which could go 133 miles per hour and had a range of 310 miles. By the mid-1930s, all three countries were coming out with aluminum monoplanes, such as the Boeing P-26A Peashooter, which could go over 230 miles per hour—roughly triple the speed of Rutland's early seaplanes from just two decades prior.

In the few years before World War II, the planes kept getting better at an astounding rate. The Mitsubishi Zero could fly 330 miles per hour, over 100 miles per hour faster than the Peashooter, and could fly over 1,000 miles before needing to refuel.

Japanese, British, and American planes were all improving at a very similar pace. There were numerous breakthroughs in design, engine power, and gasoline refinement that all contributed. The Americans had figured out how to make the aluminum structure both lightweight and strong. Lockheed made refinements to enable Amelia Earhart's Electra to cross the Pacific—these refinements were then rolled directly into later warplanes, such as the long-range P-38 Lightning. Japanese planes matched this pace of advance quite quickly.

After three days of meetings, Sonoda and Rutland made an expansive agreement where Rutland would be a key member of the JAC team. In addition to Rutland advising JAC on airplane technology, they agreed he would open a sales office for JAC products in the United States. JAC agreed to pay the rent of the office, which was across from the Douglas plant, allowing Rutland to keep an eye on the new Douglas planes by simply looking out the window. The meeting ended with Sonoda signing a purchase agreement to buy a couple of Kinner's new trainer aircraft.

Coming back to Los Angeles, Rutland collected his sales commission from Kinner. Knowing that Kinner desperately needed funds, he also offered to use his stock brokerage to sell Kinner's shares to the public. It was a good time to sell stock, he suggested, with the new orders from Japan and elsewhere. Kinner agreed.

The best way to pump a new stock offering was with a celebrity, and Kinner invited Amelia Earhart to a meeting with Rutland to see if they could use her in the promotion. She flew in to meet them at his location in Downey.

Rutland suggested to Earhart that "she would enjoy branching out into this new activity, the stock market." He noted that "the economy and the stock market was starting to come back, so that the timing was good" and that "she would be able to do well from the deal personally."

Kinner appealed more to the now-world-famous Earhart to return some favors, "since they had always helped each other in the past, and he really needed the help now."

Earhart replied that she would check on it. She had been selling her image in advertisements for everything from luggage to cigarettes, but Earhart had been using the higher-performance Lockheed planes on her recent record-setting flights. Perhaps, she said, "it would not be possible because of the current arrangement with Lockheed," so she would be unlikely to be able to promote other planes at the time.

When she mentioned Lockheed, Rutland's ears perked up. "How do you like the controls of your Lockheed Electra, Mrs. Earhart?" Rutland asked. The two of them went on a tangent about the advanced features of the plane, which she had just picked up a couple of months before. He continued by praising the designer of her plane, Kelly Johnson, and asking her about the other designers Johnson worked with.

Rutland's questions, disguised as a conversation between two airplane fanatics, were all really geared toward what the Japanese were interested in discovering. Earhart's Lockheed Electra was optimized to fly a long distance over water, which could grant obvious wartime advantages. The Japanese designers were hungry to learn what the Americans were doing to solve these problems—and, more specifically, how they were doing it.

But Earhart was a pilot, not a designer, so Rutland asked about the designers so he could talk to them directly about what they were doing. Oka had asked him to see if he could even recruit one of the junior designers to come to Japan, just as Herbert Smith had done fifteen years prior.

Rutland successfully raised the stock offering for Kinner, even without help from Earhart. This led to Rutland's popularity with start-up aviation companies trying to raise money through their own stock offerings. For example, he represented a company called Fletcher Aviation, which had an all-wood monoplane that could be made at very low cost using otherwise unemployed Midwestern furniture workers.

When Rutland called these aircraft companies, they truly believed he was interested in helping them sell stock. They never dreamed that the questions Rutland asked them about their products would actually end up in comprehensive reports for the JAC and the Japanese Navy.

Many of Rutland's espionage activities appeared to be legal under the US law of the time. In particular, as a British citizen, examining the US Navy and sending reports was in many cases fine, but he was quite likely guilty of stock manipulation.*

Rutland then started planning his next trip to Europe. He would take his family to visit the UK, and while in Europe he would see if he could sell planes from one of his clients to the air forces of various countries, including the Netherlands and Nazi Germany.

---

* The US passed the Foreign Agents Registration Act, FARA, the next year, in 1937, which would have made some of Rutland's activities for Japan illegal after that time. However, the Securities Act of 1933 was already in effect, and Rutland might have been in violation.

CHAPTER 16

THE CORONATION OF KING GEORGE VI

July–October 1937

Sir Vernon Kell, aka "K," the head of MI5, was keenly monitoring the bloody war that had just started between Japan and China. Britons in Shanghai were living in the international settlement on the waterfront—neutral territory, in theory—but the fighting didn't respect settlement borders. Just recently, a flight of Chinese bombers, trying to attack the Japanese flagship *Izumo* in the harbor, missed the ship and ended up instead killing thousands of Chinese and foreigners in the settlement.

Probably the last thing K was expecting to read about in the reports from the war zone in China was a new adventure of Los Angeles–based Frederick Rutland. The intelligence officer of the HMS *Tamar* wired that there was someone who appeared to have the code name "Shinkawa" who was working for the Chinese airline CNAC and had been recruiting some American pilots. K pondered this and thought it plausible. China did have American pilots flying for their air force and airline, and Rutland, in Los Angeles, certainly *could* have been helping recruit more.

K was not normally taken aback by greed or treachery. But this report, if true, would be quite spectacular. Could it be that Rutland was a long-time agent for Japan—but, at the moment, during a war between Japan and China, he was also working for China? Was Rutland selling out his long-term Japanese clients? If so, it clearly meant Rutland had an impressive combination of daring, greed, and low ethical standards. But to think about it, considering what he knew of Rutland, it wasn't actually all that surprising. Still, K wondered if Rutland was being smart about it. Forgetting morality for a moment, Rutland was playing a dangerous game—playing for both sides in a bloody war, while selling out both the Americans and possibly his own country, Britain.

K gave Courtenay Young the orders to have the British staff in Shanghai send any other information they found about Shinkawa immediately. Knowing who and where Rutland was, he had them make sure they didn't spend any time finding out Shinkawa's identity and location, but simply asked them to find out what he was doing there.

Young assembled all the pieces. A few months earlier, the gossip in military aviation in Los Angeles turned to the American pilots who were going to China as well-paid mercenaries. China was offering the American pilots travel to China, accommodations, good pay, planes to fly, and bonuses. Some were Chinese Americans who went for reasons of patriotism, but the rest were mostly doing it for the thrill and money. Therefore, Young concluded, Rutland was taking money from someone to help provide pilots to China, and then making more money by reporting to the Japanese Navy what the Chinese were doing.

The British must've chuckled when they read the message from Oka to Rutland, commending him on how he was able to get such an accurate report on the Chinese activity.

Young wondered when Rutland was going to take it too far and be arrested or removed, and by whom. It would catch up to him at some point. And when that happened, it would be one less thing for Young to be concerned about. Already, he felt he had spent way too much time on this Rutland character.

But two weeks later, Young sent K a report that was even more surprising. Rutland was not actually in Los Angeles. Nor was he in Shanghai. The British intercepted a telegram to the Japanese embassy in London asking them to *hand deliver* a message to Rutland. And sure enough, Rutland was found there, just a few miles from MI5 headquarters.

Rutland, it turned out, had come to London for a summer holiday with his family. He thought his American children would benefit from seeing the coronation of King George VI and Queen Elizabeth. It also turned out, as might be expected, Rutland appeared to be hobnobbing with royalty. He had written to Baron Keyes and other admirals from the Royal Navy, trying to arrange for his children to be admitted to various events around the coronation. He and his family had crossed the Atlantic on the Queen Mary in a first-class stateroom—one of the other passengers happened to be Prince Chichibu from Japan, the younger brother of Emperor Hirohito, who was also heading to the coronation as the representative from the Japanese royal family.

After a few nights in a hotel, Rutland arranged for his family to stay the summer at the Odney, a recently built private club with a large manor house on the Thames River near Maidenhead. Rutland spent considerable time chatting with friends from the Royal Navy at a much more downscale place nearby called the Cookham Club.* A major highlight for Rutland was having his two English children, Fred and Barbara, come by the Odney to see their American half siblings, David and Annabel. Fred was now twenty years old and a medical student, and Barbara was seventeen; the American children were fourteen and eleven, respectively. It was uncomfortable for Dorothy for a moment, but she breathed a sigh of relief when she realized the two English Rutland children were there without their mother. She had always been a little taken aback that Rutland's first wife was also named Dorothy. In fact, a couple of Rutland's friends in the UK complimented her on her four children, and she realized that those friends apparently didn't know she was his second wife.

Young sent an agent to the Odney to chat up Rutland and find out more about what he was doing. The agent reported back that Rutland appeared to be simply enjoying the summer in England with family and friends. Rutland told the agent and others at the club and elsewhere that he and his family had come to London at the end of April. It was perfect to have his

---

* Both clubs exist today.

two American children in London during the once-in-a-generation event of the coronation, to understand that they were actually English, and to show them the grandeur of where they came from. Rutland was able to tell his children about the times when he had met the prior King George during World War I. Rutland had joked with the agent that his younger children were transfixed by everything, but that his older daughter, Barbara, had rolled her eyes just a bit. She hadn't seen her father much since he left for America, but she had heard his stories about meeting the king many times before. She also was a bit jealous of how her father built up young Fred to the other children. But she was too young to understand how important Fred's accomplishments were to her father—the son of a laborer, having his own son on track to jump social classes and become a doctor.

K eagerly read an intercepted memo that Young dubbed as being from "the notorious Oka" to Rutland, where Oka told Rutland that he was looking forward to seeing the two Kinner planes that would soon arrive in Japan. The British realized that Rutland, on his last visit to Japan, had sold the two planes to the Japan Aircraft Company, and Oka wanted to make sure the planes would be arriving. Rutland's message to Oka was that he was sure Oka would be agreeably surprised by the quality of the planes. It appeared Oka was nervous on this point, since JAC had bought the planes on Rutland's assurances.

Young concluded in his report to K that Rutland was now a "successful aircraft salesman," so Rutland had a good reason for why he was going to so many different countries. If he was supplying planes to other countries, Young added that it also made sense that Rutland was able to help his customers hire pilots for the planes. Therefore, it wasn't strange at all that he was likely involved in helping American mercenaries get to China.

Finishing up his time in England, Rutland took a quick trip to the Netherlands and Nazi Germany before heading back to Los Angeles.

After returning to the US, Rutland sent Oka another shockingly insightful report. He said the "UK was becoming the world leader in fighter planes." In particular, he said, there was a new fighter called the Spitfire that was "even more advanced than the Hurricane," and beyond anything he had seen in the US. He suggested to Oka that it might make a lot of sense for JAC to try to license the Spitfire. Mitsubishi had created the A5M fighter and was working on the next version, which was to be called the A6M Zero. JAC had been founded partially to reduce the dependence of the Japanese Navy on Mitsubishi, so if JAC was able to license a plane from Britain, the Japanese Navy would then have an excellent yet very different fighter plane from Mitsubishi's. Even though MI5 hadn't noticed, Rutland had clearly been doing some information gathering in the UK during his summer vacation.

Rutland took his newly surfaced information regarding the latest on British warplane technology, combined it with what he was learning in California about the American planes, and put it all together as an intelligence report for the Japanese Navy.

Meanwhile, the bloody fighting in Shanghai continued, including the very active war in the air. Japanese bombers had recently attempted to bomb the Chinese capital at Nanking, and the Chinese reportedly shot down six of the Japanese planes. The Chinese successes in the air were very visible, a morale booster for the Chinese and a significant concern for the Japanese.

The Chinese had over a hundred warplanes engaged in the fighting, including relatively late-model Curtiss and Boeing planes. Although the Chinese Air Force was giving a good account of itself, they were not easily able to replace the planes that were lost, so the Japanese assumed they would be able to destroy the Chinese Air Force by attrition.

The Japanese were very alarmed to read a Chinese newspaper article that said 182 American aviators were on their way to China, each with two mechanics. The Japanese correctly believed that the Chinese press was prone to exaggerations, but they noticed even the much more reliable *New York Times* was reporting that the shipments of planes to China were continuing. More planes and pilots would be a significant threat to Japan's military position, so the Japanese were looking to get informed and stop the flow if they could. Oka asked Rutland to investigate.

Active fighting in Shanghai ended in November, with the Chinese armies withdrawing toward Nanking and the Japanese armies in pursuit. The Japanese were angry about the fierce defense the Chinese had mounted at Shanghai, and were motivated by the thought of revenge for their tens of thousands of dead. In what they thought of as an attempt to prevent another long and bloody urban battle, the Japanese Army was soon to commit the infamous barbarities of the Rape of Nanking, led by General Matsui, who had not long before enjoyed a tour of Chaplin's studio.

A few months later, just two weeks after the end of the fighting, British Intelligence in Shanghai sent K another surprising cable. Rutland was now there, in Shanghai, in person, his cover story being that he was doing business in the wrecked city. It was surprising that he could even make it into Shanghai, which hinted that the Japanese might have helped him get there.

K realized it couldn't be a coincidence that Oka was also in Shanghai in his new job as captain of the *Izumo*. Rutland was obviously there to report on what he had discovered. K and his staff assumed Rutland must have gotten info on both American pilots and planes in Los Angeles before he headed over to Shanghai. He had a cover story for the trip, since he was a businessman who was a sales agent for the planes that the Chinese probably actually did want. From there, he must have given Oka the report on British and American aviation.

Japanese Army Intelligence in Shanghai was not entirely happy with Rutland's presence there. To start, his cover story seemed fairly ridiculous. He just showed up in a destroyed city on a Japanese ship and cheerily told those he met he was here to make some sales to the *Chinese*. This defied logic. Most everyone else was trying to *leave* Shanghai, and if Rutland had really wanted to sell to the Chinese, he would have done much better had he gone where the Chinese government was in power rather than an area of the Japanese occupation.

The international settlement was teeming with spies and informers for many countries. The Japanese Navy attaché was of the opinion, through information received via his informants, that Rutland's work with the Japanese Army Air Forces was well known to the US Navy. In fact, the attaché surmised, Rutland's activities had a bit of a counterintelligence flavor, and perhaps he was working with the US Navy itself. In any event, Rutland didn't stay long, and headed back to Los Angeles.

Kell had Courtenay Young come by to discuss the matter. As Young took a seat in Kell's office, K asked, "Young, we still haven't had any communication with the Americans about Rutland, correct?"

Young replied, "No, sir."

Kell said, "Right. We should keep it that way. That Hoover is inherently not trustworthy."

Young replied, "Indeed, I agree. However, if word gets out our great war hero Rutland is a Japanese spy, it would be profoundly embarrassing. There is not much we can do at the moment, but it's obviously a risk. The man is quite a celebrity and seems to have a knack for getting in the news."

Kell stroked his mustache. "Right," he said, "but, on the positive side, the Americans wouldn't want Rutland's espionage in the news either. It would look embarrassing for them too. Perhaps, at some point, they would arrange for him to disappear and make all our lives easier."

Young rather grudgingly agreed. He was still annoyed at all the time he had spent on the Rutland case, and Rutland was still running wild, across three continents.

The lack of British-US communication wasn't only about Rutland. The British secret services hadn't communicated with their American counterparts regarding Japan at all *because* of Rutland. It seemed there was no feasible way for the British to broach that subject of Japan to the Americans without mentioning this key topic, which they'd been hiding from the Americans. But with the Japanese threat apparently increasing, at some point, the British realized, they might have to come clean.

A few months later, Young brought the news that Rutland was back in

Shanghai. The intercepted communication said that Oka arranged the usual VIP treatment for Rutland with a stay in the Imperial Hotel on the stop-off in Japan on the way. Rutland was there to meet with his old friend and business partner Kayaba, who had a new role.

The Japanese Army had found the resistance by China to be more than they had thought, and decided they needed to understand the capabilities of the Chinese military better. Kayaba had been chartered by the Japanese military to prepare an encyclopedia on the weapons used by the Chinese. While in Shanghai, Kayaba met various members of the Japanese military to interview them on their experiences fighting the Chinese. Rutland was able to tell him the capabilities of the planes the Chinese were using.

Rutland, of course, enjoyed being an expert to help his friend write his encyclopedia, and he also was happy to get paid by Kayaba. Kayaba was not able to bring the right amount of cash to Shanghai, but Rutland was able to pick some up in Japan on his way back.

Rutland was on a bit of a high from his recent successes when he got a splash of cold water on his face. The famous aviator and Kinner enthusiast Amelia Earhart had just gone missing, right as she was flying over the Mandates—the same Japanese-held islands Zacharias had been concerned about, and on which American marine Pete Ellis had mysteriously died. The Japanese still banned Americans from visiting these islands—no American had flown over these islands since their occupation. Rumors were flying that the Japanese Navy had thought Earhart was spying and had shot her plane down. Rutland realized, to his alarm, that he didn't find those rumors implausible at all. It was almost in character for them.

Had the Japanese really killed his friend and fellow famous aviator, he would be furious. But he also realized he would probably never really know.

After returning to Los Angeles, Rutland stopped by the BUSC for a dinner and met with Alan Mowbray. Rutland agreed to be the chairman of the committee for the next Armistice Day Ball. The entertainment included stars like Bing Crosby and Fanny Brice. Rutland coordinated the press coverage of the ball in the local and national newspapers, and even contacted the BBC, who was excited to cover the achievements of British actors in Hollywood. The party was broadcast on the BBC in Britain and all across the empire. The aura of glamour around Rutland was such that, even though many of the others felt him "a bit of a mystery man," they kept their doubts to themselves.

CHAPTER 17

THE SECRETS OF THE P-38

Summer 1939

Robert Gross was the CEO of Lockheed, the airplane manufacturer. The company now had 2,500 employees over a 250,000-square-foot campus in Burbank, on the site where the Burbank Airport is today. Lockheed was testing the prototype of their newest fighter plane, later to be known as the P-38 Lightning, which had an innovative twin-engine design that allowed it to fly higher and faster than anything on the market.

The FBI had come by any number of times to discuss foreign adversaries trying to learn what was going on in the Lockheed plant and stressed the unique risks to both Gross's company and to US national security should his company's secrets be exposed. In addition to the Japanese, the Germans and Soviets were highly interested, and it was clear Gross needed higher-level staff than the security guards that he had on his staff to date.

John Hanson of the FBI had been promoted to head the Los Angeles office of the FBI four years earlier, right after he had investigated the Torii case. As the FBI had taken on more of a role in protecting the American defense industry, he had met Gross several times, and the two got along well. In 1938, Gross made the unusual but logical move to hire Hanson away from the FBI to personally run his plant security, dangling a large potential paycheck in front of Hanson while also echoing the importance of the job. It turned out that FBI director Hoover had been losing some confidence in Hanson, and was looking to bring in a new special agent in charge to manage the Los Angeles office.

Once on board at Lockheed, Hanson immediately implemented more background screening of employees, and in particular, the German and Japanese employees of the plant came in for special scrutiny.

At the same time, Japanese manufacturers were also creating their new, next-generation warplanes, such as the famous Mitsubishi A6M Zero fighter, which first flew in April 1939. But from the perspective of Rutland and many other airplane enthusiasts, the most interesting new plane was in early production at the Lockheed plant. The plane was the prototype version of the twin-fuselage P-38 Lightning, and it first flew in January 1939. Rutland was also closely monitoring Douglas Aircraft, whose plant in Santa Monica was producing new planes such as the A-20 Havoc and the DC-3; Douglas's other plant in El Segundo was starting to make the Dauntless dive bomber.

The P-38 was a radically different plane than anything out there. Initially, it had been specced to be the fighter plane that flew faster and higher than any other. To make that happen, it needed to have two engines mounted on two hulls. As a by-product of the unusual design, it eventually turned out to be very well suited for many of the demands of combat in the Pacific.

Planes to be used in Europe and those in the Pacific needed to be different by design, primarily because of the distances between islands in the Pacific. As an example, the World War II British Spitfire, designed for use over Europe, had a maximum range of only 434 miles. The Zero, in some configurations, would go 1,600 miles. The Zero achieved this long range by being very lightweight and aerodynamic, with minimal armor, letting it go farther on the same amount of fuel.

The Lightning was also able to fly long distances, longer than any other American fighter in World War II, but did so in a unique way. The Zero was small and light, but the P-38 was the opposite. It was so big that it could carry more than twice as much fuel, letting it go farther than other American planes. Having two engines made the Lightning safer as well. If one engine failed, the plane could keep flying by using the remaining engine. Having a backup engine was particularly important in the Pacific, where the planes flew long distances over the ocean. Airplane engines in 1939 had up to ten times the horsepower of Rutland's plane at Jutland, but were still not all that reliable. If a single-engine plane broke down on a long flight over water, the plane would crash-land in the sea. The pilot would then have to hope he would be found by rescuers before he was found by the enemy—or by sharks.

Rutland knew well how dangerous engine failure at sea was—recalling how, at Jutland, the engine of his Short 184 seaplane had stopped working. The Short he flew at Jutland was able to land on the water, allowing him to get out of the plane and walk over to the engine to fix it, then take off and complete his mission. Given their inability to do this in modern single-engine planes, many pilots thought an engine failure in these planes in the Pacific would likely be a death sentence—and so were excited about the development of the P-38.

Two months after the first Zero flight, Sonoda from the Japan Aircraft Company arrived in Los Angeles on a ship from Kobe, accompanied by an engineer from Mitsubishi named Nakahira. They stayed at the Olympic Hotel in Little Tokyo, and Rutland came down to meet them. They met for dinner at the Ichifuji next door. Sonoda and Nakahira asked Rutland what he knew about the P-38 and about the Douglas Dauntless dive bomber.

Sonoda's agenda was substantially identical to prior times when he had met Rutland. He wanted to learn all they could from Rutland about the new generation of American planes, to inform their future development. Naturally, they had a keen interest in the Lockheed P-38. It was so different from anything else out there, and they asked Rutland for help learning more about it. Rutland didn't know many of the technical details they were asking about off the top of his head, but he agreed to find out.

Sonoda also wanted information on the Dauntless to help inform the development of the next version of the new "Val" dive bomber. Later, the Val became the plane that led the Pearl Harbor attack, but its early versions were underpowered, vibrated violently, and rolled unpredictably.

Rutland had no problem telling them much of what they wanted to know about the Douglas plane, including that it also had vibration problems, but they were being addressed by shifting the weight of the plane, adding slots on the wings, and incorporating perforated air brakes. He also told them he would dig more into the P-38 and make his full report for his next trip to Tokyo, scheduled to be in two months.

Sonoda had one request that Rutland couldn't help with as much, which was to find out more about the new Boeing bomber, the B-17, and a rumored follow-on "super bomber." There was no question that these planes could fly very high and fast. The question was, could they fly so high that a Japanese Zero couldn't defend against them? And also, if they dropped a bomb from high up, would it be able to hit a ship far below?

Rutland mentioned that Boeing was in Seattle, far away, and the B-17 was to date used by the US Army, not the navy. He didn't really have any connections in those areas, so he would try, but it would be harder to get this information. Sonoda nodded and made a note to tell Tokyo that there was need for an agent in the Seattle area.

Sonoda and Nakahira thanked Rutland, saying they looked forward to meeting him again in Japan and seeing his report. They were soon on their way back to Japan.

Lockheed was increasing its staff to produce the new P-38 and was trying to hire a large number of new workers. Hanson asked his network for referrals to potential employees. One of the people he mentioned it to was Briton and Royal Air Force officer Hugh Howatt, who was evaluating the P-38 for possible purchase by the Royal Air Force. Howatt was a good friend of Rutland's club friend Norman Glover and attended events at the BUSC.

Howatt mentioned Lockheed's hiring to Glover and Rutland at a club dinner. Eager to help, they thought of a good potential employee, an Irishman named Raymond Barry who had been working for their friend Boris Karloff on the set of the recent *Son of Frankenstein*. Rutland and Glover introduced Barry to Hanson, and Barry formally applied for a janitor position.

Barry lived in Hollywood, three blocks from Hollywood and Vine. He listed very impressive references on his job description, including Karloff and the brother of Douglas Fairbanks. Clearly, he was in the Hollywood scene, and it was curious he would then decide to become a janitor in an airport factory at least forty minutes away by car. Rutland lobbied Howatt hard on Barry's behalf, saying that his friend Barry was a good man and badly needed the job. Hanson hired Barry as night watchman and janitor.

Glover later told the FBI he should have been more suspicious of Barry. He thought of Barry as a "temperamental Irishman," but Rutland told Glover that his passion was what made Barry such a good employee. Glover and Hanson did not know that Barry had been a supporter of the Irish Republican Army before coming to the United States. It was also curious that Rutland mentioned that Barry was his friend; Rutland's friends tended to be captains of industry or movie stars, not janitors like Barry. Additionally, Barry as an Irish nationalist—was not predisposed to like Englishmen, let alone an English war hero like Rutland. Furthermore, should someone be attempting to steal industrial secrets, a night watchman or night janitor would be very convenient, since they could go all over the plant late at night, when no one else would notice them.

Hanson initially evaluated Barry's performance as mostly excellent. However, a couple of months later, Hanson became concerned about Barry's motivations, noting that Barry was highly—perhaps overly— concerned about keeping his job. The job paid decently well for a janitor, but there were any number of similar jobs in Los Angeles, so it didn't make sense why Barry would be so attached to this one. Hanson had Barry followed but didn't find anything amiss. Still, there was no need to take any chances, so he arranged for Barry to be given a different job, in the cafeteria, which was in a different building from the factory, removing Barry's ability to do any late-night information gathering.

Barry, lacking self-awareness as much as most of the other characters in this story, stormed into Hanson's office one day, asking in a very demanding tone, "Why have I been transferred?"

Hanson, surprised, didn't reply.

Barry continued, "I liked my job on the night shift. It suited me. Give it back to me, please."

Hanson denied the request, and commented that there were many reasons for job transfers, and the company needed to prioritize its own interests.

Barry, unprompted, answered a question that was not asked. He said, "I am indeed a very good security risk, and whoever had told you that I was anti-British was lying." He added, "I have never been a member of the Irish Republican Army, and nor am I a British hater. In fact," he continued, "I was a member of the conservative party that advocated better relationships between Ireland and Britain. Here is a medal I won serving in the British Army in the Great War." Hanson looked at the medal and thought it was not very convincing. For one thing, it didn't have Barry's name on it. "Unfortunately, Mr. Barry, our decision is final," he replied. "You may be excused."

Hanson made a note of this incident with Barry for the next time he had a meeting with his ex-colleagues at the FBI. There wasn't any reason to rush; Barry wasn't in a position to do anything harmful now and would no doubt soon quit. And there were any number of potential spies in the plant.

With Barry removed from the picture, Rutland tried other means of gathering information at Lockheed. Going back to his service fifteen years earlier, Rutland was a world-leading expert on landing gear. He found an inventor who had created a new kind of electric braking equipment. He stated that he wanted to discuss this landing gear with a Lockheed engineer.

He called the CEO of Lockheed, Gross, and his personal friend and Lockheed executive Cyril Chappellet to pitch the new electric brakes, which he said could have advantages in both speed of stopping and in reducing the weight of the new and larger/heavier P-38. Gross was not in that day, so Rutland got referred over to the head of engineering, Hall

A young Frederick Rutland in his military uniform, on board a seaplane carrier.

Rutland's Short seaplane. These early model, wood-and-canvas aircraft were extremely dangerous to operate, with a reputation for being "made of sticks and string."

Rutland during World War I, at age thirty, with eighteen-year-old Gerald Livock, on HMS *Engadine*. Most of the pilots of this time were closer to Livock's age than Rutland's.

Rutland's exploits during the Battle of Jutland earned him national fame, and his feat of diving off his ship to save a drowning sailor won him renown in the press, earned him the Albert Medal for Lifesaving, and was even captured in an illustration in the book *Deeds That Thrill the Empire*.

Rutland experiments landing his Sopwith Pup on the small front deck of HMS *Furious*. A gust of wind had hit the plane, but he was able to land safely, where a less-experienced pilot would likely have been killed. Rutland later implemented safer methods of landing on ships—for both Britain and Japan.

原五郎中佐（後中将・航空技術廠長）

四　ラットランド英海軍中佐

これより先き英国駐在の原五郎中佐（後中将・舞鶴司令長官在職中病没）は英海軍省航空局で空母関係を担当しておるラットランド中佐と懇意にしていたが、彼が近く離現役のうえ民間に就職する希望である事を知り、いっそのこと日本に来て仕事をするよう熱心に勧めた。

A page from the memoirs of Japanese Navy Chief Pilot Kuwabara, picturing Commander Goro Hara—who recruited Rutland—detailing the recruitment process and how Rutland secretly helped update the design of the Japanese carriers *Akagi* and *Kaga*—both used in the attack on Pearl Harbor.

Rutland's daughter Annabel in Japan in 1927. This picture was treasured by her father his entire life, and he mailed it to her shortly before his death.

Silent film star Charlie Chaplin (*third from right*), Sydney Chaplin (*second from left*), and a group of sumo wrestlers, taken just before the failed attempt to assassinate Charlie Chaplin while he was visiting Japan. Chaplin's butler, Toraichi Kono (*second from right*), later worked as a spy for the Japanese Empire.

A *Los Angeles Times* article containing details about a charity ball. Charlie Chaplin and his wife attended and are pictured here. Of note, senior US military officials would also be present. Rutland was the organizer of this ball for several years in a row, and he used functions such as these as key sources for intelligence gathering.

Frederick Rutland, dressed in finery for his journey, awaiting the takeoff of the *Hawaii Clipper* on his way to Japan.

Amelia Earhart, pictured with her Kinner Airster plane. She was the face of Kinner in advertising for a decade, but then she switched to Lockheed for her famed long-distance flights in the 1930s. Kinner struggled financially after Earhart, turning to Rutland to raise money via a stock offering. Rutland and Earhart would go on to rub elbows a number of times, although she was always dubious of his business offerings.

A stock certificate for Bert Kinner's Security Aircraft. Rutland, who had created a stock brokerage partly as a legitimate business and partly as a cover for his espionage activities, was responsible for the stock offering. Afterwards, many new aircraft companies contacted Rutland about fundraising. He would then learn about their technology and convey the information to Tokyo. Of note: the stock certificate pictured here is made out to Rutland's wife, Dorothy.

Annabel Rutland, class president *(bottom image, second from left)*, and Shirley Temple *(top image, second from left in the back row)* in the 1940 Westlake School yearbook. The society columns of the Los Angeles newspapers discuss Annabel enjoying yachting with her classmates. These were just a few of the high-class lifestyle amenities Rutland was able to provide for his family through his lucrative espionage.

Former British Flier Sees U. S. Mediation

Major Frederick J. Rutland, former British naval flier, and his daughter, Miss Barbara White Rutland, who returned on the Matsonia from a vacation trip to Japan.

—Press-Telegram Photo.

A local newspaper article written about Rutland and his daughter Barbara immediately after they came back from two weeks in Japan and a week in Hawaii. Barbara enjoyed the beach while Rutland scouted around Pearl Harbor.

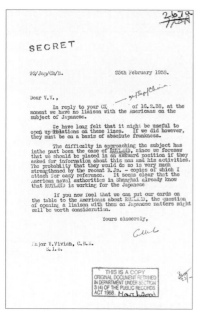

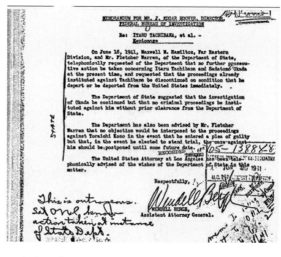

British and US intelligence didn't cooperate in trying to anticipate the coming Japanese attack, or anything related to Japan at all, for a long time. Why? As this declassified memo to the head of counterespionage at MI6 details, a large part of the reason was that Rutland's espionage was embarrassing to the UK.

A declassified memo sent to the director of the FBI, noting that the State Department had decided the apprehended Japanese agents Tachibana and Okada would not be put on trial. Of note, the FBI displays rare and emotional editorializing here, with the handwritten remark of "This is outrageous" visible in the margins.

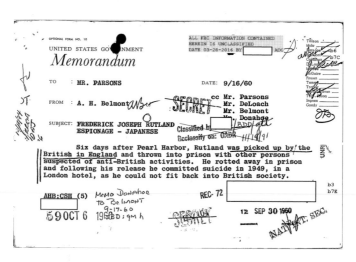

British Intelligence memos are cagey about mentioning Rutland after his release from prison, but in the declassified FBI memo pictured here, his demise is noted for the record.

Hibbard. However, Hibbard had been alerted to be careful about sharing data with Rutland by head of security Hanson. Rutland asked for an appointment, but the cautious Hibbard felt that Rutland was not really selling anything but rather seemed to be gathering information on the plane's characteristics. Hibbard looped back in the English Air Ministry representative Howatt, who also happened to have concerns about Rutland. Hanson, after chatting with Howatt, stopped the meeting with Rutland from happening.

Despite Hanson's efforts, the many secrets of the P-38 Lightning leaked fairly quickly, with information of the plane being listed in the 1939 *German Manual of Aviation*.*

Rutland felt quite confident in his updated knowledge of the new planes at Lockheed, Douglas, and more. As always, the Japanese Navy would be impressed with what he had found out.

---

* There is a reference in the MI5 files that Rutland took a trip to Nazi Germany. It would have been in character for him to have offered to sell these secrets to the Germans, but there isn't any direct evidence that he did so.

CHAPTER 18

THE SPY AS A GOOD FATHER

September 1939

There were soldiers everywhere. They were marching around Tokyo Station in tight formation, shouldering their weapons as they crossed Hibiya Park. Rutland noticed that none were smiling. So much had changed, even since his last trip to Japan just over a year prior. Gone was the feeling of optimism and the industrious spirit he had enjoyed so much. And it wasn't just Japan that seemed to be spoiling for a fight. Germany was threatening to invade Poland. He saw firsthand that Japan seemed to be eager to join Germany in an alliance, which he thought made no sense for Japan to do at all, if their primary enemy was the United States.

Compounding Rutland's sudden uneasiness was his travel companion, nineteen-year-old Barbara, his daughter from his first marriage. When she was just twelve, he had left her in England when he moved to America with his two youngest children. He had built up this trip to try to make her feel special—but, of course, he hadn't considered that a war would possibly erupt while they were on their trip. Barbara had traveled on her own from London to Los Angeles, where she had initially planned on staying for at least six months. Accompanying Rutland around his adopted city, she was initially amazed by the attention. She was the proverbial belle of the ball, described in the *Examiner* as a "dark-haired British beauty" at parties that included Karloff, Nigel Bruce, Los Angeles mayor Fletcher Bowron, commander in chief of the US Fleet Admiral Bloch, and more.

Not long after, her father offered to take her first-class to Japan and Hawaii, and she excitedly said yes. Taking Barbara on the trip would have a couple of advantages—it would be a good cover story, and also a great way to build his relationship with his daughter.

Rutland had planned this trip to Japan a couple of months earlier, after the meeting in Los Angeles, when Sonoda had requested that he find out more details about the Douglas and Lockheed planes and report back. He had obtained the requested information and had a report that impressively detailed the capabilities of those American planes, and even had specific suggestions for how the Japanese planes could be improved. In particular, he believed the information on the design of the new Douglas planes would help the Japanese dive bombers solve their vibration problems and make them considerably more effective.

In those two months, the situation in Europe had gotten particularly more tense, with Hitler threatening to attack more countries and Britain and France threatening war if he did so. Rutland decided to take Barbara with him to make his trip abroad seem more innocent—a family vacation rather than a suspicious solo excursion. Still, Rutland told people he was taking her to Shanghai, an added level of secrecy to protect his true agenda. To mark their departure, Dorothy threw the two of them a bon voyage pool party with Spanish barbeque at the house.

At its heart, the trip was to make amends. First with Rutland's daughter, then with Oka, his handler. Though these two relationships were as different as could be, he nevertheless needed to address his behavior and pacify more than a few lingering bad feelings. Oka, he knew, still doubted him. Not his loyalty—at least not exactly. He doubted Rutland's character, his integrity. Rutland picked up on this, almost immediately, and he understood that his constant requests for additional compensation hardly put him in Oka's good graces. He knew, too, that Oka—now an admiral in the Japanese Navy—had found out Rutland had used his own stock brokerage to float the public offering of Kinner's Security Aircraft Company, which only reinforced Oka's long-held belief that Rutland was only truly concerned with lining his own pockets. That this stock offering came after their come-to-Jesus meeting in London only troubled Oka that much more.

Rutland had felt distance from Barbara too. He had rarely seen her in the past seven years, mostly just doing quick check-ins when he was in London on business. He could tell Barbara was jealous of how proud her father was of her brother Fred. Fred, Rutland's oldest son and namesake, was now well on his way to becoming a doctor and was considering joining the Royal Navy's medical corps. Rutland spent significant time with his son on his visits, and Barbara felt like an afterthought.

Spending time with Barbara the summer the world started to fall apart again was Rutland's attempt to reconcile, or at least to make his daughter feel as if she was his—as much a part of his family in the States as she was a part of her mother's family in London. To win over Barbara, he understood, he needed to put in the time. Which he was more than willing to do.

The scene in Tokyo, however, revealed to Rutland that he had bigger problems than just working on the relationship with his daughter. Just after they arrived, Germany invaded Poland. It seemed very likely that Britain would declare war on Germany within days. With their country about to be at war, and with their hotel surrounded by Japanese soldiers, there was no way for Barbara to keep her mind off her family in London.

Rutland took a deep breath and assured his daughter that it was safe to enter the hotel despite the military presence, while the valet gathered their belongings. Rutland would make the best of their time in Japan, he decided, and enjoy the country's native beauty of lakes and shrines.

"Oh, Father, Tokyo is not like you described. Where are all the fashionable young men with their slicked-back hair and walking sticks you are always on about? It seems there is so little joy in the people."

Rutland smiled. "Let's look at our next destinations. I have some beautiful places to show you, and I think you will talk about this trip for the rest of your life."

"I know I will, Father. It's just that we're so far away from England. Everything feels so somber. I wish I could know that Mother and Fred are safe. And my friends."

"We beat the Germans in the last war, and no doubt we'll do so again." He said this with the confidence and authority of the war hero that he was. "All of the chatter in the newspaper about the possibility of blackouts and German bombers is a bit overdone. I know those planes very well. We have excellent planes and pilots, and I'm sure our lads will win in any airborne battle with the Germans."

Barbara leaned into her father and hugged him, welcoming his confidence.

"It will all work out. Like always," he said—though even he wasn't so sure.

When they reached the Imperial Hotel, Oka was there to welcome them. Exhausted from their journey, Barbara retired to her room, which gave Rutland an opportunity to speak freely with Oka. Together, they sat in the lounge.

"Things have changed in Tokyo, Rutland-san. It is no longer safe for you to be walking around Tokyo unescorted."

"I shouldn't think so, from what I saw from the train."

"And there is no way we can welcome you in person to the Kai Gun Sho."

"Where can we speak, then? I have much to share. The new Douglas and Lockheed planes. My upcoming trip to Hawaii, which I'm sure will unearth much about Pearl Harbor. I'm sure even you, my dear friend, will be happy with what I've been able to find."

Oka laughed and ordered a second drink. Rutland, still drinking his first, waved off the waiter's suggestion for another.

"Tomorrow," Oka said. "I'll meet you here tomorrow with a couple of my men. You can—what's the phrase—impress us all then."

"I need to ask you about something else," Rutland said. "Forgive me for bringing up a personal matter."

Oka stared at his drink, convinced Rutland was going to ask him for more money. He steadied himself against expectations.

"My daughter," Rutland continued. "I have no idea what to do with her. I dragged the poor girl halfway around the world, promising her sightseeing, and now it isn't safe for her to leave the hotel. I can't bear the idea of leaving her in her hotel room all day."

Relieved, Oka finished his drink and started listing all the places she could visit, all the things she could do. Oka assured Rutland that it would be fine, as long as she traveled with an escort and made sure she dressed modestly. "She should wear a large hat that covers her features. For an escort, I can ask my wife to take her shopping in Ginza."

"I'm sure she will love that. Thank you."

"Don't mention it. I know it's late, but I imagine you're planning on taking her to Miyanoshita? I know how much you like it there."

"Yes, I am very excited to take her to see some of the beauty of your country. We will go first to Nikko, then to Miyanoshita, and then to Kyoto before leaving Japan. On the way home, we will spend several days in Hawaii, so she can take in the beaches and the beauty of Honolulu."

Rutland leaned forward and grinned, taking pleasure in their shared conspiracy. "And, naturally, I will be able to provide an in-depth report on what's happening at the base in Pearl Harbor."

"Tomorrow, Rutland-san. Tomorrow."

Rutland caught him looking up from his drink to check out the lobby. There was no one around to worry about, not as far as Rutland could discern, at least. But the space between the two men suddenly felt heavy with Oka's reticence. He was concerned he had insulted Oka somehow, maybe by asking him to babysit his daughter. He felt as if he had overestimated his influence and mistaken his place. In the silence, which only seemed to grow heavier as Oka prepared to leave, Rutland recalled what Zacharias always told him about the Japanese and their aggression. Zacharias said that the preferred Japanese action was a surprise attack, and it was just a matter of time.

...

The next morning, Oka showed back up with two assistants and his wife, Ikuko, who was dressed in an elegant kimono.

"My goodness. That kimono," Barbara said. "It's gorgeous! See, Father, this is the Tokyo I missed yesterday. I don't care for such dour young men in military garb. But this is beauty and elegance." That day, Ikuko showed Barbara the outside of the beautiful architecture of the Frank Lloyd Wright–designed Imperial, then took her to Ginza, where they shopped and ate at one of the district's famous cafés. The cafés were somber, but Barbara was still impressed.

Meanwhile, Oka and his assistants sat with Rutland in the dining room at the Imperial. Oka said, "The information you have gotten on the American planes is extremely valuable, and I thank you for that. Yet, at this stage, we need to forget about much of your work in the past and change direction," Oka said. "As you can see everywhere, here and in the news, war is coming. We need to change your role for this reason." Turning to one of his assistants, Oka added in Japanese, "remember that in the last war, Rutland-san flew from a carrier to attack a Navy base. When we talk to him about his visit to Pearl Harbor, we need him to explain to us how vulnerable the base would be to air attack."

Rutland was somewhat surprised at Oka's tone, or perhaps by the situation as a whole, or perhaps he was just shaken by the prospect of war in Europe. Oka continued, "In the short term, we have the important task of your investigation of the defenses of Pearl Harbor. After that, we need to make firm plans for your activities after the war between Japan and the United States starts. It will be back to our original plan, where you are a sleeper, just as you and Takasu discussed in 1933. After the war starts, there will be no Japanese consulate in the US anymore, so we will need you to be ready to get the information out of the country by yourself."

Rutland nodded and said, "I understand." Although, in a way, he did not. A sleeper has a low profile, typically—far from what Rutland had been doing. But more than that, he was still in a bit of disbelief. Although there was a World War in Europe, and US-Japan relations were at an all-time low, war still seemed unlikely. As he had told others before, his belief was that if Japan was to attack the United States, it would be national suicide. They would lose, and that would be the end of Japan. The Japanese military was aggressive, to be sure, and full of pride. The pride was the dangerous part, along with the need to save face. If there was to be a war, that would be the reason, he thought. They might attack to protect their pride, even though they would lose.

"We also have a new code name for you. It's 'Miyanoshita,' after one of your favorite places."

He smiled, but with a touch of concern. "Why do I need a new code name?"

"We have reason to believe your previous code name has been compromised." Oka continued, "The sign that a war between Japan and the US has started, or will start soon, will be if we send you a telegram of exactly thirteen words. If you get a telegram of that length, collect the latest information on US Navy activity. When you have enough information, go to Mexico City and get the information to the Japanese Navy attaché there. We believe you still have a good cover story for how to get to Mexico, correct?"

Rutland nodded, somewhat feebly. "Yes, everyone knows that I have interest in a bottling plant in Mexico, so I can cross the border anytime. And yes, in the event of war, as previously agreed, I would easily be able to find valuable information by chatting up American media, titans of industry, naval officers, and more. So I am sure I will be able to be very helpful."

Rutland's eyes wandered to a newspaper being read by a foreign guest at the next table. Rutland was distracted by the headline, which said, in English, "Germans Troops Push into Poland, Britain Mobilizes."

"In fact," Rutland mentioned, "I have already focused much of my effort on these higher-level efforts, although I have been summarizing the information we received from Lockheed and Douglas recently."

"Good," said Oka. "Later this afternoon, let's discuss a bit more your plans for this high-level information collection and how you think it works."

Rutland nodded, in a bit of disbelief that the world situation had come to this point, but in more disbelief at what the Japanese Navy was asking him to do. For Rutland, personally, the worst case was if the current war in Europe expanded to truly be a World War. It suddenly seemed possible—if Japan allied with Germany, and Britain with the US, then all of a sudden there could be war between Japan and Britain, and worse, the Royal Navy base in Singapore would be in Japanese's sights. Rutland had friends on the British ships there.

He could now easily imagine his friends and patrons in the Japanese Navy ending up attacking his old ship and shipmates, in a newly improved dive bomber that had been redesigned using the information that Rutland had provided to Oka. Rutland had his own moral code, and a fight between the US and Japan was not ideal, but also not as much his concern. Even Britain—well, he was angry and bitter about his treatment by the Royal Air Force and annoyed at the harassment from British Intelligence over the years. But he was, at heart, a patriot, and furthermore, he loved the Royal Navy. The navy had given him everything, lifted him out of poverty and helped him achieve his fame. He was in touch with several of the top admirals still, who spoke about his feats in the Great War in almost worshipful terms. If it came down to the Japanese Navy attacking the British Royal Navy, well, helping the Japanese against his old shipmates was totally out of the question.

He thanked Oka and retired back to his room. He and Barbara took some Imperial Hotel stationery from the desk, and they each wrote letters: Rutland to his wife, Dorothy, in the Hollywood Hills, and Barbara to her mother, Dorothy, back in London. Rutland told his wife that in the event of war, he would send her a typewritten letter with instructions, but in any event, even with a war starting in Europe, he would very likely stay in America with her and the children.

Rutland had one more meeting at the hotel, with his friend Kayaba, who had a slightly different agenda than normal. The smartly dressed Kayaba greeted Rutland warmly, as always. After giving Rutland an envelope containing cash as dividends on his stock, he showed Rutland a book he had written for the Japanese Navy on the weapons used by the Chinese military. Rutland and he had a work session where Rutland was able to update and critique the descriptions of the warplanes the Chinese were using. The book was distributed to the Japanese forces in China and to Japanese manufacturers.

As Rutland and Barbara took the train from Nikko through Tokyo and to the Miyanoshita area, Rutland's mind wandered from topic to topic with blazing speed. He was disturbed at the events, and yet he also felt quite alive. He was in the middle of everything. How many people other than him were confidants of admirals in the US Navy, the Japanese Navy, *and* the British Navy? Probably no one else in the world. It gave him a feeling of responsibility to be so influential in world events.

But he also needed to take care of his daughter. He still felt the need to try and impress her and show her some of the excitement that he felt in working across the globe. They discussed their upcoming stopover in Hawaii, where Barbara could enjoy the beautiful beaches while Rutland "caught up with a couple of people" in Pearl Harbor. But this only returned his thoughts to the doubts he was having about his Japanese employer. He would not help Japan if it attacked Britain—and, in fact, he would come to Britain's aid. But if it was a war between the US and Japan only, then he wasn't sure exactly what would be best to do.

When they arrived in Miyanoshita, they took a rickshaw taxi from the train station to the Fujiya Hotel. But Rutland couldn't shake his uncertainty, and it cast a particular gloom over their trip. He and Barbara certainly were bonding, but he also realized that Barbara would remember her trip to Japan forever, for unintended reasons. Trying to shake his mood, he pointed west to show Barbara Mount Fuji, a sight that never failed to take his breath away.

Unfortunately, they could barely see anything. Clouds covered almost all of the mountain, and Rutland sank further into his own concerns.

CHAPTER 19

MANY STRANGE CLUES

Hollywood

Meanwhile, back in Hollywood, Alan Mowbray was also in an uncharacteristically gloomy mood. Standing in the vestibule of the headquarters of the Masquers, the exclusive comedy club for actors, he stared at the club's motto, engraved over the doors of the anteroom flanked by pictures of jesters and clowns.

We laugh to win.

His home country, Britain, had just declared war on Nazi Germany, and he recalled from his own time in the British military during the Great War just how much winning required. It was horrible and, as he approached the club's tavern, he remembered distinctly that he was only able to summon enough courage and purpose to endure such horrors because he held deeply in his heart the quiet hope that no one else would ever again have to fight a World War.

"Bollocks," he said to himself.

He straightened his tie and entered the club's tavern, reflexively ducking under its arched doorway to account for his height. To calm himself, he considered a few lines from William Hazlitt, from which the club's motto was born. "Man is the only animal that laughs and weeps; for he is the only animal that is struck with the difference between what things are and what they ought to be."

He was meeting his friends and fellow club members Boris Karloff and cement company CEO Norman Glover. Mowbray recognized that he stood in an interesting place between the Hollywood star and company owner. Known for his roles as a reliable and somewhat stocky British butler, he had become in recent years even more of a behind-the-scenes player than a movie star, though he had recently enjoyed a minor hit in Bob Hope's *Never Say Die*. He had pulled in contributions for the building of the club's new headquarters on Sycamore Avenue, and arranged for the club he started, the British United Services Club, to rent space there for its parties. As membership of both clubs continued to grow, so did Mowbray's influence, inside and outside its doors, with his cofounding, along with Karloff, of the Screen Actors Guild. Mowbray, then, was at the center of the two most lucrative enterprises of Los Angeles in the early twentieth century: celebrity and control. And, more often than not, both worked together, hand in glove. Like Billy Garland, the mastermind of the Los Angeles Olympics, Mowbray had proven adept at creating, seemingly out of nothing, an industry of influence among actors at a time when the system was decidedly against them. He was respected and wealthy beyond his wildest imagination. And yet he could never seem to shake the shadow that followed him throughout his city. The cause of his gloom, at this particular moment, was his failure to properly make use of either his fame or his power.

He spotted Glover at a table in the back of the tavern, drinking with a bald man he didn't know. As he walked over to join them, however, he realized the bald man was, in fact, Karloff, perfectly shorn like an English sheep. Unobstructed, his features were even more pronounced and even more severe. He looked young, but hardly like himself, more like a distant relative, and Mowbray could see plainer than ever Karloff's Indian heritage, which audiences often mistook for Italian or Egyptian. He looked professorial.

"You could project that bald head across Radio City Music Hall," Mowbray said. "Why on heaven's green earth would you do such a thing?"

"That will be all," Karloff responded. "I've been hearing nothing but from Hugh Hubert and Frank McHugh all day. Ronnie Reagan couldn't stop snickering throughout the SAG meeting this morning. Two rows behind him, and that's all I could hear."

"But what happened?" Mowbray asked again.

"Tell him, Boris."

Karloff looked at Glover and self-consciously ran his palm across his scalp.

"It will grow back, eventually, I'm sure. But this is the least of my worries. I shaved it for *The Tower of London*, perhaps another bad choice in a series of them with this picture. We're weeks behind and thousands in the hole. Twelve hours a day stuck out in Tarzana, waiting for Lee to get the bloody Battle of Tewkesbury right. The War of the Roses hardly took this long. Or cost this much. Thank God that's behind me."

Despite his sour mood, Mowbray couldn't help but laugh out loud.

"But that's not it," Glover said. "There's more."

"Ah, that's hardly worth mentioning. She looks darling, and I'm sure she was happy to join Dada in his silly custom," said Karloff.

Mowbray looked confused. "I don't follow."

"He cut off baby Sara Jane's hair, too, just for fun," added Glover.

"Jeezuz, no woman would be happy about that," added Mowbray.

Glover mentioned, "And with Sara Jane's first birthday coming up! Really, Boris, you should know by now there are other ways to get a rise out of a woman. Surely."

Karloff placed his hands on the table and slightly lifted himself up in the air. His back was killing him again, more and more these days, it seemed. As he neared his fifty-second birthday—a day he shared with his only daughter, Sara Jane—he began to believe this condition was becoming chronic, that he would have to deal with this discomfort and demonstrable hindrance for the rest of his life. The price he paid for the shot that had made him a star, carrying Colin Clive up the stairs of that bloody windmill at the end of *Frankenstein*. How many films had he shot without incident before that one? What was it? Seventy, or seventy-five? Maybe even eighty. Humping his way, year after year, for almost a decade, from lot to lot and bit part to bit part until a casting director spotted him in a canteen, the only guy dumb enough—he probably thought—to sit through four hours of makeup every day to play a monster. He didn't even get paid for those hours, mind you, because those hours weren't considered a part of the day. But he came out on top, earning fame and fortune behind that makeup, and collecting enough pull to form a proper union, which protected him and fellow performers from a corrupt system. *Never trust a studio head or an executive.* How many times had he told just that to people? More times than he could possibly remember. But he could surely recall when he learned these same execs, terrified of his influence, had gone so far as to bug his home phone. Nowhere was safe, which was why to this day he carried a roll of dimes on set, just so he could make calls from a pay phone, where no one could listen in.

Settling back into this seat, he felt the muscles in his lower back tighten again, and he was reminded why Mowbray had called him and Glover to the club. He and his companions were sitting on a dangerous cocktail of anger and pride and powerlessness. They were angry at the Germans and concerned for their fellow Brits, who were gearing up to take on Hitler's best, six thousand miles away from Sycamore Avenue. To help, they could raise funds for British War Relief. They also could finally address the Rutland issue, which was unfolding right in their backyard.

"The stakes are too high now," Karloff said, patting his head.

"Britain is in a fight for her life," Mowbray added.

"And Rutland is gallivanting through Asia," Glover said, "as if the world weren't on fire. With his teenage daughter."

They tried to assess whatever information they had about Rutland. Mowbray and Glover, for instance, had heard a lot from Rutland about his work with the Japanese, specifically his work with Kayaba, the firm that continued to be on the leading edge of Japanese naval air power. Mowbray also confirmed that Rutland had told him most of his income was from Kayaba's use of his patent.

In retrospect, Mowbray and Glover agreed this was all a bit irregular. And all three admitted they believed—hoped—that Rutland was most likely spying for British Naval Intelligence or MI6. "Until recently," Glover said, somewhat ashamed, "I had held him in the highest esteem as a loyal Britisher with an excellent World War record, and a first-class businessman."

"What changed?" asked Karloff.

"A few things. Just recently, we asked him to help us raise funds for the British War Relief. He said—what was it exactly, Alan?"

"He said it would be 'beneath the dignity of the British Empire to be asking its friends for money.'"

There were other clues as well. Rutland openly discussed his friendship with various Japanese admirals and, on occasion, mentioned some work he had done for them. Of course, this suddenly took on a more ominous note, thanks to recent events. So did Rutland's photography hobby. Taking pictures was one thing, but most hobbyists dropped their film off with a professional developer. Very few, if any, installed their own fully equipped darkroom in their house.

"We're now quite sure he is not a member of British Intelligence?" Glover asked, even though he knew the answer.

"That sounds unlikely," said Karloff assuredly. "That's not how MI6 works."

Karloff was no MI6 agent himself, but he'd played a secret agent on the big screen. In his latest film, called *British Intelligence*, he played a German spy, and he seemed to have picked up some knowledge of how these things actually worked.

Glover had another agenda: what he wanted most was to be part of the club, a man welcomed into the inner circle. Unlike Mowbray and Karloff and most other members of the British United Services Club, Glover was anonymous outside of construction circles. He was wildly successful and incredibly busy, as Los Angeles continued its expansion into the surrounding desert. He admired his companions and appreciated their generous bonhomie, which Glover, neither a veteran nor an actor, still feared was unwarranted. They'd shown the same warmth to Rutland, the war hero they now suspected as a spy. And now here he was trying to suss out the information with Mowbray and Karloff—making him deeply part of the inner circle.

"Did I mention what our consul general said to me," Glover continued, "when I asked if he was going to Rutland's party? Not only did he say he was turning down the invitation, but strangely, he said he would not go to the party because he didn't want anyone to think that Rutland was endorsed by the British government. That sounds like the consul also thinks Rutland is suspicious, doesn't it?"

"I realize it just doesn't sound plausible," Mowbray said. "Rutland, holder of the Distinguished Service Cross, spying for the Japanese? I fear, though, that it seems to be the only possible explanation."

Glover shook his head and finished his drink. Mowbray called for another round, and Karloff squirmed again in his seat, this time more noticeably. Glover thought he caught the outline of a back brace underneath's Karloff's suit. Ignoring it, he continued, "At his party, he mentioned again his interest in photography and showed us some slides. He showed us his darkroom. A first-class darkroom, photography equipment, radio equipment. Karloff, the spies in your movies would have those things. But if Rutland were a spy for the Japanese, it would be very surprising that he would boldly show them to us. And if he was really on a spy mission to Asia, would he really be taking his teen daughter with him?"

"If his espionage is taking place here at the British United Services Club," Mowbray added, "this is highly embarrassing, both to the Crown and to us. And to me, personally, as founder and president of this club."

"It makes me feel like a fool not to have realized earlier," Karloff said.

Left unsaid was the worst possible outcome—that they had somehow advanced Rutland's cause. Just a few years earlier, Rutland had pushed so hard to get Karloff's former employee Raymond Barry the job at Lockheed.

They continued to drink, stewing in their blind naiveté and righteous indignation. Finally, they devised a plan. They would go to the FBI—or, rather, Glover would go to their offices on Spring Street, because neither Mowbray nor Karloff could go without drawing attention.

...

On September 13, Glover visited the downtown Los Angeles office of the FBI. The FBI agents were used to crackpots with conspiracy theories contacting them, but Glover seemed worth taking seriously. The secretary ushered him into a private room in the back where two agents interviewed Glover. As soon as he mentioned Rutland, the agents stopped the meeting. They immediately called in Richard Hood, the special agent in charge who ran the Los Angeles office. Responsible for two hundred federal agents across Southern California, Hood had been fielding reports about Rutland for more than a year. *When there's smoke, there's fire*, thought Hood. He was ready to launch a formal investigation into Rutland.

Two weeks later, however, Hood received a memo directly from J. Edgar Hoover himself. To Hood's surprise, Hoover ordered him to let it go. "Stop the investigation of Frederick Rutland," the memo stated, "and do not mention the matter to any third party, including other government agencies."

What Hood didn't know was that Hoover was responding to a telegram from Ellis Zacharias, which requested that the FBI stop the surveillance of Rutland, because Rutland was "an active and key US Navy Intelligence asset." His jaw dropped. Rutland seemed as dirty as they came; he had heard as much from Hanson, his predecessor in the job and current security head at Lockheed. There was something going on, and he was itching to get to the bottom of it, which he knew he would eventually. *It's only a matter of time*, he thought—and put his Rutland file away, as ordered.

Meanwhile, Mowbray and Glover set up the British War Relief office in a swanky location in the Ambassador Hotel and proceeded to plan fund-raising events. In a quiet moment in the office, they also discussed their conversations with the FBI about Rutland.

The irony certainly didn't escape these career comedians—Karloff was playing the role of a spy in a new movie, but they felt they were partly involved in real-life espionage, thanks to their erstwhile friend Rutland, and wanted to do something about it. They, of course, didn't know that the FBI currently had the investigation on hold. For now.

CHAPTER 20

COUNTERSPIES

1940

Ellis Zacharias was alarmed at the report that had just come in. It was from a trusted informant in Mexico, and it said a Japanese suicide attack was coming soon. The informant said that the Japanese had some planes hidden in Baja California, and they would take the opportunity of the American fleet having four battleships in the port of San Diego at the same time to execute a suicide attack to try to sink these warships.

Zacharias thought it unlikely, but plausible. He'd anticipated a US-Japanese war for a long time. As always, the Japanese would start with a surprise attack at a weak point. Depending on where those Japanese planes were located, they could in theory fly over the border and reach the US battleships in as little as five or ten minutes. Even more alarming, it was unusual to have four US battleships in the port of San Diego simultaneously. The stage was set a bit too perfectly for Zacharias not to take even the hint of this threat seriously.

Zacharias, the head of ONI on the West Coast, was in charge of protecting the fleet from spies and saboteurs. He called to book an appointment with the head of the Pacific Fleet, Admiral James Richardson, and took a small plane to San Pedro. Grabbing a cab, he made it to the harbor and was escorted aboard Richardson's flagship, the *Pennsylvania*. Richardson asked if ONI had concrete evidence of any Japanese planes in position to carry out this attack.

Zacharias replied, "Well, sir, we are quite sure there are no Japanese ships around that could launch such an attack. However, we have multiple informants who are discussing the possibility of Japanese planes being hidden in the deserts of Baja California. As you know, a plane in Baja could fly over the border and be over San Diego harbor in just a matter of minutes."

Richardson scowled. "Well, it seems unlikely. But it wouldn't be prudent to ignore this warning. Plus, going on alert would be good practice for the men. I'll alert my ships." He continued, "Zack, please alert Slew McCain* and have him to put his planes on alert as well."

Zacharias saluted and left the ship to go back to his unit.

The report was, of course, false—there was no suicide attack by Japanese planes on the American ships. There were many Japanese agents in Mexico, but none of them had planes. Still, somehow Zacharias had gone on the record about Japanese suicide planes—kamikazes—before they were known to exist. Perhaps Zacharias really did have the Japanese Navy figured out.

Zacharias and his second in command, Kenneth Ringle, were frankly a bit overwhelmed with their responsibility to protect the United States from a potential Japanese attack. There were reports of Japanese ships and planes from informants up and down the coast, from Vancouver down through central Mexico. They were very concerned about the Japanese fishing village in San Pedro and Japanese immigrants who had their strawberry farms by the Douglas plant—reports of industrial espionage, monitoring the Japanese attachés, the hintings of espionage in the Japanese consulate and in Little Tokyo, the Molino Rojo in Tijuana, strange fishing activity in Turtle Bay . . . the list never ended. Zacharias talked often with Los Angeles County sheriff Eugene W. Biscailuz, who had fifty thousand index cards full of suspects, which included Japanese, Soviets, American communists, anarchists, American Nazis, German Nazis in America, Mexican fascists . . .

---

* The grandfather of the late senator John McCain.

There was no way to monitor all of these suspects with the limited manpower available. Zacharias had to prioritize ONI's efforts. Being politically ambitious, he often reacted to news from Washington, DC.

> The innocuous Japanese fishing fleet of some 1,000 boats, the Committee on Un-American Activities stated, has been locating certain strategic naval operations and could cause serious trouble if Japan and the United States severed relations. The committee asserts this fleet is ready to dynamite and bomb when and if the order comes from the Imperial Navy.
>
> —The Los Angeles Examiner, *quoting the congressional committee HUAC, July 6, 1941*

After congressmen talked to the press about the Japanese fisherman, Zacharias ordered raids on dozens of Japanese-owned fishing boats in and around Long Beach, in a location known as Fish Harbor. The raids found nothing. The one thing Zacharias, notably, did not do was loop in the FBI during the course of his counterintelligence efforts. He gave the excuse that they were few, or questioned their competence. But also, with him, it was personal.

Zacharias understood Japan and the Japanese threat very well. But he was looking for clues on the Japanese threat only in the areas under his jurisdiction—California, Mexico, and so on. There were active Japanese agents in California, such as the Furusawas and their Japanese Navy association. However, the fishermen on Fish Harbor, just like the Japanese strawberry farmers by the Douglas plant runway, were doing nothing more than trying to earn a living. It was the same with almost all of the Japanese in California.

The press and US Congress were also pushing the navy to focus on looking for a Japanese threat from Mexico. It seemed plausible at the time that Japan and Mexico would work together. In the last war, Mexico had actively helped Germany, and the rogue Mexican forces led by Pancho

Villa had attacked a border town, briefly invading the United States. Villa famously had many Japanese staff, including his doctor. Yet the Japanese in Mexico were spies, codebreakers, and the like. There was no way Japan could attack the US from Mexico.

ONI's charter was twofold. First, to deliver insights into threats to America's fleet and its decision-makers. And second, the part of ONI that later split off to become NCIS was focused on: catching spies, saboteurs, and criminals. But they were spending a lot of effort on the second part—the mission of NCIS today. The Japanese had an attack fleet of six world-class aircraft carriers, with the two first ones partially designed by Rutland. They'd built planes referencing plans they'd received from Rutland. If they were to attack the US, it would certainly be a direct attack using their navy. And that navy was not in the US or Mexico. It was in Japan, practicing for the day they would fight the Americans. When the time came, they would—for the most part—remain unobserved,* while ONI was spending much of their effort looking for spies and saboteurs.

---

* ONI had been having visiting American ships take pictures when they passed through Japanese ports, for example. But the visiting Matson and American President Lines ships didn't go to the Japanese Navy bases.

CHAPTER 21

DOUBLE AGENT

1938–39

Rutland had been hiding in plain sight very effectively. For years, British United Services Club members didn't think much of Rutland's Japanese connections, other than the occasional quip about Rutland being a bit of a mystery. On the off chance that Rutland really was a spy, people like Claude Mayo,* a club member and an officer in the Office of Naval Intelligence, defaulted to what seemed obvious—Rutland, he initially thought, was likely an agent for Britain. Rutland's cover, it seemed, was secure.

After he came back from Japan in mid-September 1939, however, Rutland felt like everything had changed. Tensions between nations continued to escalate, and they impacted him personally. Japan seemed to be actively preparing for a fight with the US. It wasn't just all the mobilized soldiers Rutland had seen when he was in Japan with his daughter—the targeted questions Rutland got from his Japanese handlers were now very war-focused. The war in Europe was spreading, with Britain now in a fight for its life.

Rutland found things different not only in Japan, but back at home as well. His friends at the club, Mowbray and Karloff, seemed suddenly serious, unsmiling, and a bit distant.

Rutland confided in his friend Claude Mayo. He stressed to Mayo that his activities were legitimate, even if they might occasionally look strange.

---

* Father of Charlie Mayo, who served with this author's father.

But a key point he stressed was that his activities had resulted in him probably being the world's leading expert on the future enemy of the USA, the Japanese Navy. He underlined how valuable he would prove to US intelligence in the event of war with Japan. Who else, he asked Mayo rhetorically, knew as much about the Japanese Navy's ships, planes, and admirals? Mayo couldn't help but notice that Rutland's spin on the situation and confidence in Japan's naval prowess sounded like the same warnings that Mayo had heard over and over from his colleague Ellis Zacharias.

Zacharias had continued to press alarm buttons about the Japanese. He was the subject of a bit of mockery among his peers in the US Navy after the false alarm he'd rung over the nonexistent San Diego kamikaze attack. Still, Mayo respected Zacharias in the same way others at ONI did. Zacharias was obsessed with protecting the US against what he thought was an inevitable Japanese attack, but he was unfocused. He recalled Hood of the FBI saying that Zacharias was dedicated, "but his feet are not firmly planted on the ground." Despite the enmity the FBI agents had for Zacharias, Mayo ultimately agreed with his position. Rutland, he thought, had a similar mind, but could anchor Zacharias's gut impulses with factual context. Mayo was well aware of espionage networks popping up throughout the West Coast—and not just Japanese. He also saw firsthand the growing evidence that ONI collected about the Russian and German secret agents who were spying in the United States.*

Mayo introduced Rutland to Zacharias, who was heading ONI's Eleventh Naval District, responsible for California and environs. Zacharias and Rutland spoke on the phone a couple of times before they agreed to meet in person. Their initial conversations were broad and casual, more feeling each other out than strategy sessions or working partnerships. But both men walked away from each meeting interested in taking these conversations further for several reasons. Firstly, they liked each other personally and had a lot in common. Both had grown up dreaming of join-

---

* Mayo, although living in Los Angeles at the time, had been put in charge of the Thirteenth Naval District, which oversaw the Pacific Northwest.

ing the navy from their homes overlooking nearby naval bases. Both had joined their respective naval officer corps through smarts and force of will, despite having backgrounds that were disadvantageous. Rutland pulled himself up from the English lower class, while Zacharias was the only Jewish student at Annapolis for the first decade of the 1900s. The two men also had similar personalities. Both had been initially promoted based on competence and because they had driven innovation in their respective navies. Both were accused of self-promotion and insubordination. Like Rutland, the headstrong Zacharias often clashed with anyone who disagreed with him, regardless of rank, and too often allowed his passion to overrule prudence. Both were passed up for promotion and both believed this slight was rooted in others' bigotry rather than their own behavior.

More importantly, however, Rutland and Zacharias both recognized what each man offered the other. Rutland knew that Zacharias could provide him some much-needed protection and potential leverage if his relationship with the Japanese grew untenable or, more likely, proved to be a criminal liability. Conversely, Zacharias saw in Rutland a possible answer to a major problem, specifically his worrisome dilemma between the signal and the noise. Zacharias had access to the massive file folder of suspects maintained by the Los Angeles County sheriff, which was so large that it defied a way to prioritize. Zacharias needed a source to tell him where to look.

Their defining meeting took place in the Del Monte Club on Windward Avenue, in Venice, close to Rutland's office by the Douglas plant.* Rutland was a member of that club as well. A former speakeasy, the Del Monte was literally built on subterfuge. Established in 1915 by an Italian immigrant named Cesar Menotti, the Del Monte was a nexus of nightlife in Los Angeles during Prohibition, hosting the city's most nefarious and infamous characters of the day, masked cleverly by Menotti's grocery store, which was built above the subterranean speakeasy. Rows of fresh produce covered a trapdoor and dumbwaiter that escorted guests up and

---

* The Del Monte Club exists in its original state and is now called Townhouse.

down throughout the night. Stocking his basement speakeasy required some creativity. Menotti hired Canadian ships to anchor three miles off the coast of Los Angeles, just outside Prohibition's legal reach. He then deployed smaller boats to transport cases of liquor through an interconnected network of tunnels through downtown Venice, which connected to his basement. Menotti's system and political connections were so well known that there was a joke that his tunnels ran all the way to city hall.

Above this once-not-so-secret network, Rutland and Zacharias finally spoke openly about matters of intelligence.

Rutland set his drink down and cleared his throat. "Mexico," he said.

Zacharias looked around the club before talking. "We can keep this between you and me, eyes only. The less people who know, the better."

"I can go to Mexico whenever I want, even if there is a war. They expect me to be there."

"Go on."

"The communication goes like this: Los Angeles. Tijuana. The Pacific. Or: Los Angeles. Mexicali. The Japanese embassy in Mexico City." Rutland traced his finger across the table, punctuating his lines with three definitive taps. "That's the way it works."

To anyone passing by, their conversation would have sounded anodyne, tedious even. But Rutland was relaying his arrangement with the Japanese Navy, how if a war broke out, he would gather information in Los Angeles and bring it to Mexico via a couple different routes, before the information got sent to Tokyo by ship.

"I play cards," Zacharias said. "Poker. A lot of people think it's a game of chance. But that's not true. You don't play the cards. You play the man. And to play the man, you have to make him believe you have a specific set of cards when, in reality, you have another. This determines the outcome."

"What's more advantageous, I assume, is controlling the deck, knowing the cards you're dealing them before even they do," said Rutland.

"Within reason and with great discretion, absolutely. The key is to make them believe they remain at advantage, which means you have to throw a few games to gain their confidence. Lose the smaller pots to win the entire pot later."

"You know," Rutland said, "I could share some trivial US Navy secrets you give me with the Japanese. Then they would trust me even more."

"Which wouldn't put you out or pick money out of your pockets."

The more they drank, the bolder they got. Each counterintelligence scheme grew more outlandish. Near the end of the night, Rutland floated the idea of capturing a Japanese submarine. "After the war starts, I could arrange with the Japanese to send a submarine to a quiet beach at night, perhaps Paradise Cove in Malibu. I would tell them I could get information to them by signaling the submarine with a lantern from the jetty. Then, when the submarine surfaces to receive the signals, you can have a destroyer pounce on it. Bang! You would be able to capture a Japanese submarine intact!"

Zacharias let out an enormous belly laugh that shook the table. "If you help me get a Japanese submarine, you can have whatever you want."

The plan to capture a submarine sounded crazy at first, but after sobering up a bit and thinking about it, they decided it just might work. The Japanese might go for it, because they wanted to be able to get information from the US mainland to Japan quickly, and this would be very quick, much faster than having Rutland try to cross the border and get information down to Mexico City. If they managed to pull this off, it would be a perfect double cross.

Rutland and Zacharias both got what they wanted from this deal. Rutland had secured his own plan B. If there was to be a war, and he was shown to be helping the Japanese, he would have the perfect alibi to keep him out of jail: Zacharias, the influential head of ONI on the West Coast, would be able to tell everyone Rutland was actually working for the Americans.

Zacharias was also thrilled. In Rutland, he had finally secured someone on the inside of the Japanese spy net, whom he believed he had turned. Rutland's story was perfect as well. Zacharias thought he had legitimately been working for the Japanese, assuming that a war would never come, but now that the world situation was edging closer toward war, it made complete sense that Rutland would want to change sides and work for the Americans.

Zacharias also realized how much he *liked* Rutland. Rutland was a man of action, he thought, unlike the bureaucrats and political animals he dealt with every day. When Zacharias thought of annoying bureaucrats, the first thing he thought of was the FBI. The FBI, he felt, still didn't give a damn about the Japanese threat. Zacharias wasn't entirely wrong, but his anger about the topic was intense and more about his personal feelings than logic. His grudge with the FBI had started with that disastrous meeting a decade earlier with FBI director J. Edgar Hoover, who had thrown Zacharias out of his office for talking about the Japanese threat too insistently.

Zacharias told Rutland that they would need to keep their partnership secret to prevent leaks. The only other person who would know about their arrangement would be his second in command, Kenneth Ringle. However, the whole arrangement had some major flaws from the start. Rutland had put all of his eggs into one basket, making a bet that the US Navy would protect him from being accused of being a Japanese spy. But Zacharias's boss, the director of ONI, had no information about this deal, and neither did the FBI. If the FBI ended up chasing Rutland, it seemed highly risky to have Rutland's alibi be in the hands of Zacharias, with whom they were having constant political battles.

In the short term, Rutland didn't need to worry about being investigated. The FBI had gotten a few reports on Rutland, but Zacharias had told them to hold off. The British knew most of what Rutland had been doing to help Japan against the US, but they didn't share that with the Americans. Zacharias and others at ONI might have trusted Rutland much less if they'd had a better idea of what he was doing. There were even issues within ONI. Zacharias hadn't told the director of ONI about Rutland, possibly because Zacharias was aiming for the ONI director job himself.

Just like the British in Los Angeles, many of the Americans who had suspicions about Rutland initially assumed he was working for *British Intelligence*. The British agencies, who had very large files on Rutland, weren't telling the Americans about it. But it was worse than that. It wasn't just that the British hadn't talked to the Americans about Rutland. The British hadn't discussed *anything* about *any* Japanese espionage with the Americans, *because* of Rutland. The reason was obvious. It would have been highly embarrassing for the British to tell the Americans that one of their famous war heroes had been in America, running a spy ring for the Japanese, now for over a half decade, and that they'd failed to mention it. MI5 had talked to MI6 about broaching the subject with the Americans, but hadn't done so. And the longer they waited to talk about things, the more embarrassing it became. A Japanese war with the United States was starting to become more and more likely, but the various intelligence agencies were all on different pages.

CHAPTER 22

TACHIBANA

1939–41

Commander Itaru Tachibana of the Imperial Japanese Navy couldn't shake the smell of brine and musk, which always reminded him of opportunity. Walking down Seaside Avenue, on a shiny afternoon on Fish Harbor, known to white Californians as Terminal Island, he passed intersection after intersection named after an aquatic animal—Albacore, Sardine, Barracuda, Pilchard—until he neared a sprawl of petroleum stations that serviced the island's industrious fishing fleets. He stared across the harbor at the ships of the US Pacific Fleet—Japan's future enemy—and marveled that he could just walk here and observe them unmolested.

He paused and removed his hat and dabbed his brow with a handkerchief, a keepsake he always made sure to store in his breast pocket, close to his heart. He was slightly winded, sweating in a handsome three-piece suit. He became increasingly disoriented from passing the identical plots of row houses, which were laid out as neatly as a sequence of Morse code that relayed on a loop a singular phrase in the same frequency, its conclusion yet to be determined. In recent weeks, he had grown weary of divining meaning in gestures and glances, rumors and hints, even declarations. He brushed the dirt off of his shoes and waited.

Of all the places he had visited since arriving in Los Angeles, San Pedro was his favorite. He enjoyed the quiet and solitude the bucolic port city afforded him, the ability to come and go in peace. He also enjoyed the city's more temperate weather. On most visits, especially in the summer months, San Pedro was often twenty degrees cooler than congested and cool-averse downtown Los Angeles, which gave him a reprieve from his cramped quarters in the Olympic Hotel in Little Tokyo.

What he loved most about San Pedro, though, was the Japanese fishermen and their families inhabiting the city, Issei (first-generation Japanese immigrants) and Nissei (their American-born children) living together on Fish Harbor, two generations of Japanese at home in this strange country. Most called the village "Furusato," a fanciful word he could never quite translate with his broken English. The closest he could ever get was "hometown," but he knew that wasn't exactly right. If he allowed himself to ponder its meaning, he knew, he would drive himself mad with frustration. English, this second language, was maddening. *Haradatashi* (infuriating).

Over the past couple of months, he had integrated himself into the community, showing up to their picnics and gatherings, sharing grilled fresh-caught fish, miso soup, mochi, and in particular, the local abalone, which was so cheap in the US. In fact, he'd eaten so many plates that he feared he'd soon grow heavy. But this was a small price to pay, he assured himself, for peace of mind. His frequent trips to Fish Harbor were more reprieve than reconnaissance. His orders included directions to use Japanese Americans sparingly, if at all, since they couldn't be trusted—many seemed more like Americans than Japanese. He was getting coaching from Toraichi Kono, who reminded him that many or most of the missions needed a white face; as open as American society was, a Japanese face drew suspicion, so that even if he could have counted on some Japanese Americans, they just wouldn't be effective.

It was ironic. There was a Japanese fishing village here, overlooking the US Navy base. In flights of paranoia, US Navy officers assumed these fishermen were going up and down the coast testing out landing beaches. Zacharias thought they were a security risk and had many boats searched. But, in reality, these Japanese fishermen weren't going to be of any assistance in Japanese espionage. If needed, Tachibana could give them direction, and they would not dare to refuse an Imperial Navy commander, but he really didn't need to. In theory, they could of course monitor the ins and outs of the Pacific Fleet across the way, but that could be done by anyone. In fact, to monitor the comings and goings of many ships, all one needed to do in this country was to pick up a newspaper.

Perhaps the real reason Tachibana liked visiting Fish Harbor had nothing to do with the people, or even the food he enjoyed. He liked that he could see the US Navy ships with his own eyes. It helped make it all real and helped him focus on his mission.

From the moment he arrived in Los Angeles in 1939, Tachibana knew he would likely become a subject of surveillance, but he didn't care. He had no formal diplomatic immunity, but he was confident he was untouchable. He had heard there was a tacit agreement between the US State Department and the Japanese Foreign Ministry to leave each other's agents alone, lest it turn into an international incident. There was no such relationship between Japan and Britain. Tachibana chuckled, thinking about the British reporter, Melville James Cox of Reuters, who had been working for British Intelligence. One day, the British embassy had gotten a call that Cox had unfortunately died from "falling out of a fourth-floor window of the Japanese police headquarters." Tachibana assumed, correctly, that at this point the Americans wouldn't dare to touch him, so he could mostly ignore the occasional person following him.

Yet Tachibana was making himself perhaps a little too visible. Guards at San Pedro and San Diego navy bases noted sightings of a suspicious car with a Japanese driver and ran the license plates. Tachibana always used a car that was registered in his name, so all of a sudden ONI had several similar reports from different bases of him acting suspiciously. After the customary report from ONI to the FBI, the FBI agents raised the issue to FBI special agent in charge Hood. Hood consulted with FBI assistant director Edward Tamm to ask if a formal investigation into Tachibana was necessary. Tamm confirmed with FBI director Hoover that the policy had not changed, but that the Los Angeles Field Office should "conduct an appropriate discreet investigation." Hoover's FBI and the entirety of the United States government was finally beginning to recognize the threat from Japan, from Franklin Delano Roosevelt's Oval Office and Cordell Hull's State Department to Frank Murphy's Attorney General's Office. In fact, firebrand congressman Martin Dies of Texas, head of the House Un-American Activities Committee, had for the first time turned his attention from communists and Nazis to address the Japanese threat in a speech.

Even Attorney General Murphy—a fierce defender of civil liberties who, as a Supreme Court Justice, later dissented in the *Korematsu v. United States* Japanese internment ruling—publicly declared that "special vigilance" was nevertheless necessary because of the number of military, naval, and aviation bases on the West Coast. The Japanese fishermen on Fish Harbor were drawing more and more attention. Hood, in his report to Tamm, stressed that the fishermen couldn't be living in a more sensitive location. Similarly, the Douglas plant in Santa Monica had Japanese farmers growing strawberries on both sides of its runway. In theory, had those farmers been spies, it would have been easy for them to use signal lights to guide a bomber to that plant, located just a short walk from the famous Venice Beach. Their location drew undue attention—not just from the FBI, but from the public at large.

Meanwhile, Tachibana—the very real spy and very real threat to America—started to relax, eager finally to clear his head for a few minutes and take stock of everything he had already accomplished and everything he still had yet to do. He removed from his pocket two pages of paper. Before opening the first piece of paper, Tachibana paused and looked around to make sure no one was watching. He knew that, on occasion, he was being followed. By this point, everyone had a tail. The FBI was beginning to monitor Rutland, and Mayo's ONI team was tracking Tachibana's subordinate, Okada, in Seattle, following him as he snapped pictures of the USS *Saratoga* around the naval base there in Sand Point. But he was satisfied that nobody was following him, not today at least, when he was by himself, miles away from any location of value, surrounded by other Japanese. The first page, which he started to peruse, was a roster of names and, marked in red and black ink, a corresponding ledger of accounts owed and accounts paid in denominations of twenties and fifties and hundreds—the ugly green currency of this shaky American brand of capitalism. Like everything else in this country, he believed, its purpose was purely utilitarian; despite the hope and ideals the promissory notes augured, they were, at heart, a receipt of transactions, a give-and-take reminder of what one put in and what one took out, a person's entire worth measured by the size of the wad in his or her pocket. Who was he to judge, though? He was an immediate beneficiary of this system, monetizing information to his advantage. These figures were the truest items he could ever hold. He scanned the list, though by now he'd committed it to memory, every syllable, and every cent. Maki, Los Angeles, $25. Nikaido, Los Angeles, $50. Fujii, Honolulu, $750. Rutland, Los Angeles, $3,000. These were his charges, the men who mattered most to him, their usefulness to him written out in his own hand. Looking at this gave him a feeling of satisfaction, and he put the paper back into his pocket.

The second piece of paper he had memorized just as thoroughly as the first, and yet he paused before reading its contents, written out in the penmanship of a young woman. He could recite every line from memory, but the words felt heavier, more substantial to him than anything else in the world. He imagined her sitting at her desk at Mills College, pen in hand, trying to give voice to her affections and frustration, finding the space at once to remain vulnerable and resolute in her expectations. How quickly things had turned, how easily his personal feelings had bled into his profession.

Like the other agents that the Japanese Navy had sent to America, Tachibana had little training or experience in intelligence. His initial assignment in the US was as a language student at the University of Pennsylvania. After graduating, he traveled around the United States and Mexico before returning to Los Angeles, where he enrolled as a language student at the University of Southern California.

He started working with Ken Nakazawa, a professor at USC, to have the Japanese Student Association help the Japanese Navy's data collection operation, pulling articles readily available at the USC library. The information was endless and everywhere. It was also ironic that for so much of this "espionage," no spies were needed—much of the information Tokyo requested was freely available. Tachibana could just tell Professor Nakazawa what he wanted, and the students would check out some journals, read some newspapers, and create a report that he would annotate and send back to Tokyo. The fishermen in San Pedro may have seemed suspicious to the Americans, but some college students in a library who were paid $20 were far more of a risk to US national security.

The motivated and energetic Tachibana was able to find, buy, or steal maps of all of the oil installations on the West Coast, diagrams of navy ships under construction, information on possible landing zones and defenses on the beaches on the West Coast, and more. He loaded up the trunk of his car and took his first trip to Mexico, dropping off both open-source and stolen information at the Molino Rojo, before sampling the roster of European and Mexican women there. The proprietor of the Molino Rojo, Yasuhara, as usual, ensured the files and reports would get to a passing Japanese ship captain to take to Tokyo.

Nearly forty years old, Tachibana had come to the US alone, leaving his wife and two children in Japan. He had gotten married young in an arranged marriage and was enjoying the freedom his position gave him to meet women. Most of his peers preferred anonymous relationships with women of a lower social status, although it was well known that Admiral Yamamoto had a relationship with a high-class geisha. Tachibana was a risk-taker in romance as well as espionage; he preferred to seduce upper-class Japanese girls who were half his age. He dated Anne Katsuizumi, whom he met through her father, who was one of Eisuke Ono's compatriots at the Yokohama Specie Bank.

Tachibana's philandering didn't distract from his espionage. However, his espionage lacked focus. Part of the problem was Tachibana's inherent recklessness and desire to impress his superiors. Additionally, however, Tachibana found the requests from Tokyo to be a little strange. The small staff of the intelligence group in naval headquarters in Tokyo just fired off a list of possible intelligence targets they thought might prove helpful down the road. One day, Tachibana got a request to send street maps of all forty-eight states and phone books from every major American city. Obtaining the phone books was easy. The hard part was hauling them back to Tokyo. Plus, Japanese Naval Intelligence headquarters had only four staff focused on the US and Canada at the time, and, with their limited time and staff available, it seemed unlikely they would use most of this information.

Helping Tachibana gather more information in the Pacific Northwest was the Seattle-based attaché Sadatomo Okada. In Los Angeles, Tachibana continued to lean on Chaplin's onetime body man Toraichi Kono—who proved invaluable, not only for his connections but for his fluency in English.

Tachibana personally ensured he was getting information on ship and plane movements from trusted Japanese agents in both San Pedro and San Diego, but relied on Kono and a couple of USC students for assignments that demanded better knowledge of English. For example, he had learned that a large percentage of the American shipyard workers were African American, and he thought it possible that these workers might be convinced to help the Japanese, or even possibly become saboteurs. Tachibana had a propaganda budget and used it to have Kono work with two students to pull together some articles on how Japan was working to free Asia from the domination of the white man. He then worked to have those published in the African American newspapers, with the idea being they would then chat with the publishers of these newspapers to see the reaction of the readers and decide if it would be possible to recruit agents from the African American community.

The navy base at Pearl Harbor started to come to the fore of Japanese thinking at this time. The base had been a bit of a backwater, but in mid-

1940, President Roosevelt had decided the US needed to show strength against Japan and ordered the US Pacific Fleet to move its home port from California to Pearl Harbor. Now, the US Fleet was closer to the Philippines or Dutch East Indies, where it seemed the Japanese might attack.

If the idea was that moving the US Fleet to Pearl Harbor would intimidate the Japanese, it had the opposite effect. For the more aggressive officers in the Japanese Navy, like Tachibana or the eventual leader of the attack, Yamamoto, the move of the US Fleet to Pearl Harbor was an opportunity. Despite the flights of paranoia in the minds of Hearst, Zacharias, and others, it would have been almost impossible for the Japanese Navy to pull off a surprise attack on Los Angeles, more than five thousand miles from Yokosuka. Now, all of a sudden, the target was just over half the distance as before, and a route to the attack could go through the freezing waters of the Arctic, which had less ship traffic, making it more likely not to be seen and therefore making a surprise much more possible.

Tachibana also felt threatened and rather angry when he heard the US Fleet was moving to Pearl Harbor. Until that moment, he had been the head Japanese agent watching the most important US base—but now, whoever was in Hawaii would have a more important job than him. His orders were to ignore Hawaii, but he wasn't going to follow those orders. If the action was in Hawaii, he was determined to work his espionage magic there and impress his superiors.

Tachibana also needed to ensure the integrity of the Los Angeles–Mexico espionage network after the war started. This role was currently assigned to Rutland, so Tachibana needed to meet Rutland and diagnose if he was dependable. After exchanging notes, Tachibana arranged to stop by Rutland's mansion.

Tachibana headed down Sunset Boulevard, noting that he needed to turn right just after he passed a whorehouse, the high-class Lee Francis brothel. It was an obvious security risk to meet agent Rutland at his house, where the FBI could be watching, but Tachibana went there anyway. He didn't care about risks, but also, he had to see if this house was as palatial as the rumors said.

Tachibana navigated increasingly narrow and windy roads to get up to Warbler Way, parking in front of Rutland's enormous house. He was astonished. It was even bigger and more luxurious than he had heard. He stopped to double-check that it was the right place, and noted the license plate on Rutland's car matched the one he'd been given. He rang the doorbell, and a butler opened the door. Tachibana quietly gasped as he marveled at the luxury of the residence, and managed to mutter the prearranged code words: "I am here from the Japan Aircraft Company." The butler let him in. American houses were usually much bigger than the small wooden houses of Japan, but he had never seen or dreamed of a house like this. The obvious question was: How much money had the Japanese Navy been paying this man?

Rutland came downstairs and escorted Tachibana to the living room for their conversation. The butler brought English tea, and they began their meeting. Rutland's top agenda item was to talk about communication networks after the war started. The current plan was still that Rutland would be getting information in the United States and going to Mexico to deliver it to Japanese agents there. However, Rutland introduced the proposal he had created—with Zacharias's help—where he would signal a Japanese submarine from a beach near Malibu. The idea was certainly bold and would be good for time-sensitive issues, so Tachibana agreed to look into it. He planned to make a trip to Malibu to see what he thought.

Ultimately, Tachibana came away from the meeting concerned about the notion of relying on Rutland during a time of war. Rutland followed up with Tachibana on his coordination with Mexico, but complained (in a letter that the FBI later obtained) that Tachibana was ignoring his calls. Meanwhile, Rutland suspected Tachibana was, if not inherently reckless, far too casual in his comportment. Tachibana wouldn't necessarily disagree with that assessment, but as far as he was concerned, the mission trumped most things, including discretion. Rutland thought Tachibana's opinion on him being untouchable by the FBI might not be wrong since Rutland had heard Zacharias complaining over and over about how unengaged the FBI was regarding Japan. But still, thought Rutland, one didn't want to take as many chances as Tachibana was taking.

Professor Nakazawa of USC had connected Tachibana with several other Japanese student clubs at other colleges and universities on the West Coast. Tachibana hired several students, usually male, at other colleges to render small tasks, such as carrying film or letters. But on occasion, the students in his employ were female, and he was asked to check in on them and provide moral guidance. A former superior from the navy wrote to him concerning his daughter, Teruko Sugawara, a student at Mills College in Oakland. Her father got a report that Teruko was smoking cigarettes in the student lounge and hanging out with American boys. He requested that Tachibana look after her. Recognizing an opportunity, he agreed, and sent Teruko a letter introducing himself and letting her know his intention of visiting the San Francisco area. He had never seen the US naval base on the island of Alameda in San Francisco Bay and wanted to get a rough idea of what was happening there. Having a young woman with him would be a great cover—they would simply look like two lovers on a waterside picnic that just happened to be near the base.

Tachibana thought it was comical that he was supposed to provide moral instruction to these girls. He wore his emotions awkwardly and did everything in his power to resist them. Not out of a gentlemanly sense of propriety—his instincts were much more selfish. He simply didn't want to think about anyone other than himself. After he met Teruko, though, he couldn't help but think of her. She had affected him, and he knew almost immediately as he laid eyes on her that she would reside in his head for the rest of his life.

Tachibana and Teruko planned a day together where he could do some work as well. Teruko packed bento lunches, and Tachibana drove them to Alameda. Staring out at the newly built Bay Bridge connecting San Francisco and Oakland, Tachibana listened to Teruko's story about how she felt freedom in America, away from her parents and the restrictions of Japanese society. Tachibana then told her about his childhood, his adventures traveling through the United States and Mexico, leaving out, of course, his exploits at the Molino Rojo in Tijuana or Lee Francis's brothel. However, in none of his stories were the traces of arrogance that most of his acquaintances—he never really had friends—associated with him. He was attentive and present, interested in what Teruko had to say, and, for the first time he could remember, eager to be liked. While he would never be confused for being pleasant, he could be charming when he wanted. He found it easier to convince people of his bona fides when he was free to speak in his native Japanese, a language that granted him greater access to the full range of emotions—something English, or at least his proficiency in it, never permitted. In this adopted language, he felt as if he could only articulate agreement or anger. Feelings as complex as joy or as practical as appreciation were beyond his grasp, and he felt limited in his ability to connect with people. Maybe this, he wondered, was why he enjoyed visiting with the Issei at Fish Harbor, who spoke even fewer words than him, in English or in Japanese.

After they finished lunch, he drove Teruko around the Alameda naval base, ostensibly to show her the US Navy fleet—but, really, he was looking for points of access, new ships, or the movement of seamen coming and going off the ships. Vigilant about revealing too much, he nevertheless couldn't resist showing off, telling Teruko that the American fleet "looked strong, but the sailors were lazy, poorly trained, and wouldn't fight." He added that it was surprising how open America was and how easy it was for them to drive around a naval base. This was incomprehensible to him. He also criticized the Americans' failure to appreciate how free they were. They could do anything they wanted—as a people and as an empire—and yet they had no idea the power that came with that. He resented their emerging dominance, but he resented even more their collective ignorance, their dim understanding of everything they held at their mercy.

He knew he was showing off and was hopeful this could somehow impress upon her that there was much more to him than she had initially thought. He was a naval officer and a gentleman, but also a man of intrigue and, perhaps, danger—a man worthy of her affection. Up until this point, he realized that he was content with trying to take down the United States in pieces. But sitting next to Teruko, he decided he would do everything in his power to take it down all at once.

"Just say the word," he told her, "and I will sink these ships to the bottom of the Pacific Ocean."

Tachibana and Teruko then drove across the Bay Bridge to Japantown in San Francisco, where they had a delicious Japanese meal with drinks. Then Tachibana—who had promised her father that he would look after her and provide moral teachings—took her to his hotel room.

CHAPTER 23

THE BLACKMAIL OF CHARLIE CHAPLIN

1938

Kono looked the part of the immigrant who had struck it rich in Hollywood. After being fired by Chaplin, he had time on his hands, which he used to drive fast cars, wear tailored suits, and enjoy the upscale restaurants in Hollywood. What he didn't have was the cash he needed to support this lifestyle.

His first post-Chaplin job was at United Artists, selling movies for distribution in Japan. But he quit in less than a year, deciding he didn't want to put in the hours or schmooze with less-than-influential people halfway around the world. The real excitement was happening in Los Angeles. He wanted to stay in Hollywood, make a lot of money, and not have to work too hard.

While he was planning his next move, he hit upon something that sounded easy. A woman named Gerith Von Ulm approached him with a not-so-humble proposal. Von Ulm, the daughter of a wealthy family, lived an upscale life in Westwood with her two Scottish terriers. To date, the screenplays she had written had all been failures, and she had turned to a new project, a tell-all book about Chaplin, she told Kono. Word had spread about Kono's quick work secreting Chaplin from the boat following the mysterious shooting death of movie mogul Thomas Ince, and Von Ulm also recognized that after working for Chaplin for almost two decades,

Kono must know enough secrets to make what would almost surely be a bestseller.

Kono was more than happy to get involved and, as the key source, negotiated to get 50 percent of the proceeds of the book. Von Ulm and Kono had some long work sessions, and she was not initially disappointed. Kono filled her in on Chaplin's many love affairs. Probably the most scandalous was the fling that Chaplin had had with William Randolph Hearst's paramour, Marion Davies, who was a star in her own right. Even more titillating was that Chaplin had his affair with Davies on William Randolph Hearst's yacht, where Ince had mysteriously died.

The book had initially been an exposé on Chaplin. It started by saying, "Kono has seen through the years Chaplin's promises broken, obligations evaded, his ruthlessness toward women, a cowardice of life," with ample coverage of Chaplin's affairs. Of course, it also took a swing at Chaplin's new wife, Paulette Goddard, who had clashed with Kono, saying that she showed "without a doubt that the way to stardom lies through the boudoir." But the book evolved into a tell-all of many of Hearst's misdeeds as well, referring to him as a "long-bodied and headed, grey-white spider who uses his tremendous and misguided power to undermine and destroy."

Had Kono and Von Ulm thought about it, they might have realized how much risk there was in taking on not just one, but two of the most powerful men in the United States. Chaplin could be ruthless, but he also feared the media. Hearst owned much of the media himself and would be an even more dangerous enemy.

William Morrow and Company was slated to publish the book—titled *Charles Chaplin: King of Tragedy*—as a steamy exposé. It was ironic. Chaplin had hired Japanese servants to help keep his private life private and his secrets a secret. He had had just one Japanese staff member who could speak excellent English—Kono—who was going to stab him in the back by going public with Chaplin's misdeeds.

Kono had what seemed like a great deal, and had signed a contract, but he eventually thought better of it. He attempted to renegotiate the deal to get even more money, which infuriated Von Ulm. "I hope the Chinese beat the hell out of Japan," she wrote to her agent in a moment of pique, referring to the ongoing Second Sino-Japanese War.

Kono, though, remained level-headed, trying to figure out how to secure the best financial return. Either he would get a bigger cut from Von Ulm, or he could possibly ask Chaplin or Hearst for money to kill and cover up the book. He conveyed an offer for monetary settlement to Chaplin.

Neither Chaplin nor Hearst blinked. In fact, both were furious, and they both stepped in to stop the book. Their influence resonated immediately. In October 1937, in a letter to her agent, Von Ulm noted that someone threatened her, which came right before an attempt on her life:

I left my car on the street one night, too lazy to put it in the garage. I got gaily in the next morning and tootled away at my usual rate of driving about forty miles per hour. Wham! A blowout on the rear left tire. The car—a large Studebaker—careened, tried to climb a telephone pole, was dissuaded by gentle twists of the wheel and tentative pushes of the brake. It balanced on two wheels and landed directly crosswise the street. I got out and looked and a neat and tidy chunk had been removed from the tire with a knife, leaving the inner tube ready for the first stone. I was more angry than frightened, as this came on the heels of a smart-aleck telephone call that if I "published the book, I'd never live to enjoy it." I advised the caller to go jump in a lake three times and come up twice.

The legal threats and thugs were effective. In December 1937, Kono advised Von Ulm that he was rescinding his agreement, noting in a letter addressed to her that he was "compelled by fear, physical force, and bodily harm to sign my name to said agreement and/or instrument; threats of death, actual assault and battery and actual physical injury done to me by two men in your home, in your presence, at your behest, aided and abetted by you." While this letter was most likely drafted by his legal team, Kono signed away his previously agreed-upon payment of $13,500 that he had been guaranteed in foreign rights sales. After this incident, Kono went directly to the district attorney's office to file a complaint against Von Ulm for an "assault with intent to do great bodily harm." The district attorney, Buron Fitts, declined to issue a complaint, but within a week he sent his chief investigator to search Von Ulm's home for a reported libelous manuscript, which had recently come to his attention—most likely thanks to Chaplin or Hearst's lawyers.

Before the calendar flipped to 1938, William Morrow and Company was already in the process of destroying every in-house copy of the manuscript, and its editor, Charles Duell, was demanding copies back from Von Ulm's representatives and foreign rights agents around the world. On the twenty-fourth of January, Fitts confirmed receipt of the "photostats, as well as copies of the manuscripts and other documents" Morrow had in their possession. His letter was written on County of Los Angeles District Attorney's Office letterhead. A day later, Duell sent a letter to Von Ulm notifying her of the book's cancellation. "We regret that our plans for the publication of your book have had to come to so unsatisfactory a conclusion."

The definitive exposé of Hearst would appear two years later—not as a book, but as a movie—when Orson Welles released *Citizen Kane*. But even then, *Citizen Kane* didn't use Hearst's real name.

Kono found himself in an unsatisfactory conclusion as well. Having burned his bridges with Chaplin, he was at the mercy of his own behavior. He couldn't turn to Chaplin for help; in fact, he had created an enemy in him and, more disastrously, in William Randolph Hearst. As far as Kono was concerned, Imperial Japan was a less immediate danger than these two nemeses. Seeking stability and a new source of income, Kono was forced to increase his work for the Japanese consulate in Los Angeles, which put him in the orbit of Tachibana, who was all too ready to take full advantage of his new asset. In Kono, Tachibana and the Japanese brass recognized a striking figure, fluent in Japanese and English, who could work his connections to help hire and run American agents in Los Angeles, and over the next three years, Kono slid in even deeper with Tachibana and the other Japanese Navy spies.

In the fall of 1940, at the San Francisco World's Fair, which was on Treasure Island, Kono ran into Al Blake, a vaudevillian actor he'd met on the set of Chaplin's 1918 World War I comedy *Shoulder Arms*. Though Blake appeared in only one scene, his performance left an impression. In the scene, Chaplin, playing a US soldier, has discovered his lower bunk is submerged in water, whereas Blake's upper bunk is dry. With the aid of a phonograph horn to help him breathe, Chaplin nevertheless lies down in his bunk. Blake watches Chaplin's antics from the upper bunk, deadpan and dry. Because Kono was responsible for drying off Chaplin in between takes, he and Blake spent most of the day together. There was a remarkable charisma about Blake, not necessarily his personality or intellect, but what was most impressive about him was how he was able to control every voluntary and involuntary muscle in his body. This allowed him to build a respectable, if odd, career as a robot—what they referred to in the Golden Age of Hollywood as a *mechanical man*. Alternately known as Keeno, the King of the Robots, he booked gigs as a human dummy. "Dressed in white tie and tails," as he was described in *Esquire*, "Al would often stand for an hour in a department store window, with a wax-like make-up on his face, alongside of a dummy dressed exactly like him. The idea was for Little Willie, standing with mama in front of the window, to decide which was Al and which was the dummy. It was never an easy task to distinguish between the two, for Blake's control over his muscles and nerves was truly remarkable. Here indeed was a man who never batted an eyelash—for as long as an hour at a stretch."

When he and Kono reconnected on Treasure Island more than two decades after their first meeting, Blake was running an exhibit at the World's Fair called the Candid Camera Artists and Models Studio. Patrons were invited to gawk at naked women for a quarter, or two bits to enjoy, as the exhibit signage promised, "a stageful of blondes, brunettes, and redheads attired only in their birthday suits." For several months after the close of the fair, Kono and Blake regularly dined together at restaurants in and around Hollywood. Blake enjoyed catching up with Kono and hearing the latest gossip about the industry, but he suspected Kono was after something. In time, Blake suspected he was a Japanese spy, largely because Kono was always flush with cash and, despite his decidedly uncertain employment status, drove around Hollywood in two custom-built cars. Blake confirmed these suspicions when Kono introduced him to Tachibana, who used the alias Mr. Yamato. Before Blake could bat an eyelash, Tachibana asked him if he had any contacts in the US Navy, a brazen question under even normal circumstances, let alone at a moment when tensions between the US and Japan were so shaky, but Tachibana didn't seem shy about asking. "We know that since your exhibit at Treasure Island closed," Tachibana told Blake, removing from his suit his ledger of accounts, "you have not been regularly employed. We know also that you are a gentleman who is not opposed to making, as you Americans say, a quick dollar. We are going to offer you a most attractive proposition. Money will be no object to us."

Blake mentioned his friend Jimmie Campbell, who was serving as a yeoman on the USS *Pennsylvania*, the battleship and flagship of the US Pacific Fleet now docked at Pearl Harbor. Blake was lying about Campbell. There was no such man, and immediately after his conversation with Tachibana, Blake reported Kono and Tachibana to the Office of Naval Intelligence.

The next morning, ONI recruited Blake to act as a counterespionage operative, a seldom-assigned role for a civilian—but, like Tachibana, the navy felt the pressure of this increasingly urgent moment. They instructed Blake to go to Hawaii, just as Tachibana wanted. In Pearl Harbor, he would find a "Jimmie Campbell" on the *Pennsylvania*, an intelligence operative planted on the ship, with recently made-up identification and service cards.

While Tachibana and Kono were arranging for Blake to sail for Honolulu, other Japanese spies kept Blake under constant surveillance. At the same time, ONI agents were trailing Blake's trailers, which confirmed everything they thought about Kono and Tachibana. Blake sailed from San Francisco on the *President Garfield*, keenly aware that a Japanese agent was keeping an eye on him. Landing finally in Honolulu, he checked into his hotel and found a dictograph planted in a seat cushion. To keep up the ruse, he phoned the USS *Pennsylvania* and connected with the US Navy Intelligence officer pretending to be Jimmie Campbell.

When the operative arrived at Blake's room, they ran through their script like expert performers, mindful of the planted dictograph that was broadcasting everything they said to the Japanese agents surveilling their every move. Their act was effective. Blake asked "Campbell" if he was enjoying the navy, and Campbell said he couldn't wait until his enlistment was up. "That's great," said Blake, "because I can show you how to make some dough—but big dough." The catch, he told Campbell, was that he had to collect information about the navy's maneuvers and capabilities at Pearl Harbor.

"Who do you want this dope for, Al—the Japs?" asked Campbell.

"That's right, and you can name your own price."

"The way this lousy navy's treated me, I'd give it to them for nothing," said Campbell.

To pull off the act, they staged a series of conversations, always close enough to the dictograph so they knew their audience could hear them. Finally, Campbell told Blake he was ready to go through with it, telling him exactly what the Japanese were looking for—or, more specifically, where he could get what they were looking for aboard the *Pennsylvania*, specifically the navy's most recent codebook. The lines were carefully considered. How to tease enough verifiable information so the Japanese didn't figure out they were lying, but not enough to let slip information they didn't want the Japanese to know.

When Campbell left Blake's hotel room, an envelope was slipped under his door. In it was a $1,000 bill with the note, "You are doing good work. Give this to your friend as a down payment." Later, Tachibana asked Blake to get even more information, this time info higher up the chain of command. In tandem with ONI, Blake devised a plan to return empty-handed. The Americans were convinced, rightly, that Tachibana wanted to see whether or not Blake was in counterespionage. Their gambit worked, and Tachibana continued to press Blake for information while he was in Hawaii.

Once Blake returned to the mainland, Ringle of ONI called Hood of the FBI to ask him to have the FBI arrest Tachibana.

Hood sent his case summary to FBI headquarters. He then had a call with Tamm. Tamm asked exactly what Hood had been thinking. "Dick," he said, "nothing would please me more than if we could arrest this individual. But, the question is, would you want to prosecute this case?"

Hood replied, "The case is rather weak, I think. You should see this fellow Blake in person. He looks just like what he is, a washed-up ex-sailor and two-bit actor. He would not be a convincing witness."

Tamm echoed Hood's thoughts, and added, "A decent defending attorney would be all over this, saying it was entrapment. And, as you say, Blake's credibility on the stand would be low indeed." He continued, "The State Department is all over me here. It is a bit outrageous, but we can't do anything on this case unless we have better evidence."

"I understand, sir," said Hood. "We have the file and will continue the surveillance and attempt to find better evidence."

"Excellent," replied Tamm. "The other thing I need your help with is to take more of this investigation back from ONI. You've seen the ONI director just turned over again, and replies from them are slow. Can you get copies of the relevant files from Zacharias's office at ONI, including their suspect lists? This way we can prepare proper prosecution when the time comes."

Blake, back in Los Angeles, also rang Tachibana to give his report and try to get some more cash. Tachibana didn't answer. He was traveling.

...

It was a Saturday evening in San Francisco. The Grill Room at the St. Francis Hotel in Union Square was full, almost exclusively with white patrons. There was quiet piano music being played when, suddenly, a loud noise rang out from one of the tables. A female voice was shouting angrily in Japanese at her dinner partner. Teruko was furious. She thought Tachibana was just using her for sex, and him paying for an expensive dinner was not an excuse for how he had been treating her. The other patrons watched, curious and amused, as she stormed out of the hotel and went to get a taxi back to Oakland. Tachibana tried to follow her, throwing some cash onto the table before unsuccessfully trying to catch up to her.

As her cab sped away, Tachibana realized that Teruko was a write-off. Tachibana went back to Los Angeles the next day, where he had both work to do and more women to chase.

CHAPTER 24

THE FBI FINALLY WAKES UP

Fall 1940

Two men ambled down Sycamore Avenue in Hollywood to the British United Services Club for its annual Trafalgar Day dinner. One of them cut a dignified figure in a tuxedo. It was Alan Mowbray, the English film actor known for playing butlers and aristocrats.

The other man, an American, was a lot more rumpled than Mowbray. Mowbray said he was a screenwriter friend; in truth, it was FBI agent Eddie Cochran. The plan was for Mowbray to introduce Cochran over dinner to the cliquish BUSC gang so he could ask the members for advice for a new movie about British fighter pilots.

Cochran said he was working on a possible sequel to the successful Warner Brothers film *The Dawn Patrol*, a World War I film about British fighter pilots. The film featured an all-British cast, including Errol Flynn, Basil Rathbone, and David Niven. With this topic, it seemed like it would be very easy for Cochran to befriend Rutland and draw him out in conversation. Then, after getting Rutland talking, he would try to draw him out about the war in Europe and the Japanese situation.

Mowbray and Cochran entered the club, greeted others, and then Cochran saw Rutland enter. It was as the file said, thought Cochran. Rutland wasn't a large man, but he had some dynamism that drew people's eyes toward him. Cochran noted his square jaw and piercing blue-green eyes that stood out from across the room as the other guests cordially greeted him.

The banter at the party was friendly. They talked about Japan, but Rutland suggested not to worry about Japan. Based on his long experience working with the Japanese Navy, he said, "the Japanese have too much sense to go to war with the United States."

It had been almost a year since the reports to the FBI about Rutland had almost kicked off an investigation. This was after Ellis Zacharias had sent a telegram to FBI director J. Edgar Hoover, requesting that the FBI back off of surveillance of Rutland, since Rutland was an active US Navy Intelligence asset. As a result, the FBI had been leaving Rutland alone.

But in that summer and fall, the FBI was getting more and more reports, including those new reports from Glover and others from British United Services Club, and pushed the matter. Zacharias sent another telegram to Hoover, which stated that Rutland was a valuable ONI informant, and requested nothing further be done until they had the opportunity to discuss. A furious Tamm called Zacharias to tell him not to push his luck. Zacharias relented and reluctantly gave his approval to the FBI to go ahead and investigate Rutland.

Relations between the FBI and ONI were generally rocky. The only reason why ONI had been able to act so independently on Japanese espionage up to that time was because, as Zacharias stressed to people he met, the FBI had other priorities. Now that the FBI was waking up, due to various political pressures and the changing world situation, the FBI would come down hard on Japanese espionage. Hoover had the Roosevelt administration formally in charge of counterintelligence within the United States.

ONI itself wasn't terribly powerful in Washington. Directors stayed for an average of under two years in the 1930s, and like in Japan, the naval intelligence group wasn't that respected by the rest of the navy either. Alan Kirk, ONI director for half of 1941, said that they were treated as "striped-pants, cookie pushers" (i.e., people who hosted parties overseas but didn't do much work) by their peers.

With Zacharias, however, the feud with the FBI was personal. He had been annoyed at the FBI since he was thrown out of Hoover's office in Washington, DC, a decade before. Since then, his interactions with the FBI had continually been rocky. He felt the FBI was getting in the way of his vital mission of protecting the US from the Japanese, and he wasn't able or interested in containing his annoyance. No one at the FBI, from assistant director Tamm to Los Angeles office head Hood, was happy with Zacharias's attitude.

Zacharias had taken matters in his own hands. He had worked with Sheriff Biscailuz and District Attorney Buron Fitts to add to their list of suspects to be arrested in time of war. In effect, he was doing the FBI's job, doing it well, and telling those around him the FBI was not only not interested in protecting the US from Japan, but not competent.

Word got back to Hood that Zacharias was telling those around him that even if the FBI did focus on the right things, they were basically structurally useless. He mentioned that "the Japanese had saboteurs and agents in Mexico working against the US," and then rhetorically asked, "How can the FBI help in this situation? Even if they were motivated, do they have the manpower to control the border? Can they operate offshore and monitor the Japanese fishing boats? What would they do if we found Japanese planes in Mexico?" The answer to these questions was that, no, the FBI didn't have the manpower of the navy, or even of the Los Angeles Police, to confront some large-scale set of saboteurs. However, the FBI were the ones chartered to investigate and arrest foreign agents and would be highly qualified to do so—and Zacharias needed the FBI to make any arrests.

Tamm had a problem on his hands with Zacharias, and the Rutland situation was his opportunity to remove this problem. The political issues and bad-mouthing of the FBI were bad, but now the FBI could show that Zacharias was apparently protecting a Japanese agent. To start, he arranged for his boss, FBI director Hoover, to give the green light to the Rutland investigation.

After the events of the prior decade, it wasn't hard for Tamm to convince

Hoover to take action, not just against Rutland, but against Zacharias as well. There was a weekly meeting between Hoover, the head of army intelligence, and the new head of ONI, Walter Anderson. Hoover demanded that Anderson remove Zacharias from his position, since he was not a team player and was preventing the FBI from investigating a Japanese spy.

The debate about Zacharias went from Anderson to the secretary of the navy, Frank Knox. Anderson and Knox agreed that, although Zacharias was a hothead who tended to make enemies, he was still likely the best intelligence officer the navy had. With tensions with Japan increasing, his skills were quite likely to be in demand.

The navy's solution was to give Zacharias an important job that removed him from intelligence duties and kept him away from the FBI. Zacharias was appointed as the captain of the heavy cruiser USS *Salt Lake City*. The ship was stationed at Pearl Harbor, so he would need to move to Hawaii. Ironically, this brought him close to Japan and put him directly in the line of fire, but totally removed him from decision-making regarding intelligence attempting to predict Japan's next move.

Zacharias always enjoyed being the captain of a warship. However, being sent to Hawaii crushed Zacharias's career ambition. Everyone knew he wanted to be the next ONI director.

Yet, it was clear to the navy that Zacharias was not the right person to be ONI director at this moment. He knew the enemy as well as anyone, of course. However, America was thinking a war in Europe or Asia was coming, and the key goal would be to hire and expand the bureaucracy of ONI, with a likely tripling or quadrupling of the staff. Not even Zacharias's allies would claim that he was a star at the politics and day-to-day management that would be needed.

The FBI took the opportunity to start the surveillance of Rutland. With the new orders from the top, special agent in charge Hood and his staff became highly motivated.

Hood and his assistant Arthur Cornelius started by contacting the postmaster, Mary Briggs, to record all letters to Rutland's house. He also sent two agents to Associated Telephone Company, going to their large building on Seventh Street in Santa Monica, and pulled his telephone records. Hanson from Lockheed informed FBI agents of the minutiae of Rutland's suspicious dealings around Lockheed, and another source discussed his office location by the Douglas plant.

Surprisingly to Hood, Rutland's intercepted calls and letters showed nothing suspicious at all. They were exactly what one would expect from an international businessman such as Rutland. There were letters and calls from Lockheed, the naval intelligence people, his bankers, accountants in the US, UK, and Singapore, and more. The only thing that seemed possibly suspicious was that there was no one from Japan appearing anywhere in any of the logs. This led Hood to conclude that Rutland must be sticking to a prudent process for contacting the Japanese via hand delivery.

On October 12, a pair of FBI agents were assigned to watch Rutland's house on Warbler Way. However, on a narrow street with limited parking that dead-ends up on the mountain just past his house, the agents would stick out like a sore thumb, so they needed to leave their car down the hill on Doheny Drive. But, since there was only one way down the mountain, they would definitely see when he left the house.

The agents watching for activity at the house reported no activity that day. Oddly, it was the same thing two days later, three days later, five days later—nothing. Rutland didn't leave the house. He'd never been known to stay in one place this long in his entire life. The agents sent their reports to Hood every day, and they were short, saying, "The subject has not left the house." Hood thought darkly that someone—Zacharias?—must have tipped him off about the FBI surveillance, causing him to stay in one place.

Dorothy Rutland was observed leaving the house. She was headed to a dog show in Santa Monica. When an informant chatted her up at the dog show, she told him that her way of raising money for Britain was much better than the regular British War Relief organization, which was "wasting $100 a month to pay for an office" in the newly built, deluxe Ambassador Hotel on Wilshire Boulevard. She named Alan Mowbray and Norman

Glover as the leaders of this organization and wasn't shy about expressing her discontent with them.

Hood had his men look elsewhere for evidence. Western Union received an order to intercept any telegrams to or from Rutland. Other agents checked post offices to see if they could find a hidden box, possibly under an alias. The FBI enlisted Bank of America's detective, who spread the word about Rutland and his descriptions and aliases to a hundred different branches, to try to find some possible hidden money trail. Hood enlisted "Confidential Informant 100," who was very close to Rutland. The informant found that Rutland was suspicious, but nothing concrete.

Meanwhile, American codebreakers in Washington had recently made good progress on their Magic program to decode Japanese communication, with distribution limited to the highest levels of the US government.

Yosuke Matsuoka was now the Japanese foreign minister. Magic intercepted a telegram on January 30 where Matsuoka instructed the US attachés to strengthen the communication networks with Mexico, since "in the event of US participation in the war, our intelligence setup will be moved to Mexico." He also ordered them to use agents "who were not Japanese or American and could thereby more easily pass over the border even after the war started." "Not Japanese or American" meant, in practice, Rutland, but Matsuoka also suggested they could investigate using "communists, Negroes, labor union members, and anti-Semites." (In a moment of prescience, he specifically also asked them not to use Japanese or Nissei, since "if there is any slip in this phase, our people will be subject to considerable persecution, so the utmost caution must be exercised.")

Matsuoka was cognizant that the regular path of communication via Tijuana was vulnerable to being cut. Therefore, his embassy liaisons set up an alternate communication route via Mexicali, a desert town far inland (a portmanteau of "Mexico" and "California"—Mexicali). Today, Mexicali is a thriving area that produces lettuce in the winter, but at the time it was quite primitive. Matsuoka likely had no idea just how bad the roads through Mexicali and the deserts of Baja California were. When it rained, they were completely impassable—far from an ideal communication route.

The FBI agents had given the update to keep Mexicali on their radar, and their sources told them Rutland was going to Mexico very frequently and was often in Mexicali, on the very same Japanese intelligence route. However, the FBI agents were confused as to what exactly Rutland was doing in Mexico. Rutland's stated purpose for being in Mexicali was that he was going to invest in a beverage bottling company called Sierra Club, a company that made ginger beer in a charming ceramic bottle. Sierra Club was considering opening a bottling plant in Mexicali. Rutland, they also found, had been looking to buy a farm in Arizona on a hill overlooking Mexico.

In the periodic scheduled calls between Hood and Tamm, they summarized that the things Rutland was doing in Mexico were highly suspicious and seemed to make it even more clear he was a Japanese asset. But they all had a cover story that was technically plausible, even if highly unlikely. Perhaps he really did have money laying around that he wanted to invest in a Mexican bottler and was interested in farming in Arizona. The direction from the State Department was as clear as always: no action without copious proof.

It also wasn't entirely clear to the Americans what the Japanese Navy was doing in Mexico either. There were breathless newspaper articles in the Hearst papers and even speeches in Congress about imaginary Japanese soldiers, planes, and submarine bases, each one sounding more paranoid than the last one. Zacharias had earlier sent a couple of US Navy destroyers to look around in Baja California, and he concluded what now seemed to be obvious—that the Japanese Navy did have a strong intelligence presence in Mexico, but there were no hidden Japanese submarine bases or airplanes. Still, one could imagine even small teams of Japanese saboteurs in Mexico could cause a lot of problems for the US, so ONI needed to keep digging.

Courtenay Young and the other agents at MI5 and MI6, on the other hand, knew exactly what Rutland was doing in Mexico. It was all laid out in the telegrams between Tokyo and the Japanese embassy in London that they were intercepting and decoding. They knew the arrangement he had with Oka was that Rutland would gather information in Los Angeles, then deliver the information to the Japanese embassy in Mexico City. If the heat was on, the San Diego–Tijuana border crossing could be difficult, so in time of war, the plan was for him to enter Mexico at Mexicali under the cover of business. From Mexicali, he would go to Mexico City, and convey this information to the Japanese embassy, after which the information would be sent to Japan via diplomatic packet.

Disastrously, MI5 had all of this information, and the evidence that the FBI would have needed to prosecute Rutland—they just weren't sharing. British Intelligence had been hoping to find some way to arrest Rutland for almost twenty years now, but the evidence of Rutland's nefarious activities was all about his actions against the US. Had they found he was spying against Britain, MI5 might have been happy to consider having Rutland arrested on one of his visits to the UK. However, nothing in their files showed that he had ever spied against Britain, so they had no way to arrest him, even if they had wanted to.

Hood submitted his report to Tamm in Washington, noting what his investigation had found about Rutland's somewhat curious visits to Mexico. His report was strictly factual—FBI files from the period do not contain personal opinions.

Tamm and Hood agreed the situation warranted deeper discussion. Hood flew to Washington with fellow FBI agent Cornelius for the meeting. Percy "Sam" Foxworth, the FBI assistant director in charge of British affairs, came down from New York to join.

After pleasantries, Tamm asked Hood and Cornelius what they thought about Rutland's activities. Hood replied, "I think we would all bet dollars to donuts that he is a Japanese agent, sir. But I have no proof."

Foxworth echoed, "In reading your report, you are saying that the evidence is strong but circumstantial. By the way, I have spoken to the British embassy about Rutland as well. They appear to be holding their cards close, but they have confirmed he is not a British agent."

Hood continued, "Yes, sir. This has to be one of the most curious cases I've been involved in. Rutland appears to be a Japanese agent, and doesn't hide much of anything, it seems. It is all quite in the open. Yet he has a potential legitimate cover story for everything. The visits to Japan. The expensive lifestyle with no apparent source of income. His stories about his friends, the Japanese admirals. His visits to smuggling routes across the Mexican border. All are suspicious but are also potentially legitimate. And, by the way, someone seems to have tipped him off to our investigation. The moment we started surveillance, he stayed in his house for days."

Tamm cursed under his breath. "I have a guess who tipped him off about our surveillance. Quite likely, someone from the navy. They seem to think he is on our side."

After a pause, Cornelius added, "We are not on the same page as the navy on many issues related to Japanese espionage, not just about Rutland. They seem to be spending a lot of time pursuing possible saboteurs in Japanese fishing boats and mystery airplanes in the Mexican desert. Not to say those things don't exist, but the clues around Rutland and elsewhere suggest a more standard espionage operation."

Hood added, "Returning to the man himself, it is also baffling that his mansion appears to be a spy's dream. It contains multiple radio transmitters and a photographic darkroom with equipment for still photography, motion photography, and even color film. But again, he not only doesn't hide this equipment, but he shows it to visitors who attend parties at his house, telling them that these are his hobbies. Again, it is plausible deniability. Barely plausible, but plausible."

He continued, "The closest thing to evidence was that he sent his Irish 'friend' to work as a night janitor at the Lockheed factory, and that friend did any number of suspicious things. For this, there is no *good* explanation. But our ex-colleague at Lockheed, Hanson, was never able to find firm evidence of a crime there either."

Tamm summed up the meeting saying, "As you know, we will need evidence that will hold up in court for this one in particular. We need to tread lightly around both Japan and around Hollywood, and Rutland is both. For now, we can't take action. But I will guess we will be back after Rutland in the future. Dismissed."

In December, the Japanese Navy sent a new attaché to Mexico City—Tsunezo Wachi. Wachi was an electronic warfare expert who had won awards for breaking Chinese codes during an earlier skirmish between Japan and China. He had also recently gotten a visit from the emperor's brother, Prince Takamatsu, for his work breaking a US diplomatic code. Wachi's trip to Mexico City included overnight stops in San Francisco, Los Angeles, and Manzanillo. The FBI was watching him during these stops.

Wachi installed his new radio intercept station in Mexico City and was soon monitoring US naval communications. He also got involved in human espionage. He sent a message saying he was able to get some new American aircraft plans, including those of a new four-engine bomber, the B-29. After the war, Wachi told his interrogators that he got the plans from someone named Sutton, "a disgruntled major who had been introduced to him from Imperial General Headquarters in Tokyo." Of all of the Japanese agents in the US that Admiral Shimada had listed in his diary a few years earlier, there was only one who was a major, and that person was also the only agent who was personally known to the Japanese Navy general staff, and that same person was known to be going to and from Mexico: Rutland.

Rutland was concerned by the FBI agents following him. But he had been trailed by the likes of MI5 before with no problem, and believed he was clean, legally. But he also knew that his protector, US Navy captain Ellis Zacharias, was now far away at sea. Fortunately, Zacharias's replacement, Ken Ringle, assured him that the US Navy would continue their arrangement and go to bat for Rutland.

Dorothy Rutland was more than just concerned that the FBI was watching her house. Her husband reassured her that, yes, there had been a couple of misunderstandings, hence the surveillance of their house, but it was fine.

Dorothy thought back to when British agents had been following her husband in London twenty years ago. He had told her not to worry that time as well. It seemed different now. And there were her children to think about as well.

CHAPTER 25

BEATING THE SUSPECT

December 1940–June 1941

Tamm of the FBI hadn't had Seattle much on his radar. This was by design. Ken Ringle of ONI, after replacing Zacharias, didn't want the FBI involved. Ringle and Mayo had their men investigating Tachibana's Seattle-based subordinate Sadatomo Okada. The ONI heads had instructed their staff to tell their FBI counterparts they would handle the issue themselves, since "it was a navy matter. Okada had been seen mostly driving around the navy base and the Sand Point Naval Air Station." Since Okada was mostly spying on naval facilities, they "wouldn't need to bother the FBI."

Two informants reported that Okada drove around clutching a Shell gasoline-stand map and black pens, marking off his targets as he went, sometimes just taking pictures, other times meeting with informants that he paid for documents. He apparently had surveyed the Boeing plants, airports, shipbuilding, Sand Point Naval Air Station, the blimp base, the army bases, naval aircraft testing, and more. In reality, Okada was going far beyond looking at naval facilities.

It wasn't like Okada was trying to cover his tracks much anyway, but it was very easy for the ONI agents to find out what Okada was doing. He was staying at the Holland Hotel in Seattle, right downtown a block from Pioneer Square, a ten-minute walk from the Nihonmachi, the Japanese area. It was such a busy area that the ONI agent just sat in his parked car with a newspaper across the street from Okada's apartment and then followed Okada when he left on his missions.

Okada's activities were fully consistent with what the ONI and FBI heads understood to be the new Japanese priorities. A recent Magic intercept showed the Japanese foreign minister Matsuoka told Japanese people in the US to no longer spend any time or money on propaganda, but to spend it on espionage, since Japan was going to be switching to a war footing.

In contrast, the FBI agents who tried to track Tachibana had a much harder time. Tachibana stayed at the Japanese-owned Olympic Hotel in Los Angeles's Little Tokyo neighborhood, where almost every guest and most of the people around the neighborhood were Japanese. The Caucasian agents in Los Angeles stood out and couldn't follow Tachibana nearly as easily.

Okada, the ONI agents reported, was out doing his espionage activities pretty much every day. Or, on occasion, he would go play golf. Either way, though—since he was out on the town all day, every day—Ringle assigned agents to break into Okada's hotel room and see what they would find there. Given the budding national emergency, the navy didn't feel constrained by the laws and political pressure that the FBI did. On April 4, two agents went into the hotel, simply flashed a badge and got a key from the front desk, went up, and looked around in his room. This wasn't legal; the US Navy badge did not give the agents the legal authority to enter private property off base, but it worked for them.

Entering the room, the agents found a jackpot—more sensitive military information than they'd thought possible. There was defense-related information, literally stacked everywhere, including info that could be used to sabotage the US Navy. The ONI men were highly alarmed to find, on the top of a stack of papers, a map showing the locations of all the oil refineries on the West Coast, with notes about the security around each. It was clear to them that Japan could easily sabotage or attack these refineries, which would cripple the ability to wage war against Japan. Taking some pictures of what they found for evidence, they made sure not to move anything or leave any tracks, backed out of the room, and reported their findings to Ringle.

The implications of what they'd found were staggering, thought Ringle.

A war appeared to be approaching, and the Japanese attachés were running wild and getting vast amounts of US military secrets. Since the ONI didn't have jurisdiction or the ability to arrest anyone off base, Ringle needed to get the FBI involved. This didn't happen as quickly as he wanted, since the FBI needed approval from headquarters in Washington. Also, ONI headquarters wasn't fully in the loop either. But at the next meeting, Ringle and his staff met with Hood of the FBI, showing the report from the ONI agents and the pictures of Okada's room. The first meeting was inconclusive; Hood needed to check with Tamm.

The follow-on meetings caused Ringle's jaw to drop when he got the reply. "The evidence," concluded the FBI, "was not enough to warrant prosecution." There was nothing the FBI would do at the moment.

Tamm, at FBI headquarters in Washington, had circled around with his counterpart at the State Department, Fletcher Warren, and Director Hoover. The answer was simple, clear, and had not changed. No one would arrest a Japanese military officer unless they had proof that would hold up in a court of law. Tamm called the new director of ONI, Alan Kirk, and told him he was disappointed that ONI would risk an international incident by committing illegal acts such as breaking and entering. Even worse, ONI was committing crimes that were not even in their jurisdiction and had lied to the FBI, apparently to keep the FBI away. There were ways of apprehending the suspect—but he stressed that they had to be done legally.

For now, the investigation would just continue as is, with the FBI now mostly in the loop as to what Okada was doing, with eyes kept open for a way to get legally obtained evidence that would hold up in court.

On June 2, the ONI agent who was on duty to watch Okada called to report that Okada was loading a mass of documents into his car. There was so much paper that it took him several trips between his room and the car. The trunk of Okada's car was full, and he was piling up so many documents into the back seat that it seemed he might have trouble seeing out the rearview mirror. The agent followed him to see where he was going. The call came later that he was heading south. It seemed obvious what was happening: Okada was likely on his way to Mexico. If prior patterns were accurate, Okada would stop at the Olympic Hotel in Los Angeles and report out to his superior officer, Tachibana, before continuing south, crossing the border and ending up at the Molino Rojo to drop off the documents.

Ringle had ordered the agents to be a bit more discreet, but he wasn't ready to tell the FBI yet. He suggested the best way would be to perform a traffic stop and have the police "discover" the evidence.

An ONI reserve officer was now the assistant chief of police for the town of Bakersfield, California, about a hundred miles north of Los Angeles. Okada was driving down Highway 99, and as he went through Bakersfield, Okada saw a patrol car behind him. The policeman put on his lights and pulled Okada over. He told Okada that he was under arrest for speeding, which Okada found very strange. He'd barely been speeding. And, normally, as far as he knew about the laws in the United States, no one is arrested for speeding. You just get a ticket. Regardless, the officers escorted him to Bakersfield Police headquarters, and his car was searched. He got a bit panicky when he saw the officers looking through his car, and things got worse when they discovered that his passport was expired. But that evening, he was released without charges. It was late. He had had a long day. He got a cheap room at a local hotel, made a quick call to Tachibana to tell him about the delay, and slept like a rock.

The assistant chief of police gave a call to Ringle at the ONI office in Los Angeles. He reported that the car was indeed full of top secret American military intelligence. Ringle then decided to call Hood at the FBI office.

The next morning, Okada left Bakersfield on the final leg of his trip to Los Angeles. The initial part of the trip was boring as he passed through the desert, with the only sight of interest the oil wells that lined the highway in the middle of the drive. The oil wells reminded him that the United States was rich with oil and was threatening not to sell any more to Japan. Okada realized that, if the US stopped selling oil to Japan, Japan's powerful navy would be unable to sail very far unless they found oil somewhere else.

As Okada passed through the town of Glendale, he saw another police car behind him. It put on its lights and indicated for him to pull over. He panicked slightly but managed to calm his nerves. *Again?!* he thought. He didn't have time for this. Pulling over, he saw country cops and thought they looked rude and uneducated. It also seemed these cops were looking for a fight.

He noticed the smirk on the face of the officer, who said that he was speeding and needed to come to the station. Okada got out of the car, faced the officer, and yelled, "You cannot do this! I'm a representative of the Japanese government! I will call my embassy!"

The police officer replied, "You're resisting arrest." He turned to his partner and said, "Cuff him."

As the officer approached Okada, Okada moved to push the officer away. The officer took a swing and hit Okada in the stomach. Okada punched back once before the other officer tackled him and put on the cuffs. The officers hit Okada a couple of additional times for good measure before taking him to the police station for questioning.

When they arrived, a couple of other men were waiting there—ONI agents who interrogated the bruised-up Okada. They grabbed a couple of choice pieces of espionage material that were on the front seat, as evidence. They had orders to find just a few more things that would convince the FBI about the sensitivity of this cache of documents. Eventually, they let Okada go, sporting a shiner on his face. He headed to the Olympic Hotel in Los Angeles.

Ken Ringle of ONI immediately conferred with FBI and ONI headquarters—before Okada even got to Los Angeles. It was a tough call, but an urgent one.

Ringle's call to the FBI office was rocky. He explained to SAIC Hood that a stash of US documents with national security implications was almost certainly being taken to the Olympic Hotel in Los Angeles's Little

Tokyo. From there, either Tachibana or Okada would drive the documents over the border, meeting at the Molino Rojo, and the documents would end up on a ship to Tokyo. Even a cursory glance would show just how sensitive this information was, and Ringle could bring over some of what they'd found.

Hood understood the threat to US national security, but his first reaction was annoyance. He replied, "Let me get this perfectly straight, Ringle. You kept us in the dark about this suspect in Seattle. Your colleague Zacharias, for all we knew, was consorting with this suspect as well. To get evidence, you committed multiple illegal acts, breaking and entering being just the first."

Ringle replied, "Yes, we bent the law a bit. However, did you see the information the suspect had? He even had stolen the plans for the new Boeing bomber. In the event of war, if that information gets to Japan, I'm sure it will mean the deaths of thousands of our boys. I'm sorry to put you in an uncomfortable situation, but this needs to be prevented."

Hood continued to unload on Ringle. He had gotten a report from Glendale already. "If there is a war with Japan, you say? Are you trying to make it happen? My men believe the suspect is bruised because he was 're-sisting arrest'? Do you want me to believe that?" Ringle told Hood that the Glendale Police had reported the suspect was disobedient and aggressive.

Hood continued, "Do you realize how bad this could look in the newspapers? Do you have any idea what the State Department would say if word got out that we're beating up Japanese government officials? There would be a major international incident. Hell, at some point, there might even be a war with the Japs. But I won't allow that war to start here, on my watch, because you don't like to follow proper procedures. The FBI does things by the book. If we are told to take out a suspect, we do. But we don't make the call."

Ringle's mind wandered to a recent report about an Australian agent, Harry Freame, who had ended up dead after being attacked on a Tokyo street just a couple months earlier. Prior to that, the Briton—Cox—had died "in a fall from a window." Japan and the FBI weren't playing by the same rules, and he needed the FBI to get with the program.

Hood also realized the documents needed to be secured, and soon, but that it needed to be done in the proper way. He needed to confer with Tamm at FBI headquarters. Hood had kept Tamm in the loop on Tachibana, back to the consulate raid in March, but the two discussed that all the evidence seized at that time was from two illegal break-ins. Fortunately, they did now have some evidence that just might hold up in a court of law: the documentation of the Al Blake and Kono incident.

Tamm still felt the evidence provided by Blake was a bit weak—but it was all they had. It would have to do.

Before Okada had even arrived at the Olympic Hotel in Los Angeles, Special Agent A. D. Horn had filed an affidavit and been issued a search warrant for violations of the Espionage Act, specifically mentioning the papers delivered by Blake to Kono, and of course not mentioning ONI or any of the illegal searches.

At five p.m. on the seventh, Hood of the FBI and his agents moved in to arrest Tachibana at his room at the Olympic Hotel. They were shocked to find that there were more documents in Tachibana's hotel room than they could easily handle, including two full metal filing cabinets and over two thousand index cards with Japanese script. They called for backup before they could go pick up Kono, which they finally did at ten p.m. at Kono's house. Other agents were able to load the documents they found in Tachibana's room at the hotel and take them to the FBI office.

Hood reported to Tamm that the documents would obviously take a while to translate. Tamm noted that there did not appear to be any press coverage yet, but any inquiries that came to the LA Field Office should be simply answered, "Yes, there was an arrest, and further details will be forthcoming soon."

Two days later, the arrests were on the front page of the newspapers. Other members of the Tachibana network were spooked and fled before they could be arrested; including a banker, a couple of local Japanese hires, and one member of the consulate, mostly to Mexico, but some to Washington to confer with the staff at the Japanese embassy.

The attaché at the Japanese embassy in Washington, Yuzuru Sanematsu, had just been surprised to find someone in Japan had just sent $1 million to his local Yokohama Specie Bank account, to be used for espionage. He realized, with all the excitement around Tachibana, that Americans might freeze his bank account at any time, and they could lose the money. Realizing that he could only withdraw $50,000 per day in cash, he sent two staff members to withdraw the maximum amount allowed per day in $100 bills. They then strapped the bills to their bodies and flew to Mexico City to drop off the money before going back to get more. It turned out a man could carry $50,000 in cash under his clothes, which equated to twenty trips.

Cornelius sent the truckload of documents to be translated. The translators, fairly overwhelmed by the amount there, reported it would take weeks. Not all of the documents related to national security, though. The translators were amused to find a letter from Tachibana's girlfriend, Teruko, apologizing for making a scene in the restaurant in the lobby of the St. Francis, but noting he should make an effort to "understand a woman's heart better." She also said she would be heading back to Japan after the end of the semester in June, and wouldn't be able to visit him in Los Angeles beforehand.

Cornelius noted with alarm the memos that showed Tachibana's approaches to the African American newspapers, where he called for the "non-white races to unite against the white man." Race relations in the US were already rocky, and what would happen if Japan poured gasoline on that fire? He didn't think Japan could create a race war in the United States. "Impossible, right?" he asked himself.

...

Rutland picked up the latest copy of the *Herald* and was highly alarmed. It said that there would be new arrests in the Tachibana and Kono case.

Hood and Ringle were quoted as flatly refusing to comment, the sole official statement being that "new arrests were coming." The article also made ominous reference to "British data." Rutland realized he could possibly be arrested at any time.

Other breathless coverage hinted that the FBI was on the track of a "mysterious, dusky-haired woman" and that Blake, who had made a living of being a dummy, was the "dummy who outsmarted the secret agents."

Weighing his options, Rutland realized that sitting around would probably be the worst option of all—and he was not one to sit around, anyhow. He considered his options. He could go to ONI headquarters and confirm he was a protected, valued agent of the US Navy. He could talk to the British embassy—specifically, find the intelligence attachés—and discuss putting himself at the service of British Intelligence. He could possibly flee somewhere else under Japanese protection. Or he could do a combination of these things. He could meet the Japanese, get them to pay him, and then do a double cross to help the Americans—and likely get them to pay him as well.

Rutland was a key player. He would be hired by one or more of these organizations. In fact, he thought, he might become a hero again, as he had in the Great War.

CHAPTER 26

POLITICAL FALLOUT

July 1941

Washington, DC–based naval attaché Ichiro Yokoyama was furious. He learned about Tachibana's arrest from the *Washington Post*. He threw down the newspaper in disgust, yelling, *"Baka!"* He knew just how badly the Japanese Navy had messed this up. What was worse, he had known nothing about what Tachibana, Kono, and Rutland had been doing at all, other than a couple of jokes he had heard about Tachibana's high-class girlfriends. Yet, as the Imperial Japanese Navy attaché at the embassy in Washington, DC, nobody would believe he didn't know what was going on. He was going to get blamed by Japanese and Americans alike. The lurid press coverage of Japanese spies would empower the pro-war factions on both sides and make war more likely.

Yokoyama's job was to help make a negotiated settlement between the United States and Japan. Yokoyama himself thought Japan couldn't win a war with the United States, and shouldn't try. Often, back home, he had been annoyed at Japanese people who said the Americans were weak, luxury loving, and would not fight. The story he told them was that, twenty years earlier, he had been studying at Yale University and attended a college football game where one of the players was knocked out cold and later died. The Americans continued the game anyhow. To him, this exemplified how tough Americans were.

Yokoyama was partnered in the negotiations with Ambassador Kichisaburo Nomura, an ex–navy admiral who had become friends with

President Roosevelt back in World War I. Nomura also left an impression—
he had an air of authority and was also missing an eye from a bombing a
decade earlier by a Korean nationalist.

The American negotiators, including Secretary of State Cordell Hull
and, on the navy side, chief of naval operations Admiral Kelly Turner,
believed Yokoyama and Nomura were making good-faith efforts and
wanted to ensure peace. Turner, in particular, socialized with his Japanese
counterparts and had a good working relationship with them. They also
realized there were hotheads in Japan, as well as the US, who were not
compromising and would be happy to go down the road to war. The negotiators were dependent on their respective governments to compromise as
well. Notably, since Turner was getting his information on Japan directly
from the trusted Japanese diplomats, he was not getting much information
from the Office of Naval Intelligence. He thought their information was
rather useless.

The headlines about Tachibana and Kono were damning, and, in read-
ing them, Yokoyama found them even worse than he had thought. The
mentions of Kono being Charlie Chaplin's butler added to the buzz, and
Kono's face in the pictures bore a confident smirk. Perhaps worst of all in
Yokoyama's mind was that Tachibana had been caught sending a spy, Al
Blake, to Pearl Harbor in Hawaii. Hawaii wasn't part of Tachibana's job.
He was not only stupid, but insubordinate.

Yokoyama and Nomura immediately called on their US counterparts
to try to gloss things over. The Americans were also angry, and realizing
that perhaps the negotiations might be doomed. Either Yokoyama and
Nomura had lied to them, or the Japanese negotiators were out of the
loop regarding what the Japanese military was doing. Either way, it was
not good. To add insult to injury, the Japanese had also just moved forces
south into French Indochina (modern-day Vietnam).

Tachibana and Kono were arraigned by the US attorney, with bail set
at $50,000 for Tachibana, and $25,000 for Kono. Hood noted Tachibana
and Kono both appeared arrogant in prison, with Kono telling his inter-

rogators that he would be out of jail soon. Hood of the FBI was a little puzzled as to why Kono was so confident. Not all of the documents were translated yet, but what they did have was more than enough to convict him and Tachibana of a crime and put them in jail for a long time.

It turned out, the Japanese suspects did know something the FBI did not know. After the flurry of visits from Nomura and Yokoyama, Secretary of State Hull decided Tachibana and the others would be set free to help keep the peace negotiations on track. Continued press coverage of the spies would empower the pro-war factions on both sides. Hood, Tamm, and the rest of the FBI were appalled, with one of them handwriting "This is outrageous" on the report to Director Hoover, but Tachibana was quickly let out of jail and left for Japan on the next ship. Out of sight, out of the news. When he arrived back in Japan, he received a very warm reception and a job offer from the group that was planning for an attack on Pearl Harbor.

That left a major risk factor: Kono. Kono was well-dressed, articulate, and known to the media from his days working for Chaplin. In traditional Japanese culture, loyalty to one's employer was one of the highest virtues; betraying an employer was perhaps the worst thing a samurai could do. But Kono had already shown himself happy to backstab his employer, Chaplin, by working with a journalist. Would Kono possibly go to the press and do something that would injure Japanese interests or further damage peace negotiations? It seemed quite possible, if he thought it might help him.

Hull deemed it fine for Kono to be prosecuted, on the condition he pled guilty to avoid the press of a trial. However, should he demand a trial, the FBI would need to drop the case and let him go, with some understanding or deal that would keep him quiet. Kono seemed to know this, and it appeared that he would drive a hard bargain.

Yokoyama received a message from the Japanese consulate in Los Angeles. They thought they could swing a deal to keep Kono quiet by paying for Kono's bail money, making it look like the money was coming from

Kono's rich celebrity friends. The consulate also informed Yokoyama that, because this royal screwup was the fault of the Japanese Navy, they would be sending him an invoice for Kono's $25,000 bail to be paid from the navy's budget. The Americans who were reading this message thought it funny.

A second Magic intercept revealed that the Japanese consulate also advised there was someone else who they would not attempt to get involved in the Kono case: Rutland. There were two reasons to avoid Rutland. Firstly, if word got out that this famous British war hero and friend of Charlie Chaplin and Boris Karloff was a Japanese spy, it would be a scandal that would again jump to the front page of the papers. Secondly, they reported that Rutland appeared to be close to US Naval Intelligence.

Tamm, realizing the potential issues if word got out, had Hoover give instructions to the Los Angeles office not to talk about Rutland with anyone (even if the request was from another US government agency) and sent a replacement version of Rutland's file to the office.

Much of the FBI was annoyed at the navy about their handling of this case. ONI's poorly thought-out actions were a risk. Beating up agents from a foreign government could result in all sorts of embarrassment. Furthermore, the FBI had tried to investigate Rutland a year and a half earlier, but they had backed off at the request of Zacharias of the navy. In addition, ONI staff was keeping the FBI in the dark on items that were in the FBI's jurisdiction. It also appeared that Zacharias and Ringle, at the West Coast office of the ONI, had been keeping their own bosses—ONI headquarters—in the dark as well, although the frequent changes of leadership at ONI confused matters.

Tamm started an FBI investigation on a new suspect: Ellis Zacharias. Zacharias had told the FBI to back off from Rutland, who they felt was very clearly a Japanese spy. It was also personal, because Tamm was annoyed that Zacharias had been apparently bad-mouthing the FBI up and down the West Coast. The FBI had (correctly) deemed Zacharias a loose cannon and PR risk* in the past—but now they also started to wonder if he was a traitor.

The documents that the FBI found in Tachibana's room had incriminating mentions of Rutland. But the submarine plot was the biggest jaw-dropper for Hood and the FBI. It was spectacular, really, to think Rutland was arranging for a Japanese sub to come close enough to the US coastline for espionage. It was not only a smoking gun, but it was evidence that would likely hold up in court. Other memos, from Rutland to Tachibana—explaining how to get to his house and the code word to say to the butler—had no good explanation, but were not clear evidence of a crime.

Had Hood and his team given the matter some more thought, they might have realized the whole idea sounded highly improbable. How would someone use flashing lights to convey hundreds of pages of facts, figures, and drawings to a sub offshore? How risky would it be for a Japanese submarine during a war to travel over five thousand miles across the Pacific before surfacing offshore of Malibu Beach, where it would likely be spotted by both the US Navy and some local surfers?

It was extremely ironic. Rutland's submarine plot was how he planned to help the US Navy double-cross the Japanese. But, the FBI, reading about the plot, decided it was the smoking gun on Rutland's plan to help the Japanese attack the US. There was nothing that Zacharias or Ringle could say that would make the FBI believe them.

The only person that might have been able to help prove Rutland was on the right side was ONI director Alan Kirk in Washington. Kirk was only three months into the job, and was ONI's third director just that year. Even before that, ONI directors were turning over in less than two years, on average, mostly because the job was a political nightmare. Upon

---

* Zacharias was indeed a loose cannon and PR risk. As just one example, in 1945, Zacharias went around his chain of command and published an anonymous piece in the *Washington Post* suggesting a change in the conduct of the war against Japan. This goes beyond "not PR sensitive" to "highly insubordinate."

landing in this new job, Kirk had gotten a quick education on why two prior directors had left the job so quickly.

Kirk had realized the rest of the navy didn't respect ONI. Structurally, at least, it was thought of as a dead-end career, with promotions going to officers who commanded ships. But he found it was worse than that. The head of naval operations, Kelly Turner, not only ignored him, but appeared to be making moves to have intelligence under his direct control. But perhaps his biggest issue was with the FBI. Kirk said after the war that he "ran afoul of J. Edgar Hoover, who maintained, within the United States, the FBI was paramount. Hoover didn't like ONI showing up the FBI as we had done in a couple of cases."

There was some irony here as well: Hoover was indeed highly politically motivated to remove competitive agencies from doing anything in the United States, to the detriment of this and many other investigations. Yet he was also not entirely wrong either. The Office of Naval Intelligence was indeed spending a lot of time looking for Japanese spies and saboteurs inside the US, and thereby not focusing on the real threat, which was the Japanese fleet itself.

Kirk knew the position was politically challenging, and that was part of the reason he got the job over other candidates, such as Zacharias. He was confident that he was good at bureaucracy and politics. His job before becoming the ONI director had been politically charged: naval attaché at the US embassy in London, where he had to deal with the demanding British during the Battle of Britain, and a tricky ambassador to England, Joseph Kennedy. Kennedy had been known as a sympathizer to the Nazis and was on bad terms with the Roosevelt administration.

Kirk had a clever way to turn Ambassador Kennedy into an ally of his. The ambassador's son, John F. Kennedy, had a bad back that had initially precluded him from service, but Kirk was able to pull some strings to get him accepted as a lieutenant in the US Navy.

Kirk had been feeling somewhat confident in his ability to manage the job going in, but was feeling less and less secure as time went on. Yet another issue he had was ONI on the West Coast—Ringle and those who had reported to Zacharias knew that Kirk had been the one who took the director job over Zacharias. They felt Kirk was just a bureaucrat, and had kept him out of the loop on many issues, including those about Rutland.

If Kirk was to go to bat for Rutland, he would need to first get proof Rutland was on the right side, and he didn't have that. He sent notes to his staff, instructing them to find out exactly what Rutland had been promised by ONI.

Rutland called Kirk to make an appointment to see him in Washington, telling him he had important info for US national security. Rutland wanted Kirk to tell everyone that Rutland was a key player in helping the US prepare against a coming Japanese attack.

CHAPTER 27

MEETINGS IN WASHINGTON

July 27, 1941

FBI special agent in charge Cornelius found a telephone at the Los Angeles airport and had the operator put him through to Assistant Director Tamm at FBI headquarters in Washington. He told Tamm that Rutland was on an American Airlines flight scheduled to land at nine p.m. at Washington National Airport. Tamm thanked him and arranged for two FBI agents to pick up the surveillance at the airport when he landed.

Rutland's head was spinning thinking about his upcoming meetings in Washington. He also planned to go to Mexico City. Mexico City was where the Japanese intelligence against the US was now being run, and if he was able to find key intelligence regarding an attack on the US or Britain, he would be able to show his value and prove he was on the right side. He didn't know yet who would pay for his trip. *But who wouldn't?* he thought. Between ONI, British Intelligence, and the FBI, someone would step up and sponsor him. Or maybe the Japanese would send him there to try to help them.

On a different note, Rutland still loved airplanes and airplane technology, and he was excited about landing at the newly constructed Washington National Airport. The airport had opened just a month earlier and had only one hangar in operation so far. One of the biggest innovations of this new airport was that the runways were lighted so well that his flight could land safely in the dark. As the plane landed, Rutland observed the brightness and spacing of the runway lighting that made it all possible, and pondered how it was similar and different to a plane landing on a ship at night.

Rutland got a cab and, surprisingly, went to a modest hotel near the National Cathedral. He had gotten used to staying at places like the Imperial Hotel in Tokyo or the Odney Club in London, with the bill usually being paid for by the Japanese Navy or, on occasion, the US Navy or one of the aircraft companies he represented. In fact, he was often paid more than once for the same trip. He hadn't paid for his own travel in years. But here he was, trying to alert the US and Britain about a coming attack by a foreign adversary, and he needed to pay for it out of his own pocket. He would tell them so.

The next morning, he emerged from the hotel, snazzily dressed as always in a double-breasted suit, and took a streetcar down Massachusetts Avenue, changing cars to go toward the navy yard. The streetcar ride reminded him of his visit to the navy yard when he first came to the US in 1933, when he took pictures there to provide information to his Japanese hosts.

With the war fast approaching, Washington was bursting at the seams. There was so much need for office space for the military that that very day, July 28, Congress had agreed to fund the construction of the world's largest office building, to be called the Pentagon, which would house US military offices across the river in Virginia. There were so many commuters heading into the navy yard that morning that it was easy for the two FBI agents to hide in the crowds, following Rutland as he walked into ONI headquarters. The agents knew that FBI and US Naval Intelligence were not always cooperating well, but they were a bit surprised that the suspect they were tailing was heading in to meet with the navy. Rutland was escorted into the director's office. Kirk greeted him cordially, but Rutland thought his eyes betrayed a bit of annoyance.

"Major Rutland," he said, "I have been in this job for just three months. In that time, I must have heard your name more than I have heard the name of the secretary of state."

Rutland congratulated Kirk on the new job, idly recalling that this pitch would be quite a bit easier if his friend Zacharias had gotten this job instead of Kirk.

Rutland began by telling Kirk that he would like the navy to hold to its agreement with him, to ensure he was properly taken care of and that the FBI and others knew that he had been an important asset to ONI.

Kirk replied, "I'm sorry to tell you this, Major, despite what you may have been told, there is no record here of any formal arrangement between you and our organization. Furthermore, recent events have not made it very easy to work with you further."

Rutland replied, "A war with Japan is indeed coming, and soon. Your president froze all of the Japanese assets in the United States earlier this week, and this makes war even more certain." Kirk nodded at this possibility. Rutland continued, "As you know, the Japanese always strike first, before any declaration of war. Their first war with China? Japan started the war by sinking some Chinese Navy ships. Japan's war with Russia? Japan started it with a surprise attack on some Russian Navy ships. Wouldn't we expect a war might start with an attack on your ships?" Waiting for an acknowledgment that didn't come, Rutland drove the point home by adding, "And finding intelligence about a future attack on the US Navy is indeed your responsibility, isn't it? In fact, isn't it your most important responsibility, for you and for your country?" Kirk nodded, slightly annoyed at Rutland's highly obvious statement, but interested where Rutland was going with the conversation.

Rutland continued, "The most important thing for the US Navy, I would assume, would be to find out when and where this attack will happen." Kirk nodded again, keeping his cards close, but leaning forward. Rutland added, "I know the Japanese Navy as well as anyone. I know their admirals. Unlike other foreigners, I've been to their houses. I've worked with them for twenty years now. And they trust me, trust me unlike any other foreigner. I can tell you why they trust me, Commander Kirk. It is because they are like animals, the Japanese. They can tell when someone likes them and respond accordingly. They know I like them." Rutland waited for acknowledgment, and continued further, "I can read their faces, so I shall know when an attack is coming. Of course, I shan't know every detail, but I'll know, and will be able to tell you." Rutland continued with his modest proposal, which was to have the US Navy pay for his travel to Mexico City, where he would be able to work with the head of Japanese intelligence there, Wachi, and be able to figure out the latest and keep Kirk abreast.

Kirk felt more than a twinge of concern. Rutland's diagnosis was, to some degree, right on the money. He knew he was indeed rather blind to the Japanese Navy's actions, and it was a structural issue in the US Navy that he had limited ability to fix. However, Rutland was not trustworthy, and he wouldn't want to put the fate of the US Navy in the hands of one documented double agent, even if there were no other considerations. But politically, it was worse than that. The heat from the FBI was too hot. Already, one important officer of ONI—Zacharias—had been removed from his post at ONI after clashing with the FBI. The FBI had ample evidence of Rutland's guilt and wanted to prosecute. Kirk told Rutland he would consider it, thanked him for coming, and showed him to the door.

Rutland left the navy yard, and the FBI agents picked up his trail.

Rutland got on a streetcar and headed back across Washington, stopping at the Alban Towers apartments, not far from the National Cathedral. He greeted the doorman, a tall African American man named Julius, who recognized him from prior visits. After pleasantries, he asked Julius if he would please call Commander Yokoyama of the Japanese Navy. He then sat in the lobby to wait. After some time, a young man in a Japanese naval uniform, Yokoyama's secretary, came down and greeted Rutland, and said that Yokoyama was not there.

Rutland asked, "When will Commander Yokoyama be available?"

"Commander Yokoyama is very busy with the peace negotiations between Japan and the United States," the secretary replied, adding coldly, "and you are British."

Rutland pressed, asking, "How about tomorrow?"

The secretary wasn't very reassuring, but Rutland said, in that case, he would take his chances and come by at nine thirty the next morning. He asked the secretary to tell Yokoyama that he had a confidential telegram for Commander Oka in Japan regarding the situation in Mexico and that he wanted them to send it using Japanese codes.

Rutland thanked the secretary, then left and walked back down Massachusetts Avenue. Julius picked up the phone at the front desk, dialed FBI headquarters, and told them about Rutland's visit.

After a five-minute walk, Rutland entered the British embassy. Two men ushered him into their office and introduced themselves as Wing Commander DuBoulay and Major Maude. DuBoulay was fully briefed and ready for the visit. The news about Rutland had reached him from the highest levels of British Intelligence.

The priority for the British embassy in mid-1941 was to do whatever possible to help influence the US to enter the war against Germany. Roosevelt was generally supportive of Britain, but US public opinion didn't support participation in any foreign war. To influence the United States, Churchill had tasked William Stephenson, the "man called Intrepid," to carry out a propaganda campaign. Stephenson was arranging for newspapers to run articles about a very sympathetic Britain that was heroically fighting for Western civilization against the barbaric Germans. The idea was that the avalanche of positive news about Britain would eventually help to convince the US to join the war, and there was evidence from public opinion surveys that this campaign was helping to move the US closer to the British camp.

FBI assistant director Foxworth had gone to meet Stephenson a few days before. His message was very direct.

"It is a smoking gun," he said. "We have enough information to shoot Rutland. Before taking such action, which would lead to headlines in the American press about the shooting of a British officer, I wish to know if the British authorities might not prefer to have him returned to the UK."

Maude, on Stephenson's orders, was ready to offer Rutland a trip back to the UK. Rutland had quite a different agenda. He asked Maude for a job—or, at least, an arrangement like he had with the US Navy, where he would get money to help the British get ready for the coming war with Japan. He could do a lot, he said, by working with the Japanese naval officers in Mexico, helping the British understand when an attack might come, and learning more about how much information the Japanese radio intercept operation in Mexico was passing to the Germans.

Maude told Rutland they would like to confer internally, and asked if Rutland would be so kind as to come back the next day. Rutland agreed, leaving the embassy and walking back up Massachusetts Avenue toward his hotel.

The next morning Rutland started his day back at the Alban Towers with a visit to the Japanese naval attaché, Yokoyama. In his briefcase was a telegram that he planned to ask Yokoyama to encrypt and send to Oka. He was waiting in the lobby for what seemed like an eternity. To pass the time, he picked up a copy of the *Washington Post* that was on the table in the lobby. The headline said "US Protests Japan Bombing of US Gunboat in China." It was clear that peace negotiators were busy trying to smooth over crisis after crisis, and didn't have the opportunity to address the core issues head-on. Twenty minutes later, Yokoyama's secretary came down and told him that Yokoyama would not be able to meet him, but the secretary offered to take Rutland for a car ride to discuss. In the car, the secretary explained that Yokoyama didn't want to meet with Rutland, because he was furious.

Yokoyama was indeed furious—but mostly with Tachibana. Yokoyama had come crawling back from a meeting with his counterpart in the US Navy, Admiral Kelly Turner, who was accusing him of stabbing him in the back. He tried to convey that he had no idea what his fellow Japanese Navy officer, Tachibana, had been doing. It was true—he really didn't have much idea what Tachibana was doing, although Turner doubted it. Now, members of Congress were calling for Yokoyama to be expelled from the US along with the Japanese agents.

Ironically, Yokoyama didn't know much about Tachibana's activities, although Rutland certainly did. But he downplayed his relationship with Tachibana in the conversation. He asked again if Yokoyama would be

able to send a telegram, a very important message for Oka. The secretary
agreed to try to get it sent to Oka, but he could not promise.

The telegram said that Rutland would likely be able to get to Mexico
City, but if not, he would send a man named Adams for him, who would
know the same password that Rutland used last time. When he got there,
he would bring the latest information on the US Navy's preparations in
California.

Tamm thought the Rutland situation was ludicrous. So much so that
it was almost funny. What kind of suspect would be meeting with the US
Navy, the British, *and* the Japanese Navy? But it was easy to figure out.
Rutland was obviously in DC to save his own skin and would talk to anyone he thought might help him. He appeared willing to work with anyone
who could give him results.

...

Tachibana, Kono, and the others who'd been scooped up for espionage had
escaped prosecution for political reasons. But there was still one Japanese
agent running around free: Rutland. The FBI would've loved to apprehend
him, but knew how difficult it would be to pull that off without the press
dogging them or the spectacle of a public trial. Worse, Rutland was highly
media savvy and was quoted often in the press. If Rutland wanted to get
press, it would be easy for him.

Tamm made a call to Kirk at ONI, who confirmed Rutland went to ask
for the navy to go to bat for him. Tamm was still annoyed that Zacharias
had told the FBI to back off of Rutland a year earlier. Kirk grudgingly
reiterated to Tamm that ONI was not going to protect Rutland.

Rutland walked back down Massachusetts Avenue to the British embassy and met again with Maude and DuBoulay. DuBoulay had an interesting pitch for Rutland, as coached by Young back at MI5 in London. It
was the best kind of deception—not entirely truthful, but not exactly full
of lies either. He explained that Rutland was in trouble in the US, with

the FBI on his trail. This was clearly true. He also suggested that Rutland would do better out of the hands of the FBI, specifically in England. His pitch to Rutland was that Rutland's experience with the Japanese would very likely be helpful to British Intelligence. With a war with Japan likely coming, it would be great for Rutland to serve the empire again. Perhaps, he even suggested, Rutland could be of great assistance to British Intelligence.

Rutland bought it, suggesting his knowledge of the Japanese Navy could save British lives in the future conflict with Japan. Rutland, as was par for the course, then requested some expensive VIP treatment. At the time, a cheap ticket across the Atlantic was very dangerous. German submarines were sinking British ships in the Atlantic, and a passenger from Washington to the UK stood a decent chance of being on a ship that would be torpedoed. The only other way to get to the UK was by plane, and at this point in the war, a trip on a plane across the Atlantic was a very rare commodity not available for any price.

Rutland suggested to DuBoulay that, as a key intelligence asset, he be flown back to England on a military flight, such as a bomber. He told DuBoulay that if the Japanese knew that Rutland was getting the VIP treatment, they would assume he was important, boosting his credibility and helping him get more info from them.

DuBoulay agreed to look into the matter, thanked Rutland, and showed him to the door.

Rutland checked out of his hotel and boarded an Eastern Airlines plane headed to Texas. FBI agents at the airport observed where he was going and called ahead to the local offices in Houston to help pick up the surveillance. After a couple of plane changes, Rutland landed in the border town of Brownsville, Texas, with a ticket to fly to Mexico City from there. Unfortunately for Rutland, the border controls had recently been strengthened, and he was not able to get a proper visa to go to Mexico and then come back to the US. He was stuck and running low on cash. He went to a bank to pick up a $200 money order from Dorothy. There was nothing he could do about Mexico, so Rutland booked his flights back to Los Angeles.

Landing in Los Angeles, Rutland picked up a newspaper. The headline said "Roosevelt Cuts Off Oil Exports to Japan." Rutland knew what that meant. War was almost certain now. The Japanese Navy that he knew so well needed American oil to do anything. He was able to calculate, in his head, about how much oil the Japanese had—and it wasn't much. Japan had the options now of either backing down or making a move to capture some oil. He didn't think the Japanese would back down—once they had started in a given direction, it wasn't in their nature to retreat. In particular, their pride would not let them retreat to a threat or insult that was made in public.

Rutland took some time and considered his options. Like Japan, he was pushed into a corner. Staying in the US was clearly not an option. FBI surveillance was all over him. If the US Navy wouldn't go to bat for him—and it clearly wouldn't—then Britain was his only and best option. The only option he could consider was defecting to Japan—and with war on the horizon, that seemed out of the question, even for Rutland. Rutland therefore contacted the British attachés in Washington to arrange logistics for the trip, stressing again that a VIP plane ticket would be key.

Rutland was still a bit short on cash. He met Leon Lewis, head of a group of Jewish researchers who were investigating American Nazis and other threats, and sold him a list of Japanese spies.

The FBI also went into cover-up mode. Tamm destroyed the index card with Rutland's info in the "Custodial Detention Index" and ordered Hood in Los Angeles to personally go find that same card in the LA office and destroy it. Tamm then sent Hood a replacement file.

Later, a memo from FBI headquarters informed the LA Field Office that they were not to discuss Rutland in any memo or communication that anyone outside the FBI would see (even other American agencies) to prevent embarrassment.

Rutland left his family in Los Angeles and headed back to the UK on a bomber that Maude had arranged.

...

Tachibana had arrived back in Japan. Upon arriving, he was taken to naval headquarters in Ichigaya, where he was greeted by Vice Admiral Minoru Maeda, the new head of naval intelligence. Maeda and his staff spent two days intensely debriefing Tachibana about his time in the United States.

Tachibana liked that the questions were focused and intense. When he was in Los Angeles, he had found this group eager, yet impractical. Smiling, he thought about what happened when he sent aerial photos of the massive Ford plant known as "The Rouge." Rutland had just had those pictures in his house, so he sent them on. But more to the point, the Ford plant was in Detroit, more than two thousand miles from Los Angeles. It seemed impossible enough for the Japanese Navy to pull off any kind of attack on the US West Coast, so the chance Japanese planes could bomb Detroit was nil. He had been roundly praised for getting these pictures, and it made him wonder if the intelligence staff was uneducated or unfocused— but seeing the team so focused now was reassuring.

Maeda and his staff member Eizo Hori asked Tachibana about the vulnerability of US Navy ships in port to an attack. Tachibana immediately answered, "The American ships in port are not expecting anything. The men are not as well trained as our men are. They spend a lot of time on leave off the ship."

Maeda, impressed by Tachibana's knowledge and even more by his aggressiveness, decided to hire Tachibana into his group right away. Tachibana leapt from his seat when Maeda later told him that his top secret new job would be to help plan an attack on Pearl Harbor.

Maeda's group quickly leaned on Tachibana for the knowledge he had gained watching the US Fleet in Los Angeles. They had an efficient agent on the ground in Hawaii to help them with their efforts.

The new Japanese agent, Takeo Yoshikawa, had been sent to Hawaii earlier that year, and immediately showed himself to be far more dependable and effective than the existing agent in Honolulu, a German who had been dubbed "Agent Fujii."

Yoshikawa had been surprised to be given his assignment in Hawaii. He had recently come back for an extended sick leave after a bad case of appendicitis. During his recovery period, he was sent home to rest and spent that time intensively studying English with a tutor who had him read Sherlock Holmes short stories. He felt a bit like the iconic detective, but the stakes were far, far higher.

Tachibana prepared a multitude of other questions and tasks for Yoshikawa. There were daily requests to report the numbers of ships in Pearl Harbor, what ships were in port each day, what times of day the ships typically sailed from the port, when the ships in the harbor had the most sailors aboard, and more. Yoshikawa said the number of questions were "as numerous as snowflakes in winter." He found the number of requests a little annoying, since he clearly couldn't observe the locations of the American ships twenty-four hours a day.

At first, Yoshikawa had pretended to be an unemployed Filipino dishwasher and was hired to wash dishes at the US Navy officers club. When he wasn't observing the US Fleet from that club, a nearby restaurant, or some nearby sugarcane fields, he swam in the waters near the American fleet, diving to the bottom to measure the depths of the water and to check if the ships were surrounded by nets. He performed this operation by breathing through a bamboo tube.

No one told Yoshikawa that his country was planning to attack Pearl Harbor, but he found it obvious from the content of the questions. Tachibana had been the one to ask Yoshikawa to find out about the depth of the water and if there were nets around the ships—questions that would only be asked if they were planning an attack using torpedo planes.

One key request from Tachibana was to report when the largest number of American ships were in Pearl Harbor at once. The answer was just after dawn on the first and third Sunday of every month. This would be the perfect timing for a surprise attack.

CHAPTER 28

LOOKING FOR SPIES IN ALL THE WRONG PLACES

October–November 1941

Rutland walked into the office of Sir John Godfrey, director of British Naval Intelligence, in the Admiralty Building in London. Escorting Rutland into Room 39 was Godfrey's personal assistant, a young officer named Ian Fleming, whom Rutland was familiar with from his time writing for Reuters.

Rutland was nervous, still very much leery about this meeting and his return to England. Under a constant state of surveillance, Rutland knew his government was highly suspicious of him, despite the assurances he received in Washington before he agreed to return. The men at the British embassy in Washington had lied to him, it seemed.

They had sent him back to the UK on a bomber, on a ticket better than first class. But even before he'd made it back to London, things went awry. When his plane landed to refuel at Foynes, Ireland, immigration inspectors pulled him aside to search his bag and examine his traveling papers. When they found the Japanese visas in his passport, they pressed him about his visit, asking for specific names of people he was visiting and places he intended to go. Satisfied with Rutland's answers, the inspectors waved him on, but refused to return his papers, which they wanted to verify and research independently. They told him that he would get them back at some undetermined date. Rutland expressed his anger as best he could, but even he knew underneath his righteous indignation was a grave concern about returning, which suddenly felt like the wrong move.

"Welcome home, Squadron Leader," Godfrey said. "Please take a seat."

Rutland pulled out his chair and arranged himself in a position that appeared deferential but not too solicitous.

"Thank you," Rutland said flatly. "I'm happy to be back in England."

"Yes, I imagine it's quite the return from Los Angeles, that oasis in the desert. We may not have many movie stars or trolley cars, but you and I both know in our bones that as a destination London is hard to beat, even during a war."

"Well, as I said, I'm happy to be back."

Rutland was unsure if Godfrey's propriety was perfunctory or a ruse. He knew Godfrey's résumé just as well as Godfrey knew his. In the parlance of Rutland's adopted country, they had *come up together* during the war, though Godfrey was positioned more advantageously on their ascent, a fact made clear by the green baize adorning his office door—a conspicuous demarcation between the stately and their subordinates. A Staffordshire man, Godfrey had been educated at the elite, four-hundred-year-old King Edward's School in Birmingham.

He had served on the *Euryalus* in Gallipoli and, after surviving a battle in Egypt, he got staffed up with the commander in chief in the Mediterranean around the same time Rutland was washing out of the Royal Air Force. Now he was at the head of a key British Intelligence center. Through it, Godfrey regularly communicated with the Secret Intelligence Service—more popularly known as MI6—the Special Operations Executive MI5, the counterespionage department, and Combined Operations, which gave him wide and deep access to the British Intelligence services.

Whether his greeting was mannered or sincere, Rutland couldn't yet divine, but it bothered him nevertheless, and he made sure to keep his guard up as he tried to figure out Godfrey's intentions.

"How long have you been abroad?" Godfrey asked.

"I first left for Japan in 1922. Since then, I have lived four years in Japan, nine in America."

Fleming jotted down these dates in his notebook. He was a curious man with a long face and a furrowed brow and a pair of stonelike eyes that seemed to search for every detail, no matter how minute. Rutland got the impression that Fleming was the one he had to win over, the one who would compile the minutes of this meeting and translate them into a narrative that would either recommend Rutland or, as far as British Intelligence was concerned, cast him out.

"I have worked closely with many of the top officers in both the Imperial Japanese Navy and the United States Navy. My priority now, of course, is to help Britain in any way I can."

Fleming leaned forward.* His uniform, which was neatly pressed, bunched around this Windsor knot. For the first time, Rutland noticed the lack of medals across his breast—odd for a commander in his midthirties. "And who would you say you have been working for over this time, Squadron Leader?"

"I initially was one of the dozens of Britons who were helping the Japanese in the early 1920s. But you most likely know that. You probably know, too, that I was there with Lord Sempill and Herbert Smith of Sopwith. At the time, the British government was supportive of these efforts. They were quite keen on fostering an Anglo-Japanese partnership, which . . ." Here, Rutland paused for effect. ". . . again, as you know, dates back decades. Perhaps most relevant to this discussion is how well I learned about the Japanese Navy. I became friends with many junior officers in the early 1920s, who are the leaders of the Japanese Navy today. There is no one else in Britain or America that knows and has the trusting relationship with general staff of the Japanese Admiralty as I do."

"Noted," Godfrey replied as Fleming continued to write in his ledger. "And I shan't hold your service in Japan during that period against you."

Rutland was relieved to hear this, and he felt himself relax a bit. That

---

* Fleming said his fictional character James Bond "was a compound of all the secret agents and commando types I met during the war." Rutland was a glamorous, well-dressed agent that operated in many countries, splitting his time between espionage and going to glamorous parties. Rutland may well have been part of Fleming's inspiration.

and the invitation to speak freely about his own importance and experience was when he always felt most like himself. He welcomed back his confidence.

"And how about afterwards? Who did you work for later?"

"The Japanese requested my help again in the 1930s. I visited Japan on business—I had a trading company—and they were interested in my experiences in America. However, after tensions started building, I began to work for the United States Navy. They were very pleased to receive my insights."

Fleming asked, "What type of work did you do for the United States?"

"That's classified. I am sure you understand."

Fleming nodded and marked something in his ledger.

"What I can tell you—and I probably shouldn't even share this, mind you—is the United States Office of Naval Intelligence is the only American intelligence agency with the proper priorities. There are so many intelligence agencies in the United States. Some Americans told me that it is a bit like a chicken coop. Agents from one agency run out the door, just at the same time agents from a different agency run in the door, all chasing after the same intelligence."

Godfrey and Fleming mostly agreed with this statement. By this time, Britain's Navy Intelligence and ONI were indeed starting to cooperate. MI5 had kept its intelligence from the Americans for a very long time, but the intelligence officers from the US and Royal Navies had shared information out of sheer necessity. In a way analogous to the relationship between ONI and the FBI in the United States, and for very similar reasons, British Navy Intelligence and MI5 weren't entirely on the same page. Their priority was to ensure British ships stayed afloat. ONI's priority was to ensure American ships stayed afloat. A possible Japanese attack on British ships might very well necessitate extreme methods, even those that MI5 would not condone, like taking a risk on sources.

Sensing his story was beginning to sit with them, Rutland straightened in his chair. "An attack by Japan is coming," he said. "Sooner than you think. Where the Japanese will attack isn't certain. But there is a strong chance our Royal Navy ships in Singapore will be in their crosshairs. I should remind you—I joined the Royal Navy at age fourteen. As the Indians say, the Royal Navy is my father and mother. I see that HMS *Repulse* is heading to Singapore now, and I flew a biplane off of its rear turret in 1917. I shall do my utmost to protect it and our shipmates. I ask only that you consider letting me do so."

Godfrey and Fleming took in Rutland's statements. They knew MI5 didn't trust Rutland. However, he seemed sincere at the moment, for what it was worth.

"What are you suggesting?" Godfrey asked.

"I imagine Britain would prefer to be ready for an attack, and I think my skills and my contacts can both be uniquely helpful in this regard."

"Go on, then," Godfrey said.

"After the FBI rolled up the Tachibana spy ring in the US, the Japanese moved that intelligence network to Mexico City. There are at least a dozen Japanese naval officers in Mexico, all of which are involved in planning espionage and sabotage against the US and Britain."

"Look here, we're tracking Nazis in Europe, not Japanese networks in some backwater."

"When the Germans sink a British ship in the Atlantic, did it ever occur to you the location of the ship might have been tipped off to the Germans by the Japanese? The Japanese radio intercept team in Mexico City is sophisticated and precise, just like everything else they do. Mexico City is at high altitude, perfect for intercepting US radio traffic from Virginia. They often know where our ships are."

Godfrey and Fleming were leaning forward. A focus of their department was tracking German warships, especially in the North Sea and North Atlantic, the major shipping lanes surrounding the British Isles. Fleming was already working with an Australian pilot to photograph the German fleet at anchor, hoping to gather in the near future the same kind of intelligence Rutland was offering them at this very moment.

"And you can infiltrate this network?" Godfrey asked.

"I already have. It is what the Japanese asked me to do, visit and coordinate with their Mexico City operation. I've been there numerous times. They trust me. Send me to Mexico City. The Japanese there will welcome me, and I will be able to know when the attack is coming and tell you." Pausing for effect, and with his voice actually cracking with emotion, he continued, "I beg you to understand, there is nothing in the world more important to me than protecting the Royal Navy and this country."

Fleming asked, "And how, pray tell, will you divine this imminent attack?"

"I know the Japanese Navy better than anyone. I have worked closely with Admirals Shimada, Yamamoto, and Takasu for almost twenty years. The junior Japanese officers, when they hear that I am being sent from the Japanese Admiralty, tell me far more than they would any other foreigner. I won't know all of the details, of course—in fact, the Japanese in Mexico themselves won't even know all of the details of the attack. But I'll know the state of preparation and the timing. And I shall be able to let you know."

No one said anything for a few moments. To break the silence, Rutland chimed in, "I should add that I can help you with coordination with the Americans, too, should you desire. I'm quite friendly with ONI director Kirk."

Fleming continued to write in his notebook, occasionally looking up to study Rutland's countenance. Finally, Godfrey nodded and stood. "I want to thank you, Squadron Leader, for this insight. Your assistance has already proved instructive. You understand, of course, that we need to discuss this new information. We'll be sure to be in touch as soon as humanly possible. Commander Fleming will see you out."

Rutland stood, surprised by the meeting's sudden conclusion. His desire to receive at least verbal assurances that the British government would hire him hadn't been met. On the other hand, he hadn't been thrown out—or, worse, detained. His freedom remained, and as Fleming wished him well before returning to Godfrey's office, he took great comfort in knowing he had made the best possible case for his utility. His fate was still unknown, but he felt his safety was nevertheless assured.

Once Fleming returned, Godfrey had one of his staff, Ewen Montagu, contact Courtenay Young and Dick White at MI5 to set up a meeting. He wanted to discuss the next steps about Rutland, but he also wanted to convey a strong message to MI5. Fleming typed up his notes and sent them to Young and White in advance. From the start, the meeting was contentious.

"Rutland is a national hero," Godfrey asserted. "Why was MI5 so aggressive in its questioning of him?"

Immediately, Young dismissed Godfrey's cautious endorsement of Rutland as an asset. "With all due respect, Godfrey, that is in the past. We need to talk about the future. It would be frightfully dangerous to send Rutland to Mexico or to the United States."

"Rutland appears to be possibly quite useful. It might not make sense to send him back to the Japanese in Mexico," Godfrey countered. "Perhaps, though, he can help us somewhere else, something with lower risk and less visibility. It would be a shame not to take advantage of Rutland's particular talents. As a mere suggestion, if there is to be a war, who would be better to interview prisoners?"

"Rutland ought to be in prison himself," Young said. "On my desk is a large file documenting Rutland's activity. One thing that is clear is that he's an unscrupulous liar. In fact, the only reason he isn't in prison right now is because the Americans have not been forthcoming with their communication." Young paused, and then continued, "It's rather exasperating. The message we received from the FBI in September was that they had enough evidence to shoot him, and they threatened to do so if we didn't take him back. We thought perhaps they weren't being literal, but they did seem uncharacteristically angry. I don't know if they are angry at Rutland or at us. But either way, we lack evidence of illegal activity against this country, and we have not yet been able to bring him to trial."

"That appears to be exactly the point," growled Godfrey. "If you've no evidence that the man's committed crimes against this country, all the more reason to treat him properly." Godfrey's attitude was not surprising. He was a Royal Navy man.

Young and White were trying to return the conversation to the near-term priority of what to do with Rutland. They needed to keep Rutland out of the news. It was critical, because British prime minister Winston Churchill's priority was to have the United States join the war on Britain's side. If word got out that a British war hero had been running the Japanese spy ring in Hollywood for a decade, and the British hadn't mentioned it to the Americans, the press coverage would be very damaging to Britain. The PR effort they'd been running would be set back noticeably.

Young had orchestrated Rutland's return to avoid this exact scenario. He wasn't about to let Rutland do anything in the name of the British government, let alone let him run wild. If they couldn't legally arrest him, they could at least keep him under surveillance and prevent him from talking to the wrong people as much as possible.

The discussion continued, though no one believed it would make much of a difference. The spirit rather than the substance of the meeting was to finalize a decision and ensure they'd shared exactly what each agency knew.

"Before he returned," Godfrey said, "Rutland wrote to Maude in Washington, explaining that the Japanese strung him along for years. Rather than paying him for his past work, they continued to demand more and more from him, which sometimes pushed him into dubious legal areas. Mind you, I haven't seen this letter."

"Rutland was on the run when he wrote that letter," Young countered. "He would have said anything to cover his own arse. He was flailing. The last thing you do with a drowning man is grab him, or he's sure to bring you under with him." Godfrey was annoyed that MI5 would treat a hero from the Royal Navy poorly, but he also knew that Young was potentially right. What kept him going was the recent success he had found in counterintelligence operations. In September 1939, he issued his "Trout Memo," a directive for how to conduct deception operations against the Germans.

"The Trout Fisher," he wrote, "casts patiently all day. He frequently changes his venue and his lures. If he has frightened a fish he may 'give the water a rest for half-an-hour,' but his main endeavor, to attract fish by something he sends out from his boat, is incessant." In the memo, Godfrey listed fifty-four ways that the enemy may be fooled or lured, just as the fisherman lures trout. Rutland was good bait, he believed, and so desperate for cover he would likely give the Japanese any intelligence, no matter how uncredible, to save his own hide. Godfrey wanted to use Rutland. The idea wasn't entirely outlandish. Later, a more outlandish scheme grew out of this memo, which involved both Fleming and Montagu. "Operation Mincemeat" involved planting false intelligence on a British corpse for the Germans to discover to throw them off England's planned invasion of Sicily in 1943.

But for now, the Royal Navy would take no such action. A new national emergency law allowed MI5 and other services to arrest suspects affiliated with countries that Britain was at war with and keep them in jail indefinitely without trial. But this law couldn't be used to arrest Rutland yet, not until Japan and Britain were at war. Young prepared orders to have on hand, so that when war with Japan did start, he could have Rutland arrested immediately.

MI5's decision to keep Rutland out of sight and out mind had worked for them, but it certainly didn't help the FBI or ONI in the United States, which were still very much in the dark about the details of Rutland's activities, how the Japanese were preparing their espionage for after the war started, and any details about Japan's impending attack. Rutland might not have offered the British a smoking gun, but he did proffer a loaded gun with its hammer cocked. He knew *what* was coming and offered a plausible way to find out *when* it was coming.

Unfortunately, even if the British had gotten any details and warned the Americans, or had used Rutland in some way, it's not entirely certain any US agency was ready to receive it, let alone act upon it. It wasn't that there weren't clues—there were many clues. The issue was putting them together, and there was disorganization at the top. The visionary of ONI who knew the most about the Japanese and had predicted the Japanese attack was coming, Zacharias, had been removed from intelligence at just the wrong time.

ONI had made two mistakes in managing Zacharias. They kept him around for too long, then they got rid of him too soon. The bellicose Zacharias had been sounding the alarm about Japan for over a decade, irritating and embarrassing his colleagues and superiors. His constant warnings about the Japanese threat were widely dismissed as crackpot conspiracies rather than actionable intelligence, but his concern was warranted and, ultimately, prescient. Yet the constant warnings from Zacharias and others felt like the boy crying wolf, and likely contributed to the ability of the Japanese Navy to pull off the attack. As Admiral Bull Halsey said, "So many false reports being received from unknown sources concerning presence of enemy ships, carriers, transports, and submarines that it is very difficult to glean the true from the false."

But in any event, when the attack finally happened, Zacharias was away from intelligence and at sea, and Rutland had been removed to England. The navy had installed Kirk as head of ONI over Zacharias because they believed Kirk had the political, organizational, and diplomatic skills needed, and it was thought that he could get along with the other intelligence agencies. Getting along with all of the other agencies was going to be impossible, though—there was nothing any head of ONI could do to make Hoover cooperate with them.

ONI continued to struggle, embroiled in battles with the FBI and naval operations. Kirk had tried to do what had long been neglected—to boost up information gathering in Japan and around the Japanese Navy itself. ONI had been able to recruit a couple agents in Japan, at the Tokyo Lawn and Tennis Club, where foreigners and Japanese citizens had been socializing since its founding in 1900. One of the tennis-playing agents was a young man who appeared to be Japanese. He was not. He was Korean and happy to risk his life to help the US against Japan, and periodically observed several Japanese Navy bases, including Yokosuka and Maizuru. The US spies were able to confirm the construction of a new battleship, which appeared to be over 250 meters long and was relatively easy to notice when they passed by the shipyards—but they didn't get much more. Had ONI sent an agent to the southern Japanese city of Kagoshima, they would have seen an interesting sight. Hundreds of Japanese planes were practicing low-level attacks in a harbor that is quite similar to Pearl Harbor. But, overall, the scale of what ONI did in Japan was quite limited.

Kirk was deemed unable to do what was needed to scale up and improve ONI to where it needed to be for the approaching war. He spoke to Admiral Chester Nimitz and was replaced as head of ONI by Theodore Wilkinson on October 15, less than two months before Pearl Harbor, with Wilkinson becoming the *fourth* ONI director of 1941. Wilkinson was a talented officer who had placed first in his class at the US Naval Academy, so in Kirk's mind he was leaving the agency in as good a shape as possible.

Wilkinson was indeed competent, but was hardly in a position to do anything, let alone act on nebulous intelligence to prevent an attack. On joining, he asked his team for the latest from their agents in Japan. One of ONI's tennis-playing agents went to the main Japanese naval base at Yokosuka and reported that the security had been increased, and so he wasn't able to get close enough to get any information. He couldn't tell if any ships were in port and had no clues as to where the Japanese fleet was.

In mid November, the US codebreakers "lost" the Japanese carrier fleet. The codebreakers would usually not be able to read actual messages, but could still identify ships by their call signs. The Japanese carriers had stopped using their radios at all, which to an astute observer was yet another clear sign of an upcoming attack.

And there were other clues.

In Hawaii, the commander of the US Fleet, Admiral Kimmel, asked his intelligence officer Edwin Layton where the Japanese fleet was. The answer was, the Americans didn't know. Kimmel asked, rhetorically (or so he thought), "So the Japanese fleet could be right here, rounding Diamond Head as we speak, and we would have no idea?"

Layton nodded.

CHAPTER 29

PEARL HARBOR, REDUX

About 250 Miles North of Hawaii, December 7, 1941, 5:30 a.m.

The sea was rough. The ocean waves splashed the bows and water flew up onto the decks. The planes—Zeros, Vals, and Kates—were positioned on the decks of the ships, wings unfolded and ready to take off. The maintenance crews were working hard to hold on to the planes to ensure they weren't rocked too much from the pitch of the ship.

On board the lead carrier, the *Akagi*, the flight leader of the Pearl Harbor attack, Mitsuo Fuchida, hit the Kayaba starter on his Nakajima torpedo bomber (called "Kate" by the Americans) and heard the engine come to life. Fuchida saw the air operations officer wave the white flag from the bridge. His deck crew unchocked the wheels, and he gunned the engine and felt his neck jerk back as the plane took off and rose into the air.

The modern Japanese planes traveled the distance to Oahu in an hour and a half. The planes of just five or six years prior would not have been able to pull off an attack from this distance. The updates to these planes had been carried out using the information that Frederick Rutland had provided to their designers.

The carriers themselves had been updated based on meetings with Rutland, and even the starter on the Kate was manufactured by Kayaba—a company in which Rutland remained a major shareholder.

As Fuchida assembled the planes in the attack position, he opened his windshield and fired a Kayaba flare pistol to signal that surprise had been achieved.

Meanwhile, in Mexico City, Commander Wachi of the Japanese Navy and his men were monitoring US communications, as they always were. They had not been able to decode the US radio transmissions recently, but they were tracking signal locations and strengths as well as call signs of US warships. All of a sudden, they intercepted a US Navy radio message that was not in code—it was in plain text. The message said "Air raid, Pearl Harbor. This is no drill." They looked at each other in shock before they realized exactly what it meant. Wachi realized that it was only two a.m. in Japan. They were almost certainly the first Japanese not in the strike group to hear the news that the war had started. Excited, Wachi led his men in three cheers of "*Banzai!*" for the emperor.

He had hoped he would have an intelligence network in Southern California to activate to support the war effort, but he didn't. Rutland—and all of the rest—had either been expelled or jailed or were in hiding.

When the attack started, Captain Ellis Zacharias was not at Pearl Harbor, but at sea roughly 230 miles west. His ship, the *Salt Lake City*, had left a few days earlier, and had escorted the aircraft carrier *Enterprise* on a mission to deliver planes to Wake Island. They were sailing on their way back to Pearl Harbor when, as he rose early that morning in his cabin, there was frantic knocking on his door. The communications officer burst in, saying, "Captain! A message about an attack on Pearl Harbor, and that it's not a drill!"

Zacharias turned the radio to station KGU. A prerecorded voice was reading a statement: "We are having a sporadic air attack. Everyone should keep calm and remain indoors. Do not go into the streets as it will interfere with military going to their posts. There is nothing to worry about." It was especially jarring for him to hear this announcement, as he himself had written it a couple of weeks earlier at the request of his friend Lorrin Thurston, the radio station owner. It was not just frustrating, but eerie, to hear his own words repeated back to him.

Zacharias put his men on battle stations as *Enterprise* launched planes to try to find the Japanese ships that he knew were somewhere not far away. They found none, and the ships needed to head back to Pearl Harbor anyhow due to lack of fuel. Zacharias's strike group was probably fortunate not to have found the Japanese, since they had just the one carrier.

The Japanese had brought six.

Zacharias entered Pearl Harbor a day later and saw pure devastation. He was angry but, in a way, fulfilled. Stepping ashore briefly, he had a friend cable his wife to say he was okay. He also called Thurston of KGU.

"Zack!" he exclaimed. "Thank God you're all right! Can you come over?" Zacharias replied that he was unfortunately going to be busy for the foreseeable future. "The Japanese attack! It was just as you said. How's your ship?" asked Thurston.

"She's fine, Lorrin. And just you wait till she starts shooting. You'll hear about it."

"Good luck, and Godspeed, Zack." Thurston hung up the phone, and Zacharias returned to his ship.

...

Meanwhile, in California, a call came from an FBI agent in Hawaii to the Los Angeles office of the FBI. Special agent in charge Hood was on duty and picked up the phone himself. The agent was explaining about the surprise attack, and Hood's eyes widened as he heard an explosion in the background. The normally calm Hood felt his blood pressure rise and told the agent there had been no attack in Los Angeles that he knew of as of yet, thanked him, and hung up the phone. He immediately activated the plan that had been rehearsed with his men, contacting the port, the police, the Department of Water and Power, the oil refineries, and the phone company, and had them all go to the highest level of security. He didn't think it likely the Japanese would bomb Los Angeles, but it seemed quite possible that the Japanese would activate saboteurs who could bomb or disable these key facilities.

Hood had several suspects at top of mind as most likely to be controlling any saboteurs. He immediately sent men to pick up Kono and Furusawa, who were arrested even before all the Japanese planes had gotten back to their aircraft carriers.

Kono was interned without charges. Six months later, innocent Japanese American civilians—also interned without charges, as over one hundred thousand Japanese Americans soon would be—joined Kono in Manzanar. The movie-loving Kono ended up running the camp movie projector, just like he had done at Charlie Chaplin's mansion.

Chaplin himself was conflicted. He was dismayed that the US would be fighting against Japan, yet he was resolute in his belief that Hitler needed to be stopped and therefore was pleased that the US would be joining the war against Germany.

In Washington, J. Edgar Hoover went into full damage-control mode. He knew that someone would take the blame for the Pearl Harbor attack, and he needed to ensure it was someone—anyone—other than the FBI. The obvious first candidates for taking the blame were the officers in charge in Hawaii, and he quickly stated as much in a memo to President Roosevelt a few days later. He issued orders to keep quiet on all topics where the FBI could be blamed—the Rutland case being a major one.

...

The day of the attack, Rutland was just about to sit down for dinner when a news flash came across the BBC. It was exactly as he'd forecast—a surprise attack by Japanese planes on the American fleet at Pearl Harbor. He had spent the last six months trying to explain that this would happen and had been roundly ignored—been treated, in fact, as an enemy.

There was not much detail on the radio reports, but he knew the Japanese had pulled off an attack without declaring war first, and was certain many of his good friends from Japan were involved. Kuwabara was there for sure, he thought. He wondered what Zacharias was doing that moment, but he knew his friend on the American side was likely trying to maneuver his ship to avoid bombs. Singapore was on his mind as well. Perhaps the attack was on the United States Fleet only, but it was also possible that Japan was going to attack the British warships in the Far East. Knowing his Japanese friends, he feared and assumed the latter.

After his anger had briefly settled down, Rutland's mind returned to figuring out how to rejoin the Royal Navy. Getting into the war would allow Rutland to redeem his honor—and, in fact, he could perhaps become a hero again. He would never admit to himself, out loud, that he had done anything wrong—but perhaps subconsciously he felt he could make amends.

He was optimistic, despite all of the recent issues with MI5. It would make sense for the Royal Navy to take him now. He had his expert knowledge of the new enemy, and, if the crown wanted him away from Japan, he would then be extremely qualified to be a regular Royal Navy officer again. Either way, his skills were desperately needed, and he had many friends at the Admiralty. Certainly, it would work out.

Skipping dinner, he composed a quick letter to the Lords Commissioners of the Admiralty:

I have the honour to submit that I may be permitted to rejoin the Royal Navy at a rank of Lieutenant. I submit that I am particularly suited for commanding torpedo carrying motorboats or other boats that land troops. I am an experienced and fit Navy veteran who appears young for my age.

He signed the letter: *Frederick Rutland, DSC.*

First thing in the morning, Rutland walked to the post and mailed the letter. He returned to his brother-in-law's house and turned on the radio, hoping to hear more about the attack. He was sitting on the couch when there was a very sharp double knock on the door. He knew immediately what it was. As he feared, when he opened the door, there were two constables standing on the porch.

"Mr. Frederick Rutland?" asked the lead constable.

"Yes."

"You will be coming with us. You have five minutes to get any personal belongings you would like to bring with you."

Rutland was taken to Brixton Prison and put in a cell with no further information. As the metal doors slammed shut, he demanded the jailor tell him what he had been arrested for and what the charges were.

There was no immediate answer, but later, one jailor told him that his detention without trial was authorized under Defence Regulation 18B, reserved for those "who presented imminent danger to the realm"—a special law passed by Parliament because of the national emergency. For anyone arrested under this law, there would be no charges filed, no trial, no habeas corpus. Simply put, Rutland would be in prison until the crown decided he would not be.

He tried to calm down and get a better sense of the situation. The inmates were allowed out of their cells for dinner, and as he walked out the first evening, he gasped as he saw a fellow inmate he knew. It was Barry Domvile, a British admiral who had apparently been helping the Nazis. There was Oswald Mosley, head of the British Union of Fascists, who had also been a flyer in World War I. He greeted them, but cautiously. Almost all of his fellow prisoners were either fascists or Nazis, and he thought of himself as a British patriot. He was shocked when he learned that several of the other inmates had broken into a chorus of "Deutschland über Alles" when it came out that the British battle cruiser HMS *Hood* had been sunk by the German battleship *Bismarck*. To Rutland, it felt wrong—very wrong—for him to be included in this group.

Rutland eagerly read every newspaper he could find. A few days later, he was dismayed to read two British ships had been sunk by Japanese Navy planes near Singapore. One of them was indeed HMS *Repulse*, the ship from which, in 1917, Rutland had demonstrated the safety of flying a plane off of a warship turret. He was in shock—from his perspective, he'd been punished, was still being punished, even though he had tried to warn both the British and Americans that this was coming.

. . .

Not long after, Rutland was called into a private interrogation room. Two well-dressed men walked in and took a seat. They didn't introduce themselves, but the leader was Courtenay Young of MI5, who had been tracking Rutland for several years. Young crossed his legs and brushed a spot of dirt from his spats. He removed from his vest pocket a tin of snuff, which he laid on the small table between him and Rutland. With his left hand, he pinched the powder and sprinkled it across the fleshy pad between his right thumb and index finger, then inhaled the powder in both nostrils. Looking at Rutland, he adjusted his monocle and wiped his nose with a pressed handkerchief. Then he offered the tin to Rutland. "Go on," Young said. "You shouldn't be deprived of every pleasure."

Rutland refused.

A Cambridge man, Young couldn't resist holding court. He held an instinctual appreciation for what, at heart, an interrogation truly is: a performance, planned in advance, to unsettle a suspect, as well as a fact-finding mission designed to sift through half-truths and innuendo.

"At ease, Squadron Leader Rutland," said Young. Rutland thought the look on Young's face conveyed disdain. There were very few pleasantries exchanged.

"You're holding me here with hooligans and fascists," Rutland said. "Bloody Nazi sympathizers. I deserve better."

"We've heard from the Americans. They said, and this is a quote, that 'they have enough evidence to shoot you.'"

"Nonsense," Rutland said. "I was helping them. It shouldn't be a problem to confirm this. Why don't you speak to the US Navy and ask them yourselves? The contacts are Captain Ellis Zacharias, Commander Kenneth Ringle, and Captain Claude Mayo of US Naval Intelligence. They will let you know of my help to the United States. When you say 'the Americans,' who pray tell did you hear from?"

Here, Young turned to his colleague, J. L. S. Hale, MI5's senior legal advisor, with a quizzical look on his face. They didn't answer Rutland's question.

Rutland continued, "It is the same in the United States as it is here in Britain. Just as you don't always share information with Godfrey, in the US the FBI and ONI do not always have the same information either. I'd simply ask you to confirm with the US Navy directly, rather than with the FBI."

Ignoring Rutland's request, Young commented, "We respect your prior service to the crown," adding, "In reading your background, it mustn't have been the easiest of roads out of Weymouth. Yet, look at your history post the Great War. Infidelity. Wife swapping. Insubordination. Espionage. And treason. It is really quite a shame."

Rutland turned away—embarrassed or further enraged, Young couldn't quite determine. Rutland finally replied, "Not only was I helping the Americans, but I have never once acted against my home country. And I suppose you know that. Else, you might have charged me with a crime, perhaps?"

"You seem to have lived quite the life in America. Your Hollywood lifestyle. Your mansion overlooking Sunset Boulevard. Your children's private schools. Your club memberships. Your butler and nannies. All paid for by the Japanese Navy. So why don't you tell me, Squadron Leader Rutland, what did the Imperial Japanese Navy receive from you in return?"

"Nothing," Rutland stated flatly.

Hale, who'd been silent up to this point, found his voice. "We need you to come clean, Squadron Leader. Otherwise, you will be here a very, very long time."

Young and Hale studied Rutland, searching for any sign of resignation. All they saw was anger and a palpable bitterness. Neither man could figure Rutland out, despite their experience getting information out of suspects. He was the most difficult of suspects: slippery and stubborn, intelligent and arrogant.

Rutland was getting a good sense of where this was going. He had a very good idea why the MI5 representatives were asking him for some kind of confession. Yet he had done his work for the Japanese Navy in Japan and in the United States—not in Britain. Therefore, despite their blustering, it was obvious they could not have any evidence that he had committed any crime against his country. Logically, MI5 wanted him to confess, in case they needed to cover themselves.

Rutland asked, "What is the endgame here? Do you think you can keep me, with my powerful allies, in prison forever?" There was no answer. He continued, "Look, I think we can reach an agreement here. I have done nothing wrong, but if you want to keep me away from Japan, that is all very well. The Royal Navy is short of trained officers. Grant me release, and I shall simply rejoin the navy and serve the crown faithfully. As you know, the Royal Navy has such a dearth of experienced ship captains that at Dunkirk, they needed to depend on fishermen to pilot the boats. I'm a very experienced navy officer, exactly what they need. Let me help this country, and you shan't hear from me again."

The MI5 agents were stunned into silence. It seemed clear to Rutland that the offer was not going to be considered.

Rutland added, "I have many powerful allies at the Admiralty. Not only will they likely accept me back into the service, but if you do not let me I'd be able to make your lives rather exceedingly troublesome."

Young didn't like being threatened and ended the interrogation there. Rutland was escorted back to his cell.

Rutland wasn't entirely bluffing. He knew that many in the Royal Navy continued to have interest in the famous Rutland of Jutland, and that included perhaps half of the Lords Commissioners of the Admiralty. Just as his young flyer friends in Japan in the 1920s were now running the Imperial Japanese Navy, those in the top positions in the Royal Navy knew about Rutland's service in the first war, and many knew and respected him personally.

Rutland became, in the words of his captors, an "indefatigable correspondent," penning letters to nearly every person of influence he could. He wrote letters to his family and lawyers to try to get out of prison, more to the USA to try to get a statement that would exonerate him, and others to various admirals to try to get the Royal Navy to accept him into the service. At one point, Young was highly alarmed to find Rutland preparing a letter proclaiming his innocence to be sent directly to 370 members of Parliament.

Sometime later, Young checked the letter box at his home and was annoyed to find one of Rutland's handwritten letters addressed directly to him. He had no idea how Rutland had found his name, let alone his home address. He suspected a frequent visitor, Rutland's daughter Barbara, had helped him. Or perhaps someone in naval intelligence may have been leaking information to him.

...

Sir Roger Keyes was an ex–Royal Navy admiral and a member of the House of Lords. He was the founder of the British Commandos, and he and Winston Churchill had been perhaps the loudest voices against Prime Minister Neville Chamberlain's appeasement policy toward Adolf Hitler. Keyes and Rutland had worked together on a couple of daring missions against the Germans in World War I, and Keyes was shocked to get a letter from Rutland, bearing the return address "His Majesty's Prison, Brixton."

Baron Keyes called Godfrey of naval intelligence. Godfrey had been initially angry at MI5's treatment of Rutland before the Pearl Harbor attack, but now, he was particularly stuck on the fact that Rutland had been trying to warn the British about the coming attack, and MI5 had actively silenced him. He followed up with calls to MI5 for clarification, but was rebuffed.

Keyes then called Winston Churchill directly, asking him about the gallant Rutland being in Brixton Prison. Churchill reportedly admonished Keyes, "Leave it alone, Roger. There were reasons." Keyes then wrote an apologetic letter to Rutland, apologizing for not being able to do more.

In July 1942, there was a debate in Parliament about the Britons who were being held without trial. The members of Parliament had been expecting a more theoretical debate, and were riveted when Baron Keyes stood up and made an angry speech, starting by reminding the listeners that there was only one living Briton who could wear the Albert Medal, First Class, in gold. He continued that the Briton in question was ex–Flight Commander Rutland, and he was in Brixton Prison. Keyes added that Rutland had initially been working for the Japanese, before having a change of heart and then collaborating with specific US Navy Intelligence officers, whom he could name. Keyes stated that he wasn't defending the officer, saying that Rutland had apparently been "hunting with the hounds and running with the fox" (that is, playing both sides) but had Rutland— with his unique knowledge and high competence—been allowed to help the Royal Navy, many of the early disasters might have turned out differently.

The story broke in the British papers, and then ran in the New York *Daily News*, the *Washington Post*, and elsewhere. There was some mild panic at the FBI and MI5 about the bad press, and Hoover issued a memo instructing FBI agents not to mention anything about Rutland working with the US Navy to anyone outside the agency, "to prevent future embarrassment to the bureau." Fortunately for the FBI and MI5, the war was dominating the news, and Rutland didn't stay in the public eye.

The FBI kicked off a more detailed investigation to try to understand exactly what Rutland had been doing. Dorothy Rutland and her two children could no longer afford to live in the palatial house in the hills, and had moved to Pasadena. The FBI raided her house and confiscated a box of Rutland's most sensitive files—these included his correspondence with Kayaba and the Japan Aircraft Company; his letters with Mrs. Rutland detailing instructions on what to do if a war was to erupt, dated as far back as 1939; and one file where the FBI has redacted every word (but could presumably be his agreement with Zacharias). The agents also spoke again to Mowbray, Glover, and Karloff, and asked them about Dorothy. They assured the FBI agents that "Rutland was not the kind of man who would confide his affairs with a woman," and despite the evidence in the letters, concluded she was blameless.

Rutland's next interrogation by Young started with no pleasantries, no handshake, just an icy glare between the men. Young made a few things very clear to Rutland. He was not going to allow Rutland to be in the press again. And Rutland was not to talk about the specifics of his case anymore, to anyone. Young said they would be uncompromising, "merciless, even," if Rutland "pursued his vendetta in the press."

Rutland replied that he was being held in prison for political reasons only and should be freed forthwith. He followed by mentioning to Young that putting citizens in prison without trial didn't sound very British—and pointed out, in fact, that it was more something Nazi Germany would do.

Young repeated to Rutland that "if you want to have a chance of us setting you free, you will need to give up your letter-writing campaign and will need to come clean and provide a full reckoning." Rutland countered with nearly the same story that Baron Keyes had presented to the press. He stated that MI5 ignoring his help in 1941 had been a "blunder of the first magnitude."

Soon after, Rutland and other political prisoners were sent to a jail on the Isle of Man, a location that was so remote it seemed to be as much exile as prison. Letters were tightly controlled, and visitors rare. He attempted to get sent back to Brixton, using Barbara to write and deliver letters, with a focus on getting a deposition from Zacharias or Ringle. Zacharias was not reachable—understandable, as he was fighting battles at sea. But it was also likely that he had been told by his superior officers not to make any more waves. Rutland even came up with the idea to have his wife, Dorothy, in Los Angeles sue Zacharias in court for damages. That way, Zacharias would be put on the stand and be forced to testify.

By mid-1943, more than half of the other prisoners had been freed, but Rutland remained behind bars. MI5 had other tricks up their sleeves to keep Rutland quiet. Rutland's wealthy brother-in-law, Rupert Hood-Barrs, was arrested for tax evasion and sentenced to twelve months in prison for perjury. Evidence used at Hood-Barrs's trial included paperwork confiscated from Rutland on his arrest. Specifically, Inland Revenue had mentioned that money going back and forth between Hood-Barrs and Dorothy Rutland was likely part of an elaborate money-laundering scheme, which was substantially correct.

Young mentioned in a memo that Rutland's brother-in-law was "if anything, a nastier piece of work than Rutland, who, at least, has the benefit of a charming personality that his brother-in-law, Rupert, certainly lacks."

Meanwhile, Rutland's older children were contributing to the war effort, each in his or her own way. His eldest, Fred, was now a doctor and had joined the Royal Navy with the rank of surgeon lieutenant. Frederick was assigned sea duty as the doctor on the HMS *Relentless*, where he joined the battle against the German and Japanese Navies in the Indian Ocean. Barbara Rutland worked for the Royal Air Force at one of the air bases, but she still corresponded often with her father. She was later given clearance by MI5 to work for the RAF in Canada, despite the association—or, perhaps, MI5 found it advantageous for her to be farther away from her father.

By mid-1943, the British were letting more and more of the Nazi sympathizers out of prison, and the Home Office concluded that Rutland should be released. They were "rather surprised by the decision of MI5," which agreed that Rutland was no longer a threat to British national security but asserted that he should be kept in detention anyway. However, Young of MI5 realized that Rutland would need to be released at some point. The bad blood between Young and Rutland was such that Young asked his colleague, J. L. S. Hale, to try to make a deal with Rutland.

Hale told Rutland, "Your activities in America have caused us much embarrassment vis-à-vis the American intelligence services. Should the Home Secretary agree to release you from prison, you would need to assure us that you will do absolutely nothing to put us in any position of embarrassment."

"Yes, I fully understand," Rutland replied. "Should I be released, I shan't do anything that would cause any problems. My word is gold here."

Hale repeated, "This is a position where we will not entertain any negotiation."

Rutland nodded and agreed, allowing himself a smile. He told Hale, "If I were to be released, I would likely take a position back at Scammell, building equipment for the military. Or I would be pleased to take any position anywhere where I might contribute to the war effort."

Hale nodded. "Any release would be subject to conditions such as registration of address with the police, with restrictions on moving. Practically speaking, that would mean you could not go to America." Rutland was happy to agree to anything at this point, and did so.

In December, Hale contacted Rutland with the news Rutland had hoped for. Rutland would indeed be released. But there would be additional conditions—specifically, Rutland would not be able to enter any restricted military area. This was quite a blow, because it meant Rutland would not be able to take any job related to helping the British war effort. He wanted to be involved in the war and stated that it was appalling that he was being treated this way, as if he were an alien, not British. He agreed to abide by the restrictions for the time being, but in no way would he commit to following them in the future. Hale agreed, and Rutland was released on December 20, 1943.

Despite his promises, Rutland backed out of his deal to be quiet almost immediately. He tried to get the provisions of his release reversed. He also had his lawyers threaten MI5 and Young and Hale personally to have some confiscated possessions returned. The MI5 files get sparse after that, but Young of MI5 was arranging for continual police monitoring of Rutland, which was not related to national security, and therefore must have been due to Rutland's potential to embarrass MI5.

...

After the war, Rutland initially lived in a cottage in the small Welsh village of Beddgelert, spending his time typing the memoirs of his naval service. He eventually moved a bit closer to civilization, and lived in a series of small apartments, but told his children that he would, for the most part, stay away from them, because he didn't want the stigma or accusations about him to impact their lives or careers. But he was always excited to meet with his children when he could. His son Fred came to Wales to take some long walks with his father. He mentioned his father was a "very bitter and angry man, but that he was very excited to talk about" the younger Frederick's service in the Royal Navy. The son pointed out to his father that it was a bit ironic that, although he had also joined the Royal Navy and served overseas in a World War, his service had been quite unlike his father's—very uneventful, and that they had sailed around the Indian Ocean looking for Japanese or German submarines, but hadn't found any. His father brushed that off, claiming that the medals he had won were just a matter of luck and being in the right place at the right time.

Dorothy visited him from Los Angeles in about 1947, taking along with her their daughter, Annabel. Twenty-one-year-old Annabel hadn't seen her father in six years, and was emotional on their visit. He told her that he would do his best to let her and his other children, all now young adults, live their own lives without being haunted by his problems. She pushed for a different tack, pleading with her father "to fight the accusations, clear your name. That would be best for all of us, but you most of all."

Rutland explained to his daughter that clearing his name was impossible. "If you have never been charged with a crime, it is impossible to prove your innocence," he noted. It was frustrating, but there was nothing to be done.

Not long after returning to the United States, Annabel got married, and took the opportunity to change both her first and last name, hoping to leave the scandal behind. She and her husband were living quietly in Los Angeles, when one day a large package from England arrived. Opening the package, on the top, was the snapshot of Annabel, less than two years old, in a kimono with an umbrella. With it was a note from her father stating that it was a treasured memory. Underneath the photo in the package were her father's files, family pictures, wartime pictures, and more. He said that he wanted her to have these files, since he would have no more need for them.

...

Before the package arrived in Los Angeles, Rutland's son Fred also received a letter. He opened it. It read:

Dear Fred:

This letter may come as a surprise to you, although it shouldn't, really. You know my views on life and death.

My life has been an adventurous one, always full of excitement. But I have probably bored you and the rest of the family enough already about that. The point is, I have always told myself that so long as life was worth the living, I would live it to the full and when it no longer held any real interest, it would be time to go.

I feel that time has now come.

You are a doctor and I think you will understand. This is not an impulsive decision. For as long as I can remember, I have known I could not drift into an inactive old age, dependent on you and the family.

This letter will probably by now have distressed you. But you are the elder son and I feel you are the only person I can ask to do what I want doing.

So when you get this, will you go down to Dorking. Take the Leith Hill Road. About two miles out, you will cross a stream. On the far side of the bridge, you will find a footpath on the right. You will find me about thirty yards down this path amongst some bushes.

This may all seem rather dramatic, but it is not meant to be. I want to avoid being found by some stranger accidentally, or by some child.

With much love,
Dad

Fred Rutland panicked and tried calling his father, but there was no answer. He then did as his father had requested, but when he got to the location in the letter, he didn't find a body. He looked everywhere, but eventually gave up and went home. Sometime later, the phone rang, and it was the police. They asked him to come to his father's home. He drove to his father's place as quickly as possible. When he arrived, he found some constables. They asked him to identify a body they'd found in the apartment.

The body they had found in the apartment was, indeed, his father—Frederick Rutland, DSC—who had apparently died from inhaling gas from the stove.

EPILOGUE

I started the quest to understand the story of Frederick Rutland and the implications to Pearl Harbor during the COVID-19 pandemic that began in early 2020. Like most people, I was stuck in my house and bored to tears. My initial encounter with the Rutland story was accidental.

Initially, I had started poking around in the FBI files to find out more about my recently deceased father, who had worked in counterintelligence for the US Army in the 1950s, and his father, who seemed to have been involved as well. Dad's job had been chasing communists around the Los Angeles area. The little I was able to find out about his career has very substantial overlap with the Rutland story. Dad worked at both Douglas and Lockheed, on introductions from his father. As far as I know, Dad didn't chase Charlie Chaplin, but he was tailing the "communist" Harpo Marx. He had originally applied to work at ONI. My father's best friend lived in the house of Rutland's best friend, but fifty years later, which must be just a coincidence. And Dad is clearly rolling in his grave that I am discussing any of this in print.

Much of the background for this book came not from academia, but firsthand, in stories I heard as a child from my father, his family, his tight-knit group of friends who had worked in US intelligence, and friends. I am one degree of separation from most of the characters in the story. The most gripping tales I heard were the ones told by the journalist Theodore H. White (who warned me never to go to Japan), the Domoto family (who worked at Yoko Ono's father's bank), and the Barbosa family. My grandmother must have met most of the characters as well, since she ran the family lunch counter, located next to the Hearst building and a block from the Japanese consulate.

I was, frankly, very lucky to stumble across so much of the Rutland story that had never been seen before. Part of it was timing. When I filed some Freedom of Information requests with the FBI, I found that Rutland's file had recently been declassified. There was some chance I was the first person outside of the bureau to see it.

More recently, my work took me to Japan, where I was advising Japanese companies on uses for artificial intelligence. I realized that my advising these organizations was, in concept, almost identical to what Rutland had been doing in the 1930s—funneling technical innovations from California to Japan. The major difference was that, today, Japan and the US are allies.

The Japanese Naval Intelligence archives had been burned in 1945, and the Japanese side of the story was thought not to be recoverable. However, I was fortunate to meet Commander Kusunoki of the Japan Maritime Self-Defense Force, whose house is crammed with old books and documents regarding pre–World War II Japanese Naval Intelligence. He uncovered documents that shed light on the Rutland story and that even Japanese historians have mostly never seen—none of which have been translated into English. They include the memoirs of Director of Naval Intelligence Shimada and Head Pilot Kuwabara, and the records of Shiro Kayaba and his company.

Implicit in my assumptions in this book is that I believe Rutland really was trying to help the US in the year or so before Pearl Harbor. When I tell people about the Rutland story, the first question is often "So, was he a bad guy?" My short answer is that he was absolutely a bad guy. However, he was also complicated—like most of us—and I also believe his efforts to warn the US and Britain of the attacks were genuine. Initially, he felt very smart—from his point of view, he was taking Japanese money to help them prepare for a war that he didn't think was possible. He did— undoubtedly and substantially—contribute to the naval aviation capabilities of the Japanese Navy, without which the Pearl Harbor attack might not have been possible. Yet, once it became clear a war would happen, I believe he had a change of heart and truly did attempt to help the Americans and the British. It is just not possible he cheered when the Japanese planes sank the *Repulse*, his old ship. Although he was bitter and angry at the FBI and MI5, there is no evidence he disliked ONI, and quite a lot of hints he remained in his heart loyal to the Royal Navy. Had MI5 allowed it, it seems likely he could have been a very successful captain of one of the landing craft that landed troops in France on D-Day.

The FBI cover-up about the Rutland case is very clear from the documents that have been declassified. It would have been political dynamite for Hoover had word gotten out that a famous British war hero had been helping the US Navy and was trying to warn about the attack, but the FBI had him silenced and threatened to "shoot him." The recently released FBI files not only confirm that Rutland was in fact a US Navy asset, but that the director of the FBI had told his agents to take extreme care not to mention Rutland working with the US Navy, *because it could possibly be the basis of future embarrassment to the bureau.*

The FBI was very frantically trying to cover up everything it could about Rutland, Zacharias, and the ONI relationship. As late as 1960, a British journalist contacted the FBI on a mission that had been instigated by Baron Roger Keyes. It turned out the original Baron Keyes had died fifteen years earlier, and the new Baron Keyes involved was the son and namesake of Rutland's ally. The younger Keyes was carrying the grudge into the next generation. The journalist said that Keyes had told him the famous Rutland of Jutland was innocent, and he therefore wanted to check with the FBI. Furthermore, the journalist had recently contacted the retired US Navy captain and TV host, Ellis Zacharias, who had also told him Rutland was innocent.

The FBI is professional to a fault. FBI files from the period report only facts, not opinions. Considering this, it is striking that the FBI file says that the agents told the journalist that they would not be able to help in any particular way, and that "we don't like Zacharias." The FBI also held a long grudge.

It appears that most of the US Navy's files on Rutland are gone, but there are many more FBI files out there that have not yet been declassified. I am excited that the file of So Yasuhara, the man who ran the Japanese Navy–affiliated whorehouse in Tijuana, has been approved for declassification on my request and has been placed in the highest priority queue. Currently, declassification is taking about forty-two months, so this file will be available around 2025, assuming it doesn't get caught in the wheels of bureaucracy.

There are many blacked-out parts of the FBI file on Rutland that clearly pertain to Zacharias. It's humorous to note that the FBI redacts by blacking out names, and names are often in alphabetical order, so with his name beginning with Z, it makes it easy to surmise that many of the redacted parts are about him.

The FBI did successfully avoid taking blame for the Pearl Harbor attack. The blame was shifted to the commanders in Hawaii, Admiral Husband Kimmel, and army general Walter Short—although Kimmel and Short's reputations have been substantially rehabilitated over the years. Pulitzer Prize–winning author John Toland said there had been disappearance of evidence as part of a cover-up to purge intelligence records damaging to officials high up in the Franklin D. Roosevelt administration, but he didn't know what all that evidence was. The Rutland case is one part of that puzzle. Recent research has shown the FBI ignored not only Rutland, but also other clues about the coming attack, such as those from "Agent Tricycle" and the Aussie MI6 agent Dick Ellis.

MI5 was also trying to cover up and keep the Rutland case quiet for the exact same reasons as the FBI. Yet Rutland was a very angry and motivated man with nothing to lose, who was continually going after both MI5 the organization and the MI5 members directly. The MI5 files on Rutland total over one thousand pages, but they get rather sparse in the immediate postwar period when it appears that he was continually causing trouble for them.

It has always made me wonder. Rutland was embarrassing and a political threat to intelligence services on two continents. His activities were the subject of a cover-up, and many people wanted to keep him quiet. It doesn't seem totally impossible his death was not suicide but murder.

I feel incredibly blessed to have been able to uncover the story of Frederick Rutland. Somehow, I ended up following in so many of his footsteps, and for that reason, I felt I was uniquely able to tell the story. I won't minimize his negative impact, but I am particularly happy to be able to share the positive parts: his idealism, his love for his family, and his late-breaking attempt to make up for his sins.

ACKNOWLEDGMENTS

I have an outpouring of gratitude to a large number of people who helped make this book happen. I'll list them here, knowing that I am going to miss some, who I hope will forgive.

The actual book itself came to fruition thanks to Mark Tauber, Mauro DiPreta, Miles Doyle, Andrew Yackira, and Janet Rosenberg.

As a first-time author, I'm grateful to the following people who encouraged me in my research and in the writing of the book. Bradley Hart, Fumio Iwasa, Jan Goldman, Ken Kotani, Koichi Kusunoki, Paul Carr, Sarah Lacy, Seth Abramovitch, George Anders, and Jean-Louis Gassée.

The research of the book has been rather all-consuming. I'm thankful to Alexis Arinsburg, Hamilton Bean, Nicholas Beyelia, Julia Bricklin, Jessica Buxton, Richard Carrico, Kim Cooper, Admiral Sam Cox, David Castillo, Villy Dall, Mike Digby, Bill Malin, Hearst Communications, Jesse Fink, Norman Friedman, Lance Gatling, Benjamin Goldstein, Jan Goldman, Evie Groch, Ikuo Hiraishi, Brian Kenney, Nicholas Kitto, Yasushi Kodama, Ian McConnaughey, Jürgen Melzer, Yukinori Nikaido, Nate Patch, Eric Pratt, Justin Pyke, Nat Read, Laura Rosenzweig, Steve Ross, Colin Rowat, John Sbardellati, Richard Schiave, Elizabeth Spiller, Clay Stalls, Noriko Taji, Carlos Uscanga, June Vayo, Paul Glyn Williams, Bill Yenne, and Keimei Yamazaki.

There was a lot of inspiration from family: Michael Drabkin, Nina Drabkin, Adin Drabkin, Aliza Drabkin, Noemi Drabkin, Davina Drabkin, and a whole pile of Drabkin and Levant cousins who heard the stories growing up. Friends who patiently heard my ranting about the story include: Mike Alfant, Fiona Birchall, Rob Claar, Linda Cuccinata, Chris Hall, Chris Harris, Henry Hirose, Tom Fellenz, Jonathon Knight, Eric Lennane, Amy Lennane, Hank LeMieux, Owen Mannas, Miyako Ozaki, Cary Pugh, Jim Weisser, Jim Fink, Jerome Mead, Carrie Pendolino, Danny Rozansky, Don Steul, Arndt Voges, and Mitsuhiro Kodama, Jacqueline

Kehoe, Isabelle LaFreniere, Taylor McDonald, Ben Strauss, Ben Garton, Lowell Sheppard, Motoko Nakazawa, Steve Wasserzug, Elizabeth Pierson, and Simon Jones. I would say they were all also strong contributors to keeping me sane during COVID lockdowns.

I also think about my history teachers in school. In particular, I was thrilled by the lectures of Daniel Gavaldon and William Steele.

SELECTED BIBLIOGRAPHY

Archival Material
Columbia University Archives, New York

   Oral history interview with Alan G. Kirk, 1961

FBI files (via FOIA)

   Files of Frederick Rutland, Ellis Zacharias, Harry Thompson, John S. Farnsworth,
   Toraichi Kono, Sadatomo Okada, Toshio Miyazaki, Tsunezo Wachi, Tamon
   Yamaguchi, Takashi Furusawa, Tasuku Nakazawa
   Awaiting declassification of files of So Yasuhara, Ken Nakazawa, Leigh Karaki,
   Shio Sakanishi, and Japanese Radio Operators

Japan Center for Asian Historical Records, Online (JACAR)

   Records of the Sempill mission
   Records of Shiro Takasu

National Archives (UK), Kew

   MI5 KV files, including Personnel files of Frederick Rutland, Lord Sempill, CHC
   Smith, and Herbert Smith
   Secret packs of the commander in chief, Grand Fleet, volume LVIII, pack 0022,
   section L

National Archives (US): Riverside, CA; Washington, DC; St. Louis, MO

   Files of the Eleventh Naval District
   Records of U.S. Citizenship and Immigration Services
   Naval records on Rutland and others

National Diet Library, Tokyo (国立国会図書館)

   Files of the navy's radio service
   Kayaba records, the 80-year history of the Japan Aircraft Company (Nippi)

The National Institute of Defense Studies, Tokyo (防衛研究所)

   Y. Sanematsu memoirs

Pritzker Military Museum & Library, Chicago, Illinois

   William Hudson Collection, Tsunezo Wachi interviews

Smithsonian, National Air and Space Collection, Winfield B. "Bert" Kinner Collection

Stanford University, Hoover Institution Archives

International Military Tribunal for the Far East records
Hoji Shimbun records

University of Pittsburgh, Archives & Special Collections department

Donald M. Goldstein Collection, Itaru Tachibana interviews

University of California, Berkeley, Bancroft Library

Fang family, *San Francisco Examiner* **photograph archive negative files**

University of Southern California, Los Angeles, East Asian Library

Pedro Loureiro Collection

California State University, Northridge: Oral histories

Roos papers

University of Texas

Thayer Hobson Collection
Sam Houston Regional Library and Research Center, Martin Dies Collection

Books

Asada, Tsuyoshi. *Kaigun Ryotei: Komatsu Monogatari.* Yokohama: Kanashin Shuppan, 1996.

Basave, Daniel. *El samurái de la Grafle.* Mexico: Fondo de Cultura Economica, 2019.

Benson, Robert Louis. *A History of US Communications Intelligence during WWII: Policy and Administration.* Fort George G. Meade, MD: Center for Cryptologic History, National Security Agency, 1997.

Chaplin, Charles. *Shoulder Arms.* Directed by Charles Chaplin. Los Angeles: Charles Chaplin Productions, 1918.

Clausen, Henry C. *Pearl Harbor: Final Judgment.* New York: Crown, 1992.

Department of Defense. *Magic Background of Pearl Harbor.* 4 vols. United States Navy, 2022.

Dorwart, Jeffery. *Conflict of Duty: U.S. Navy's Intelligence Dilemma, 1919–1945.* Annapolis, MD: Naval Institute Press, 1983.

Drea, E. J. *MacArthur's ULTRA: Codebreaking and the War against Japan, 1942–1945.* Lawrence, KS: University Press of Kansas, 1992.

Hill, Robert A. *The FBI's RACON: Racial Conditions in the United States during World War II.* Boston: Northeastern University Press, 1995.

Hori, Eizo. *Daihon'ei sanbō no jōhō senki: Jōhōnaki kokka no higeki.* Tokyo: Bungei Shunjū, 1989.

Fahey, John. *Australia's First Spies: The Remarkable Story of Australia's Intelligence Operations, 1901–45.* Crows Nest, Australia: Allen & Unwin, 2019.

Farago, Ladislas. *The Broken Seal: The Story of Operation Magic and the Pearl Harbor Disaster.* New York: Random House, 1967.

Friedman, Norman. *Fighting the Great War at Sea: Strategy, Tactics and Technology*. Annapolis, MD: Naval Institute Press, 2021.

Gage, Beverly. *G-Man: J. Edgar Hoover and the Making of the American Century*. New York: Viking, 2022.

Goodman, Walter. *The Committee: The Extraordinary Career of the House Committee on Un-American Activities*. New York: Penguin Books, 1968.

Gunjishi Gakkai. *Kaigun Taishō Shimada Shigetarō Bibōroku Nikki 1* [Admiral Shimada Shigetarō's Memoirs, Volume 1]. Tokyo: Kinseisha, 2017.

Hart, Bradley. *Hitler's American Friends*. New York: Thomas Dunne Books, 2018.

Hemming, Henry. *Agents of Influence: A British Campaign, a Canadian Spy, and the Secret Plot to Bring America into World War II*. New York: PublicAffairs, 2019.

Hynd, Alan. *Betrayal from the East: The Inside Story of Japanese Spies in America*. New York: Robert M. McBride and Company, 1943.

Jacobs, Stephen. *Boris Karloff: More than a Monster: The Authorized Biography*. South Yorkshire, UK: Tomahawk Press, 2011.

Johnson, Clarence "Kelly." *More than My Share of It All*. Washington, DC: Smithsonian Books, 1979.

Kayaba Industries, 50 Years of History, 1935–85. KYB (カヤバ工業５０年史), 1985.

Kayaba, Shiro. *The Weapons of the Chinese Military*. Tokyo: Modern Japan Publishing, 1938.

Koshiba, S. *Shina Kinmu no Kaisōroku* [Memoirs of Service in China]. Tokyo: The National Institute for Defense Studies, unpublished.

Kotani, K. *Japanese Intelligence in World War II*. Oxford, UK: Osprey Publishing, 2009.

Kotani, K. *Nihongun no Intelligence; Naze Jōhō ga Ikasenai no ka* [Japanese Military Intelligence; Why Japan Doesn't Use Intelligence Well]. Tokyo: Kodansha Senshomechie, 2007.

Kurono, T. *Teikoku Kokubō Hōshin no Kenkyu, Riku-Kaigun Kokubōshisō no Tenkai to Tokuchō* [A Study of Imperial National Defense Policy: Development and Characteristics of the National Defense Thought of the Army and Navy]. Tokyo: Sōwasha, 2000.

Kushner, Barak. *The Thought War: Japanese Imperial Propaganda*. Honolulu, HI: University of Hawai'i Press, 2007.

Kuwahara, Torao. *Naval Aviation Recollections*. Tokyo: Shinkuu Publishing, 1964.

Layton, E. T., R. Pineau, and J. Costello. *And I Was There: Breaking the Secrets—Pearl Harbor and Midway*. New York: William Morrow and Company, 1985.

Livock, Gerald E. *To the Ends of the Air*. London: Stationery Office Books, 1973

Loftis, Larry. *Into the Lion's Mouth*. New York, NY: Berkley Caliber, 2016.

Lowman, D. D. *Magic: The Untold Story of U.S. Intelligence and the Evacuation of Japanese Residents from the West Coast during WW II*. Twickenham, UK: Athena Press, 2001.

MacIntyre, Ben. *Operation Mincemeat: How a Dead Man and a Bizarre Plan Fooled the Nazis and Assured an Allied Victory*. New York: Crown, 2011.

Macintyre, Donald. *Jutland*. London: White Lion Publishers, 1975.

Mank, Gregory. *Hollywood's Hellfire Club: The Misadventures of John Barrymore, W.C. Fields, Errol Flynn and the Bundy Drive Boys*. Port Townsend, WA: Feral House, 2009.

Matthews, Tony. *Shadows Dancing*. New York: St. Martin's Press, 1994.

Melzer, Jurgen. *Wings for the Rising Sun: A Transnational History of Japanese Aviation.* Cambridge, MA: Harvard University Asia Center, 2020.

Miller, R. *Codename Tricycle: The True Story of the Second World War's Most Extraordinary Double Agent.* London: Pimlico, 2005.

Nasaw, D. *The Chief: The Life of William Randolph Hearst.* Boston: Mariner Books, 2001.

Ono, Hiroyuki. *Chapurin no Kage* [Chaplin's Shadow]. Tokyo: Koudansha, 2009.

Peattie, Mark. *The Rise of Japanese Naval Air Power, 1909–1941.* Annapolis, MD: Naval Institute Press, 2013.

Powers, Richard Gid. *Secrecy and Power: The Life of J. Edgar Hoover.* New York: Free Press, 1987.

Prados, J. *Combined Fleet Decoded: The Secret History of American Intelligence and the Japanese Navy in World War II.* Annapolis, MD: Naval Institute Press, 2001.

Prange, G. W. *At Dawn We Slept.* New York: Penguin Books, 1991.

Reeve, Commander Richard, USNR, et al., *The United States Strategic Bombing Survey (Pacific),* Japanese Intelligence Section, G-2. Washington, DC: United States Government Publishing Office, 1946.

Rosenzweig, Laura. *Hollywood's Spies: The Undercover Surveillance of Nazis.* New York: NYU Press, 2017.

Rutland, David. *Behind the Front Panel: The Design and Development of 1920's Radios.* Philomath, OR: Wren Publishers, 1994.

Sanematsu, Y. *Kaigun Daigakkō Senryaku Senjyutsu Dōjō no Kōzai* [The Naval War College: Accomplishments and Sins of the Strategy and Tactics Dojo]. Yokohama, Kōjinsha: 1975.

Sanematsu, Y. *Nichibei Jōhō Senki* [Military History of Japanese-U.S. Intelligence]. Tokyo: Kojinsha, 2009.

Security Aircraft Company (Bert Kinner), Stock Certificates.

Seth, Ronald. *Secret Servants.* New York: Paperback Library, 1968.

Spivak, John. *Honorable Spy.* New York: Modern Age Books, 1939.

Stevenson, William. *A Man Called Intrepid: The Incredible WWII Narrative of the Hero Whose Spy Network and Secret Diplomacy Changed the Course of History.* Guilford, CT: Lyons Press, 2009.

Summers, Anthony, and Robbyn Swan. *A matter of honor: Pearl harbor: Betrayal, blame, and a family's quest for Justice.* New York, NY: Harper, 2017.

Prince Takamatsu. *Takamatsunomiya Nikki* [Prince Takamatsu's Diary], volume 4. Tokyo: Chūō Kōronsha, 1996.

Terasaki, T. *Reimei; Nihongaikō Kaisōroku* [A Memoir of Japanese Diplomacy]. Tokyo: Chūo Kōron Jigyō Shuppan, 1982.

Toland, J. *The Rising Sun: The Decline and Fall of the Japanese Empire.* New York: Random House, 1982.

Urabe and Shinsato. *For That One Day: The Memoirs of Mitsuo Fuchida, Commander of the Attack on Pearl Harbor.* Kamuela, HI: eXperience, inc, 2011.

Wachi, T. *Tsushin Chōhō no Gaiyō* [Overview of Imperial Japanese Navy's COMINT]. Suikoukai, 1963: 11–15.

Warner, Guy. *World War One Aircraft Carrier Pioneer: The Story and Diaries of Captain JM McCleery RNAS/RAF.* Barnsley, UK: Pen & Sword Aviation, 2011.

Westlake School for Girls. *Vox Puellarum (Yearbook).* Los Angeles, CA. 1938–42.

Wilhelm, Maria. *The Man Who Watched the Rising Sun: The Story of Admiral Ellis M. Zacharias*. Mountain View, CA: Ishi Press, 2013.

Yamamoto, T. *Rikugun Nakano Gakkō "Himitsu Kōsakuin" Yōsei Kikan no Jitsuzō* [The Japanese Army Nakano School; the Reality of a Secret Agent Training Agency]. Tokyo: Chikuma Shobō, 2017.

Yamazaki, Keisuke. *Intelligence 1941*. Tokyo: NHK Press, 2014.

Yenne, Bill. *Lockheed*. Lincoln, NE: Bison Books, 1987.

Yokoi, Shunsuke. *The Imperial Japanese Navy Secret Intelligence Room. The Hidden Background of the Pacific War*. Tokyo: Shinseikatsusha, 1953.

Yoshikawa, T. *Shinjuwan Supai no kaisō* [Memories of a Spy in Pearl Harbor]. Tokyo: Mainichi Wanz, 2018.

Young, Desmond. *Rutland of Jutland*. London: Cassell, 1963.

Zacharias, Ellis M. *Secret Missions: The Story of an Intelligence Officer*. Annapolis, MD: Naval Institute Press, 2014.

Newspapers and Periodicals Referenced

Bellingham Herald

London Gazette

Long Beach Press-Telegram

Los Angeles Daily News

Los Angeles Evening Post-Record

Los Angeles Examiner

Los Angeles Times

New York Times

Nichibei Shimbun

San Francisco Examiner

The Times (London)

Washington Post

Select Newspaper Articles

"Naval Airman's Heroism." *The Times* (London), August 12, 1916, 6.

"Englishman Travelling through US, Canada and Japan Seeks to Represent Manufacturers." *New York Times*, September 3, 1933. Business Connections section.

"Bail Is Reduced. Flyer Gets Reduction in Campfire Forest Case." *Bellingham Herald* (WA), August 24, 1934, 7.

"Rutland to Leave on Trip to Japan." *Los Angeles Times*, November 25, 1936, 38.

"Britons Will Give Dance. Chaplin Buys Charity Ball Tickets." *Los Angeles Times*, October 11, 1936, 50. Accessed June 2, 2023. https://www.newspapers.com /image/380280078.

"Bon Voyage Fete for FJ Rutland and Daughter." *Los Angeles Examiner*, August 19, 1939.

"Former British Flier Sees U.S. Mediation." *Long Beach Press-Telegram*, October 20, 1939, 2. Accessed June 2, 2023. https://www.newspapers.com/image/703977284.

"Japan Navy Officer Head in Spy Plot." *Los Angeles Times*, June 10, 1941, 1.

"New Arrests Loom in 'Spy' Round Up Here." *Los Angeles Examiner*, June 10, 1941.

"US to Deport Tokio Officer." *San Francisco Examiner*, June 21, 1941, 2.

Ringle, Ken. "What Did You Do before the War, Dad?" *Washington Post*, December 6, 1981.

Articles

"Passenger Lists (for the Rutland Family.") Ancestry®. Accessed April 16, 2023. https://www.ancestry.com/search/categories/img_passlists/.

British United Services Club "British United Services Club History." Accessed May 24, 2023. https://busc.clubexpress.com/content.aspx?page_id=22&club_id=599365&module_id=406508.

Jakobsen, Knud. "Jyllandsslaget: og Første Verdenskrig i Nordsøen." Sea War Museum Jutland, 2018.

DeFrance, Smith J. "The Aerodynamic Effect of a Retractable Landing Gear." The National Advisory Committee for Aeronautics, March 1933. Accessed May 24, 2023. https://ntrs.nasa.gov/api/citations/19930081304/downloads/19930081304.pdf.

A picture of a Lockheed Altair purchased by the Mainichi Newspaper is here: https://aucfree.com/items/s841237286.

DeLeon, Andrew. "Martin Dies Jr., the House Un-American Activities Committee and Racial Discrimination in Mid-Century America." Thesis at Sam Houston University.

DeFrance, Smith J. "The Aerodynamic Effect of a Retractable Landing Gear." The National Advisory Committee for Aeronautics, March 1933. Accessed May 24, 2023. https://ntrs.nasa.gov/api/citations/19930081304/downloads/19930081304.pdf.

Drabkin, Ron, K. Kusunoki, and Bradley Hart. "Agents, Attachés, and Intelligence Failures: The Imperial Japanese Navy's Efforts to Establish Espionage Networks in the United States before Pearl Harbor." *Intelligence and National Security* 38, no. 3 (2023), https://doi.org/10.1080/02684527.2022.2123935.

Drabkin, Ron, and Bradley W. Hart. "Agent Shinkawa Revisited: The Japanese Navy's Establishment of the Rutland Intelligence Network in Southern California." *International Journal of Intelligence and Counterintelligence* 35, no. 1 (2022). https://doi.org/10.1080/08850607.2020.1871252.

Fujifilm. "The History of Fujifilm. The Challenge of Making Pictures in Japan." Accessed May 24, 2023. https://www.fujifilm.co.jp/corporate/aboutus/history/ayumi/dai1-01.html.

Fujiya Hotel. Accessed May 24, 2023. https://fhr.fujiyahotel.jp/.

Hynd, A. "Mr. Kono and Mr. Blake." *Esquire*. January 1, 1944. https://classic.esquire.com/article/1944/01/01/mr-kono-and-mr-blake. FBI files note that this article is almost entirely accurate, other than that Blake inflated his own importance and cut a few things that were sensitive (such as the Rutland reference).

Kahn, David. "The Intelligence Failure of Pearl Harbor." *Foreign Affairs* 70, no. 5 (1991): 138–52. https://doi.org/10.2307/20045008.

Koontz, Giacinta. "Bert Kinner: The Ups and Downs." AviationPros. Accessed May 24, 2023. https://www.aviationpros.com/education-training/article/10381193/bert-kinner-the-ups-and-downs.

Johnson, K. W. "The Neglected Giant: Agnes Meyer Driscoll." Washington, D.C.: National Security Agency, 2015.

Kimmel, Thomas K., J. A. Williams, and Paul Glyn Williams. "The FBI's Role in the Pearl Harbor Attack." *American Intelligence Journal* 27, no. 1 (2009): 41–48. http://www.jstor.org/stable/44327110.

Los Angeles County Registrar - Recorder. Property Deeds.

Masquers Club. "History." Accessed May 24, 2023. http://www.masquersclub.org/.

Nørgaard, Hans E., and Villy Dall. "Britisk Krigshelt Fra Agger Blev (Nok) Japansk Spion." Historisk Årbog, 2013, 39–56. Accessed May 24, 2023. https://arkivthy.dk /images/Aarbog/2013/4britiskkrigsheltfraagger.pdf.

US Navy Office of Naval Intelligence. "Japanese Intelligence and Propaganda in the United States during 1941." December 4, 1941. Accessed May 24, 2023. http://www .mansell.com/eo9066/1941/41-12/IA021.html.

Oleo Company History. https://www.oleoinc.com/about/story.

Ortega, M. "Reseña: Entre la Historia y las Relaciones Internacionales: Lothar Knauth 45 Años de Magisterio sobre Asia en la Facultad de Ciencias Políticas y Sociales, UNAM." *Saberes Revista de Historia de las Ciencias y las Humanidades* 1, no. 2 (2017). Accessed May 24, 2023. https://www.saberesrevista.org/ojs/index.php/saberes /article/view/74.

Pfeiffer, D. "Sage Prophet or Loose Cannon?" *Prologue Magazine* 40, no. 2 (2008). Accessed May 24, 2023. https://www.archives.gov/publications/prologue/2008 /summer/zacharias.html.

Rekishi ni nemuru: Tamarein (Sleeping in History, the Tama Spiritual Cemetery.) "Torii, Takuya." Accessed May 24, 2023. http://www6.plala.or.jp/guti/cemetery /PERSON/T/torii_ta.html.

Schultz, Fred. "Resurrecting the Kimmel Case." *Naval History Magazine*, US Naval Institute, August 1995. Accessed May 24, 2023. https://www.usni.org/magazines /naval-history-magazine/1995/august/special-report-resurrecting-kimmel-case.

Thompson, Kate. "KYB Tells Its 100-Year Story." *Garage Wire*. November 22, 2019. Accessed May 24, 2023. https://garagewire.co.uk/news/company/kyb/kyb-tells-its -100-year-story/.

Townhouse Bar. "History." Accessed May 15, 2023. http://www.townhousevenice .com/history.

Uscanga, C. "Tsunezō Wachi: De Espía a Monje Budista." Discover Nikkei. April 30, 2021. Accessed May 24, 2023. https://www.discovernikkei.org/en/journal/2021 /4/30/tsunezo-wachi/.

United States Government. Naval Intelligence Manual, ONI-19, 1933. Washington, D.C.

INDEX

ABOUT THE AUTHOR

Ronald Drabkin is the author of peer-reviewed articles on Japanese espionage. His obsession with espionage history started when he was a child in Los Angeles, where he vaguely understood that his father had been working for the US military in counterintelligence. Later, he discovered that his grandfather had also been in "the business," and it drove a voyage of discovery into previously classified documents on three continents.

His career prior to writing was at early stage start-ups in the US, where he was an early adopter of Google and Facebook advertising. He currently lives in Tokyo.